The Ripper's Children
Inside the World
of Modern Serial Killers

The Ripper's Children
Inside the World
of Modern Serial Killers

by Raymond Cornell and Ilene W. Devlin

The Ripper's Children: Inside the World of Modern Serial Killers

© 2021 Raymond Cornell and Ilene W. Devlin

ORDERING INFORMATION: Additional copies may be obtained from Raymond Cornell at cornell47cornell@aol.com or 641-781-0436 and Ilene W. Devlin at ilenewd@icloud.com or 210-854-6593.

ISBN – 978-1-7357340-7-1

Cover photo by Marek Piwnicki on Unsplash.

DEDICATION

To Jan Johnson and Leo Oxberger who judged me and found me worthy and to the late Iowa Governor Robert D. Ray, one of the last good guys.

Raymond Cornell

Table of Contents

PREFACE

Why would anyone read a book like this, let alone write one? I wrote this book because I had to do so. Only you know why you are reading it.

This is not a murder novel, nor is it a psychology text. It is an attempt to define a phenomenon of modern life in terms understandable to those most likely to be touched by it: average, everyday people who are suddenly caught up in horror. There is no fiction here, only overwhelming, bloody death.

We can never really know what is going on in the mind of a John Gacy or a Ted Bundy. The best we can hope to achieve is to look at the things they do and to try to gain some insight into what makes them what they are.

Violent death has become an intrinsic part of life in America. We ingest massive doses of it from morning until night: newspapers, books, movies, and, most of all, television. From cradle to grave, we are taught that killing is an acceptable way to solve problems and to fulfill our needs. Yet we are surprised when some among us carry those fantasies into reality.

Having come from a family of criminals of one kind or another, I have always been aware of the attitudes and behavior making up that lifestyle. My years as a prisoner and more than a decade as a specialist in criminal justice have brought me into contact with hundreds of killers of one kind or another.

This book is the culmination of a decade of murders that touched me personally. In 1976, my brother was convicted and sentenced to life in prison for murder. In 1978, my friend, John Gacy, was charged with thirty-three murders. Finally, in 1980, a few weeks after John was sentenced to death for his crimes, my sixteen-year-old sister was brutally raped and killed by a person suspected of being a serial murderer.

In the years since, I have devoted myself to an effort to understand serial murder and its place in contemporary society. This book is the result of that effort.

Raymond Cornell

ACKNOWLEDGEMENTS

To thank all the people who helped and encouraged us with this book would take many pages. People from every walk of life have played a part; the only thing they hold in common is that all of them have been touched by crime. Straights and gays, criminals and victims, prostitutes and cops, lawyers and judges, convicts and parole board members have all assisted to make this project work. Their names are not listed, but they know who they are. They also know the depth of our gratitude.

We would like to especially thank Dean Janet Johnson of the Pace University Law School.

To our editor, Lillie Ammann, many thanks for your guidance.

INTRODUCTION

In the late summer and early fall of 1888, the city of London was gripped by a terror like none the world had ever seen. A silent, deadly force moved through the streets of the East End, killing with impunity and disappearing like smoke.

History knows him as Jack the Ripper. He was the father of the most horrible phenomenon in modern crime—serial murder. Many great killers struck before him, but they murdered primarily for reasons of politics, conquest, financial gain, and religion. With the appearance of Jack, for the first time, the reasons for killing became locked into the changing nature of society itself.

After he had concluded his gruesome, solitary business, Jack disappeared as suddenly as he had come. Even today, nearly a century later, speculation still exists as to his identity. Literary detectives, called Ripperologists, carefully sift and resift the evidence looking for the final clue.

Although his victims numbered no more than seven, and probably only five, an insignificant number by modern standards, the full impact of this new kind of criminal is only now showing its bloody blossom.

Yet, with the little we know, we can conclude much. In many ways, Jack set the stage for all those who came after him. The care and precision of the crimes, the taunting of police, and the virtual impossibility of apprehension by normal police procedures are all part of a pattern to be seen again and again.

Jack and his "children" have a great deal in common. Identifying and defining a few of these similarities may make this type of criminal a little more understandable. In this book, we will create a general profile of modern serial murderers and highlight areas for future study into what creates these killers.

The Human Predator

Murder is as old as mankind. "Cain rose up and slew his brother Abel" and invented murder. That set the pattern for most murders from then until now: uncontrollable anger erupts into a killing rage directed at a family member. A leavening of drugs or alcohol may be added to lower inhibitions and make the deed easier. Nothing much has changed.

Anthropologist Robert Ardrey suggested in his book *The Territorial Imperative* that man is descended not from some harmless omnivore ape but from a highly specialized "killer ape" whose aggressive drive lives on. While impossible to prove scientifically, this theory still holds considerable attraction for those who deal with the criminal aspects of human beings.

Many established members of the anthropological disciplines have taken strong issue with Ardrey. In one area, however, his viewpoint seems quite valid: crime.

If Ardrey had been a criminologist rather than an anthropologist, he would probably be a legend instead of being accused of being a crackpot.

Certainly, his approach is as applicable as any of the theories of thinkers such as Freud, Maslow, or Yochelson and Samenow. Freud thought criminality was a function of sexual aggression. While possibly true, that was a simplistic perspective. Maslow in his hierarchy of need attributed criminality to the search for identity. Yochelson and Samenow took the approach that criminal behavior was a matter of personal choice. Yet none of them seemed to succeed in comprehending the role of criminals in society or how changes in society lead to changes in types of criminal behavior.

As soon as early humans banded together and began to make rules for living as a group, they routinely began breaking those rules. It is important to keep in mind that people who violate the laws established either by a majority or by those in power are, by definition, criminals. Laws are written to reflect the attitudes and views of those who make them and often have only a limited relationship with what goes on in the real world. Laws are not made by the poor or disenfranchised, rather, by the affluent, the educated, and the articulate. The much-misused term "silent majority" defines the vast group of people who have no role in the making of the laws by which they must live. This explains to some degree why it is easy for those who feel they have no stake in a society to violate the rules of that society.

As civilization became industrialized, the individual became anonymous and lost his/her place in the world. Social philosophers call this alienation of the individual by technology "anomie." One result can be an attempt to create identity through violence. As society has changed and moved away from the stable family unit and the resulting internalized behavioral controls, those restrictions have not been replaced with anything of equal strength. This has left a void in the values and motivations of many human beings.

Given that context, the taking of life as a problem-solving device has become more convenient. When faced with frustration, one simply bypasses all the lesser options, such as talking, negotiating, and bargaining, and goes immediately to the ultimate solution—murder. For thousands of years, indeed, to some extent still today, murder was the accepted and approved method for solving the problems of society and the individual.

The idea that murder is wrong is a rather recent development. Prior to the early writings, such as the Code of Hammurabi, c. 1750 BCE, few social restrictions on murderous conduct had been formulated. At that time, when one took the life of another human being, a blood debt was incurred. That debt was satisfied either in the form of some payment to the family/clan of the victim or that clan would take a life in return. The practice lives on in the form of the feud. However, rulers eventually saw that the approach was impractical. Hence, the beginning of laws controlling such behavior was developed. Murder became an offense against the ruler and all the people.

Take a moment and reflect on the other party involved in the transaction of murder: the victim. When Thomas Beckett was slaughtered in Canterbury Cathedral by the knights of Henry II, it was necessary for them to come close enough to feel his last breath on their faces. Murder was a personal, if not an intimate, act between two people. In modern times, actual physical contact is no longer necessary for murder. Guns and other weapons that kill at a distance have sanitized the act. It is no longer necessary to touch or even look into the eyes of one's victim.

In addition, what by rights should be the most private act of a person's existence, his or her death, becomes the center of a public spectacle. In modern times, not only are the actual circumstances of the death shown and discussed by the various media, but every aspect of the victim's life becomes available for public debate. By virtue of being a victim, the person has his/her passage from life debased to the level of a circus sideshow. Thus, the murderer is the ultimate invader of personal privacy.

Western man has elevated this celebration of violence to the level of art. Walk through a museum and look at the great paintings. You will be amazed at how many portray scenes of violence and death. From the great masters and the deaths of saints to Picasso's *Guernica*, art reflects our attitudes. Murder, like beauty, is in the eye of the beholder. If a Fascist were to look at *Guernica*, he would merely see soldiers doing their job, which is killing. The people lying on the ground saw themselves as being murdered.

It is also extremely important to be aware of the semantics of death. The word used to describe the act or circumstance sets up a psychological frame of mind that justifies the deed. Killing is to cause the death of another. Killing becomes murder by the breaking of society's rules and the addition of malice or premeditation. Killing in self-defense or in the defense of others is homicide, but, according to the law, lacks malice and is, therefore, not murder.

With the possible exception of sex, as many words for killing exist as for any human activity. The words roll glibly off the tongue, leaving one sadly ignorant of the reality of the act: murder, homicide, manslaughter, genocide, fratricide, matricide, suicide, kill, waste, blow away, and—that all-time favorite—terminate with extreme prejudice. Each of these in its own way is defining the same act. The variations on this theme are caused by the adding or subtracting of components: premeditation, malice, and so forth. In each case, we are, in fact, talking about the taking of a human life by another. Thus, murder by society's definition involves the denial of another being's right to exist.

During war, the term "killing" is used to release the military

4

from the personal responsibility and social strictures against taking another human being's life. The group being fought is wrong and should not exist. However, noncombatants are not considered part of that wrong group and usually are off limits for killing. The term killing lowers the status of the person whose life is taken to that of a nonentity and involves no lingering guilt for the taker.

How many times have you heard one little boy say to another, "I'll kill you"? Even in early childhood, people are subjected to society's process of making the act of taking a life acceptable and appropriate. Several studies have estimated that by the time the average American child finishes elementary school, he has seen 8,000 murders on television. By the age of eighteen years old, he has witnessed 200,000 violent acts on television. Literally from every direction, we give our young the idea that murder, like baseball, is acceptable social behavior. The dichotomy between what we preach from the pulpit and what we view and enjoy in the living room is incredible.

One of the most amazing of all man's attributes is his ability to justify anything he chooses to do in terms of a greater good. The rationales and rhetoric can be as varied as religion, nationalism, and the good of the group. This ability goes all the way down to the serial killer who murdered and mutilated ten people, because he was convinced it would prevent the San Andreas fault from collapsing and dropping California into the sea. He saw himself as taking a few lives in order to save millions. Another example would be serial murderers who have taken the lives of large numbers of prostitutes. They may very well be thinking to themselves that they kill not because they enjoy killing, but because prostitution is wrong.

As the twentieth century closed, senseless murder became a matter of national concern. More than two-thirds of all murders are committed by family members and acquaintances. The perpetrator usually surrenders or is apprehended within twenty-four hours. Often this is an average citizen who loses control of his or her behavior and murders someone. Criminal behavior but not necessarily a criminal personality.

The other nearly one-third are murders committed by strangers. These are much more difficult to solve and to prosecute successfully. They are often the result of a felony that may not be related to the actual homicide, such as robbery or rape. Mass murder usually falls into this category.

The phenomenon of group murder threatens to become commonplace. Two types of group murder exist: mass murder and serial murder. Mass murder is usually considered the act of one individual killing four or more people at one time. Serial murder is the act of one individual killing several people with a waiting period between the murders. The variations within these definitions are almost endless. For example, in the San Francisco "Zebra" killings, several individuals banded together to commit a long string of murders. Some individuals killed several people on one occasion and several more on another occasion. Technically, this would make them serial mass murderers. However, the basic definitions remain valid.

A tiny category is the province of the serial murderers. The FBI defines serial murder as the unlawful killing of two or more victims by the same offender(s) at separate times. Other authorities define a serial murderer as someone who kills a minimum of five people over time.

The FBI in its Uniform Crime Report speculates at least thirty-five serial murderers are active at any given time. The Murder Accountability Project, a nonprofit that compiles homicide data, calculated some 2,000 serial killers were at large in the United States in 2017. Using the FBI definition and numbers, serial murderers kill at least seventy-five people a year. Using the nonprofit's numbers of 2,000 killers and a minimum of five victims each, that equates to over 10,000 victims a year. Although these, like any other law enforcement statistics, must be viewed with a grain of salt, we, the authors, are inclined to agree with the higher numbers. This is based on analyses of crime trends, homicide trends, and research into the behaviors of serial killers. These statistics are even more dramatic when one considers that these crimes are the handiwork of a small number of individuals.

Some would say that mass and serial murders reflect compulsive consumerism. It is not enough to kill your enemies; it has now become necessary to kill anyone who reminds you of your enemies. When a man walks into a post office in Oklahoma and kills fourteen other postal workers basically because they are wearing the same uniform, he is not really killing the boss who intended to fire him; he is killing the system. It's nothing personal to him.

In the minds of many, the serial murderer is definable as a sort of human rogue. A rogue is an individual who, for whatever reason, is ostracized by or separates himself from the body of the herd or group. A human rogue is not content merely to be separate. As a result of his isolation, he may turn on the group and kill. The motive for this violence is vengeance.

These marauders have always been with us in one form or another. Historians conjecture that individuals of this type may be at the root of many of the myths and scary tales of our childhood. It is not a difficult leap to go from the behavior of a Dracula to a Ted Bundy: striking from the dark, mutilating the victim, and disappearing.

In our struggle toward civilization, we have brought this creature from the dark along with us. The serial murderer as we now know him has become a sort of technological boogey man. *In* society but not *of* society, he moves through the darker places of our culture, doing what his predecessors did: killing and frightening. We are far too sophisticated to take the poor old vampire count seriously, but a Ted Bundy frightens us as much as Dracula would have frightened a seventeenth-century peasant and for the same reasons.

In examining the serial murder phenomenon, we went back to late 1888 and the father of them all—Jack the Ripper. By modern standards, Jack, with his five victims, would be penny-ante stuff. However, Jack laid the groundwork for most of what has followed. Many people consider him to be the first true, recorded sex criminal. Before the end of the nineteenth century, the concept of the sex crime did not exist. People who committed offenses like that were usually considered to be "morally insane." The concept of sex as a primary motivator for criminal behavior was incomprehensible. Thanks to Jack the Ripper, all that was about to change.

Between 31 August and 8 November 1888, five of the most gruesome murders ever encountered to that time were committed in the East End of London. The first four victims, prostitutes and women of the lower class, were killed in the byways of the poverty-stricken Whitechapel district. The women's throats were slashed and their genitals mutilated. The fifth victim, another prostitute, was a woman named Mary Kelly. Photographs of the death scene reveal mutilation almost beyond belief. All five were disemboweled with a skill that made police certain they were dealing with either a butcher or a doctor who had gone insane.

The killer has, at different times, been called Leather Apron, Bloody Knife, Red Jack, and Jack the Ripper. The killer and these crimes have been the subject of literally thousands of books, short stories, treatises, and articles. With all that, we still know next to nothing about the person who committed them.

Jack has been credited with several speculative motives. He has been accused of being a social reformer speaking out against the appalling conditions of the poor of Victorian England. Perhaps he was a Russian anarchist attempting to create political unrest among those same poor. One of the most popular theories has been that Jack was an insane member of the Royal family. Whatever the truth is, the atmosphere of terror created in that three-month span dramatically affected life in Great Britain and set the pattern for serial murderers who followed.

Jack was the first serial murderer also to be his own public relations man. He took great amusement in sending snide and insulting letters to the police and the newspapers, creating a tradition that continues today. On one occasion, he sent a police official part of a kidney from one of his victims. The accompanying letter said in part, "I ate the rest and it was delicious."

He also has another distinction that, for better or worse, continues: striking from out of the dark then disappearing forever. The terror he created remained as his legacy. No one felt safe, and many suspected friends and acquaintances of being the faceless monster. After the murder of Mary Kelly on 8 November 1888, Jack disappeared. He was never apprehended.

As Jack faded from center stage, his successors seemed to concentrate on the western side of the Atlantic. The following decades would see occasional instances of serial murderers. Men appeared like Carl Panzram, whose basic philosophy of life was that most human beings were too ignorant to be allowed to live. He killed twenty-one people and sodomized over one thousand males. Executed in 1930, he laughed on the gallows. Earle Nelson, who traveled around the United States and Canada, raped and murdered twenty-two women. His crimes were so brutal the press dubbed him "The Gorilla Killer." Crimes of that type occurred but infrequently. Most of the killers were never apprehended, and those who were have long since been obscured by time.

Serial murder is largely an American phenomenon. In the span between 1900 and 2010, 4,479 serial murderers were identified worldwide. America, with a little over four percent of the world's population, produced 3,092 (sixty-nine percent) of those—over twice as many as the rest of the countries on earth combined.

A number of factors have converged in America to create this climate for murder. First, they include the absolute freedom of movement enjoyed by Americans. No checkpoints in the United States block passage from state to state. The vast distances making up the American landscape allow a murderer to kill victims hundreds, if not thousands, of miles apart within a day or so. Second, the obsessive respect for privacy upon which we insist, combined with our rights under the First Amendment, handicap police efforts to collect intelligence data that could lead to apprehension in crimes of this type. Lastly, the over 17,985 autonomous law enforcement agencies in this country are simply too numerous and communicate too poorly to work well together. Given these and other factors, it is conceivable that a fully developed serial murderer could take literally hundreds of lives and stop only when incarcerated or dead.

The very things that go into making up the so-called "American character"—our willingness to trust others, our reliance on authority figures, our fondness for helping those we consider disadvantaged, and our almost limitless gullibility—are also the things that make it possible for these killers to identify and take their victims with ease. Tragically, most victims thoughtlessly place themselves in jeopardy. They pay for their trust with their lives.

Beginning with Albert DeSalvo (the Boston Strangler) and continuing through the current search for the Long Island Serial Killer, serial murderers have become a part of our everyday lives. Probably every American can name four or five serial murderers. Their names roll off the tongue as readily as movie stars: Juan Corona, Wayne Williams, the Hillside Strangler, Gacy, Bundy, Son of Sam, and the Green River Killer. These are some who have been apprehended.

Although we, the authors, have serious reservations about

the guilt of some of the individuals mentioned, they all have been convicted of several homicides and are believed to be guilty of many more. Each of these individuals has been linked to at least five victims. For our research into serial murderers, we primarily have used the period between 1971 and 1981, because a vast amount of material is available on these criminals, and Kenneth Bianchi and Wayne Williams are still living as of 2021.

For over two decades, those murderers littered the streets and countryside of America with bodies. Why? Who are they? From where do they come? How can they be stopped? These questions have answers; some of them are unpleasant. In researching this work, we, the authors, were confronted not only with the statistics of unsolved homicides but with an indictment of law enforcement agencies and their techniques. Serious questions were raised about the effectiveness of the judicial system and its stepchild, the corrections system. We also found that public apathy toward violent crime has facilitated the creation of an environment where killers like these not only exist but thrive.

Murderers, like their victims, do not exist in a vacuum. To understand them, we must understand their world. To understand the shark, you must learn something about the ocean. Because we do not know who the uncaught ones are, we can only use what we know about those who have been apprehended to speculate about the others. In the succeeding chapters, we will examine as much as is known about a number of these individuals. Some factors to watch are child abuse, sexual deviance, lack of identity and feelings of alienation, opportunity, mobility, drugs, alcohol, and media attention. We then will create a general profile of modern serial murderers. The origins, motivations, and techniques of these individuals comprise the most frightening mystery of our time. Whatever the cause, be it physiological, psychological, or spiritual, the result is a new variety of human predator.

JUAN CORONA: UNANSWERED QUESTIONS

Nineteen seventy-one was a good year for murder. The year-long trial of the Manson family continued in Los Angeles. In March, Lieutenant William Calley was found guilty of the mass murders at My Lai in Vietnam. The Texas Strangler killed his eleventh victim in August and disappeared. The Zodiac Killer took his last victim in San Francisco and also disappeared. But the biggest event of that year was the arrest and indictment of a Mexican immigrant in Yuba City, California.

The questions inherent in the matter of Juan Corona are engrossing and more than a little frightening. Years after his arrest and conviction for twenty-five murders, the case of Juan Corona remains as baffling as it was then.

Juan Vallejo Corona was born in Autlan, Mexico, in 1934. One of ten children, his mother affectionately called him "Juanita," little Juan. Autlan, situated 120 miles south of Guadalajara, is a small town whose only industry was a sugar mill. Poverty in Mexico in the 1930s was even more dramatic than it is today. Rearing a family of ten on the meager income made from picking crops or working at the mill proved extremely difficult. The despair, malnutrition, and hopelessness of abject poverty were simply facts of life. Like so many Hispanics before and since, Juan Corona at an early age began looking north to the United States.

In 1950, Juan followed his older brothers, Natividad and Felix, across the border as an illegal alien. He was sixteen and spoke virtually no English. He found himself in America doing exactly what he would have done in Autlan—picking crops. His only saleable attributes were a strong back and a willingness to work.

By 1952 at age eighteen, he obtained a better job driving a truck for one of the construction companies building Folsom Dam. Life had begun to look up for young Juan.

Corona, now reaching maturity, was a stocky, muscular, young man with flashing dark eyes and a ready smile. The long

11

hours driving the gravel truck did not stop him from enjoying life in his new land. Weekends and evenings were spent socializing and dancing. Five feet eleven inches and 185 pounds, Juan was a talented dancer and attractive to women. Despite the temptations and attractions of the new land, Juan remained loyal to his family. He sent part of his paycheck home every week and usually made the two-thousand-mile roundtrip journey to Autlan for the holidays.

In January of 1953, Corona met and fell in love with a girl from Sacramento. Also Hispanic, her family had been in the United States for many years, and she had been educated in the Sacramento school system. Their attraction for each other quickly led them into difficulty. Like teenagers before and since, they stayed out late and sneaked around to see each other. Under pressure from her family, they were told to marry. Driving to Reno, they wed in the early spring of 1953.

His new bride did not want to leave her family and live at the Folsom construction site. Juan gave up his gravel truck job, and they moved to Sacramento. She found a job as an office worker and he as a common laborer. Within weeks it was obvious that, love match or not, the marriage was doomed. Urged by her family and Juan's brother, Natividad, the couple went to a priest, and the marriage was annulled.

Leaving Sacramento, Juan again found himself working in the fields. He found better employment working in a gypsum plant in the winter. Living with his brother, Nat, near Yuba City, Juan scraped and saved every penny for the day when he could head his own company. During that period, his older brother also taught Juan the contract labor business.

Contract labor, or casual labor as it is sometimes called, is a tradition in the farm industry. Because of the vast size of many California produce farms and the need for intermittent labor-intensive work, this practice is common. At certain times of the year, labor contractors, who are state licensed middlemen, provide large numbers of seasonal workers. These are usually unskilled workers obtained by recruiting in skid row areas. Working from dawn to dark for several weeks, they are then idle until the next seasonal demand. The labor contractor makes his income by charging a fee to the farm owner, then paying the laborers the absolute minimum and pocketing the difference.

Two days before Christmas 1955, as the brothers prepared for their annual journey to Autlan, one of the worst rainstorms in California history broke a levee in the Yuba City/Marysville area. The region was flooded, and reports of drowned bodies were common. By mid-January, the area remained largely under water, but those who had been evacuated began to return.

On 11 January 1956, Natividad petitioned the court for an involuntary civil commitment against Juan. He said that Juan, who had a lifelong fear of water, thought that the people he was seeing on the streets of Yuba City were dead and that a calamity of biblical proportions had taken place. It was later established that forty people had, indeed, drowned. Nat said Juan had gone mad and was spending all his time praying and reading the Bible.

At Nat's urging, Juan saw two doctors who indicated that they thought he was schizophrenic. Those physicians were not psychiatrists, but the mental health law at the time allowed them to certify him as incompetent. Juan was transported in handcuffs to the DeWitt State Hospital in Auburn, California. The decision was made to deal with his alleged malady using ECT, electro-convulsive therapy, commonly known as "shock treatment."

The incident was typical of the primitive level of mental health treatment in America during the mid-1950s. A man with a limited command of the English language was alleged to be mentally ill, certified as ill by individuals with no competence in the field, transported in handcuffs by armed guards to a secure hospital facility, diagnosed as schizophrenic and combative, and given ECT—all within a period of one week.

During the next several weeks, Corona was subjected to a cycle of twenty-two shock treatments. That technological approach was much in vogue in the United States in the 1950s. Little-known side effects like memory loss and muscle spasms later brought ECT into disfavor with the psychiatric profession. Today, it is used very rarely and then only with individuals who are suffering from the most acute forms of psychosis and/or depression.

Juan was released from Auburn on 18 April 1956. He was freed with the understanding that he would return to Mexico and reside there with one of his brothers. Juan would later say he knew he had been ill but could remember nothing of the events leading up to and including his hospitalization.

Within months, Juan returned to the United States, that time with a valid resident alien work permit. Returning to Yuba City, Juan again moved in with Nat. Apparently, the hospital incident did not cause any ill will between the brothers.

Juan, now twenty-two years old, had changed dramatically. He no longer drank and was interested only in business. When he went to bars at all, he drank coffee. His quiet, courtly demeanor generated many acquaintances but no close friends. Back working in the fields again, he filled his idle hours with odd jobs around the community.

The next three years were largely uneventful. Juan and Nat lived together in the house they were jointly buying, and life was quiet for both. During that period, however, Juan's suspicions about his brother's sexual orientation began to increase. For years, he had heard Nat was a homosexual. Now he strongly suspected that was, indeed, the case.

In 1958, Nat signed over his labor contracting business to Juan for a percentage of the profits. Nat, in partnership with a local man named Ray Duron, opened the Guadalajara Cafe in Yuba City. Some local people suspected Duron was sexually involved with Natividad Corona. The speculation has never been proven. However, it is known that Duron had co-signed the commitment documents used to hospitalize Juan.

The following year, 1959, Juan met and married Gloria Moreno. Gloria, also a resident alien, had been working as a cook in one of the nearby labor camps. The courtship and marriage were old world: love and romance were minor issues alongside practicality, hard work, and the desire to start a family. As is often the case, their practical marriage survived as romantic marriages failed all around them.

Juan took marriage as seriously as he did his business. Gloria was protected and sheltered to the degree that she never had to learn English or to drive a car.

Juan and Gloria also undertook the task of buying Nat's share of the house and vehicles the two brothers had purchased jointly. For many years, Juan had been rankled about the price his brother charged him for those items.

In 1960, the first of the four Corona daughters was born. Juan and his family were well on their way to middle-class affluence. Within a few years, he had become a reputable businessman. Widely respected by both growers and workers, he specialized in

Native American and Hispanic labor.

Unlike his brother, Juan made a serious attempt to screen his laborers for honesty and reliability. Juan also avoided using women and children because of his concern for their safety. The only time Anglo laborers were hired was during the brief peach harvest in August and September.

By the middle 1960s, Corona was well established. In 1966, he received the labor contract for the Sullivan ranch, a large commercial fruit growing operation. As part of the contract, he also gained unlimited access at no cost to a bunkhouse and kitchen for his laborers.

In 1970, he joined a prestigious Mexican American group known as La Association de los Charros. The group, although ostensibly an organization to promote horsemanship, was, in fact, a loose brotherhood of successful California-based Mexican Americans.

Life was not going as well for brother Nat. In February 1970, another local Hispanic, Jose Raya, was found in the men's room of the Guadalajara Cafe. A large portion of his face, including his lips, had been hacked away with a meat cleaver. The incident occurred between midnight and one in the morning, and no one in the establishment admitted seeing anything. Police investigators were told by Natividad Corona that his brother, Juan, had been the one who discovered the injured man. He attempted to imply Juan was responsible and mentioned Juan's so-called "nervous breakdown" fifteen years earlier.

Raya subsequently filed suit against Nat and Juan. He swore Nat was the one who had actually chopped him.

The reason for the attack was never clarified, but a persistent rumor said it occurred when Raya rejected a sexual overture by Nat. In October, Nat quickly sold his property and belongings to another brother, Pedro, and fled to Mexico. He allegedly never returned to the United States. Evidence arose later that indicated Natividad Corona was then suffering from the tertiary stage of syphilis. That stage of the disease, sometimes called paresis, causes insanity and eventual agonizing death. This is the same disease from which Al Capone suffered and died in 1947.

As a result of the lawsuit, a default judgment of a quarter million dollars was levied against Nat. The court dismissed all allegations against Juan. After Nat's departure, life for the Corona family resumed its familiar routine. It is unknown whether Juan and his family went to Autlan for Christmas that year. If they did, they would undoubtedly have seen Uncle Nat. Persistent rumors stated Nat had been seen in the Yuba City area in early 1971.

On 20 May 1971, an orchard owner named Garo Kagehiro found a hole dug among his peach trees. The hole was the size of a grave. At the time, he thought nothing of it and assumed soil testers from the California Department of Agriculture had made the hole. By coincidence, he returned to the orchard later in the day. The hole had been filled in and now definitely looked like a grave. Kagehiro immediately called the police.

The first officers on the scene excavated the hole and uncovered the remains of forty-year-old Kenneth Edward Whitacre. Whitacre, a California native, had been seen in Yuba City in early afternoon the previous day. An Air Force veteran, Whitacre took up a transient lifestyle after his discharge. He had worked as a casual laborer in the Yuba City area for a long time.

The cause of death was a large stab wound in the left chest that severed the aorta. Cuts on his hands and cheek were consistent with what pathologists call "defense wounds." These are usually incurred when the victim attempts to protect his body with the hands and forearms. Numerous postmortem wounds were largely confined to the head and apparently were made with a heavy-bladed instrument, such as a machete or meat cleaver. A machete is more probable as it also could inflict a stab wound, where a cleaver is not designed to cause a penetration cut. Whitacre had been attacked so savagely that one of the head wounds penetrated the scalp and both layers of the skull, exposing the brain.

The bottom of the grave had been lined with the victim's overcoat. The corpse had been carefully laid out, then covered with dirt. The grave was a considerable distance inside the perimeter of Kagehiro's orchard. Tire tracks were discovered and preserved from a nearby dirt road.

The body was removed and taken to a local funeral home for autopsy. The next day, police investigators, struck by the similarity of the injuries between Whitacre and the Raya case the previous year, began looking at Juan Corona as a suspect. Natividad Corona, although the one thought to be guilty of the Raya slashing, was not considered a suspect as he was allegedly out of the country.

The succeeding days became occupied by the initial attempts of the authorities to lay the Whitacre killing at Juan's feet. A mysterious informant, who has never been identified, contacted police and made a statement to the effect that Juan Corona's temper was so bad he frequently had fits of rage that were only curtailed by his family forcibly restraining him until he calmed down. The allegation was later proven to be completely false.

On 25 May, five days after the discovery of the body in the Kagehiro orchard, the storm hovering over Juan Corona finally broke. Workers on the Sullivan ranch, the primary contract for Corona, had found another grave the night before. Uncertain as to what to do, they waited until six the next morning to report the find. The foreman to whom they reported was none other than Ray Duron.

Following the workers back to the site, Duron determined something was, indeed, amiss. By seven o'clock, he had contacted ranch owner Sullivan, who came out and looked at the shallow grave. Sullivan instructed Duron to call the sheriff immediately. By eight, Sutter County Sheriff Roy Whiteaker arrived on the scene. At that point, what must be considered one of the poorest crime scene investigations in the history of American justice commenced.

In a situation like this, the standard approach is to secure a perimeter of many yards around the site of the grave. Excavation would then begin but only to the point of determining whether or not the site in question did contain a body. At that time, additional resources would be brought to bear. These could include a medical examiner or coroner, evidence technicians, forensic photographers, and possibly pathologists or forensic specialists. In some jurisdictions, a representative of the local prosecutor's office would also be summoned. The crime scene would be secured, and only professional law enforcement personnel allowed access. The number of people in the perimeter would be severely limited, and every effort made to preserve the scene and any potential evidence therein. This approach is especially important in serial murder cases where the evidence may be jumbled, confusing, and inadequate. None of this was done.

Rather, Ray Duron and a Sutter County detective simply began to dig. The shallow grave quickly revealed its contents. The body was later determined to be that of sixty-seven-year-old

Charles Fleming. The body was removed from the ground and transported to a local funeral parlor. There is no indication that the crime scene was secured or that any search for peripheral evidence was conducted.

By midafternoon, the sheriff was back in his office. The autopsy revealed the death wounds were very similar to those of the man found on the Kagehiro property. Sheriff Whiteaker, apparently, began to suspect that he had a "wino slasher" on his hands. Whiteaker also learned of a missing persons report on another transient, Sigurd Beierman, a long-time resident of the Marysville "wino park."

In late afternoon, Whiteaker decided to conduct a comprehensive search of the area where the second body had been uncovered. That portion of the Sullivan ranch abutted the Feather River on the east and a flood levee on the west. By six p.m., Whiteaker and a number of deputies arrived back on the scene. Overhead, the gray spring skies promised a rainy night.

Searching south to north in the narrow strip of land, they discovered dried blood on the grass in a prune orchard. Within a half hour, another body was brought to the surface. The body, later identified as Melford Sample, was searched before it was even removed from the grave. Documents, including two meat purchase receipts, were found in the pockets. The name on those receipts was Juan Corona. They were dated 21 May 1971, the day after the discovery of the first body. By now, the dark skies and rain began to make the search difficult.

During the time the third grave was being excavated, four more graves were discovered in quick succession. It appears at that point simultaneous searches and excavations occurred in the dark in the rain by a large number of untrained people. The possibility of untainted evidence recovery was now lowered to nearly zero.

The fourth body to be recovered was a white male who has never been identified. The fifth and sixth, Donald Smith and John Haluka, were out of the ground by nine-thirty that evening. Within an hour, another unidentified victim had been recovered. Five bodies had been uncovered so far, and deputies had discovered two more graves. The rain increased in intensity. The scene that night must have resembled something from an Alfred Hitchcock film.

By ten-forty-five, Sheriff Whiteaker and the district attorney began the process of requesting a search warrant for the home of Juan Vallejo Corona. The request was based on the signed receipts found in one of the graves, the fact Corona was in the area almost daily, and the similarity between the death wounds and the injuries inflicted on Jose Raya the year before.

Both the rain and the digging continued. By a little after eleven p.m., victim number eight, Warren Kelley, had been uncovered. Shortly after midnight, Sigurd Beierman, the only one of the victims ever to be listed as a missing person, was no longer missing. During the previous hour, three more graves had been discovered, bringing the total for that night alone to ten. In six hours, ten graves had been discovered and seven excavated.

Finally, a little before one in the morning, the decision was made to stop and wait for daylight. The delay was based on the lateness of the hour, the weather, the exhaustion of the searchers, and the large number of corpses already found.

The decision to stop proved a wise one. No one will ever know what evidence either for or against Juan Corona was destroyed by the frantic, haphazard, and unprofessional approach used during the evening. The conditions for proper recovery simply had been ignored. Large numbers of people moving back and forth, around, over, and sometimes inside the grave sites themselves; adverse weather conditions; and the continual handling by untrained personnel of the material removed from the graves leave one convinced that evidence that would have been revealed by an orderly search had been lost forever.

Shortly after two a.m. on the morning of 26 May, a judge authorized a search of the home of Juan Corona. Mr. and Mrs. Corona had been living for some time in the small community of Live Oak, roughly halfway between Yuba City and Marysville. The search warrant was executed at three-fifteen a.m. The Coronas were roused from their beds and the search began. A bilingual interpreter did not arrive until nearly four. By the time he arrived, the search was underway. The interpreter never read the terms of the search warrant to Corona. At four-forty-five a.m., he did, however, read Juan his Miranda rights. Corona later recalled the only thing he could remember the man saying to him was he should get a lawyer as soon as possible.

The search of the house produced a number of items: kitchen

knives, a crowbar, a machete, a meat cleaver, some ledgers and check stubs, a checkbook, and a posthole digger. A wooden club and two pairs of men's shorts were also taken.

The search warrant also included the bunkhouse at the Sullivan ranch. The search revealed a loaded 9mm pistol, cartridges, and several knives. A little before five a.m., Corona, now formally under arrest, was handcuffed and taken to jail.

By then, the press became aware of the large number of bodies already uncovered. By noon on the twenty-sixth, the city began filling up with reporters. Unlike most major serial murder cases, the local citizenry seemed remarkably unconcerned. None of the usual hysteria or fear associated with cases of that type occurred. The victims were not members of the community as such and were viewed as so much disposable human trash.

Back in the orchards, the digging resumed. Between nine-thirty and eleven-thirty a.m., three additional bodies were uncovered. Of those, only one would ever be identified. Victim number eleven, William Kamp, was also the only one who died of gunshot wounds.

Shortly after noon on 26 May, Juan Corona was arraigned on ten counts of first-degree murder. The total included the body found in the Kagehiro orchard six days before and nine that had now been excavated on the Sullivan property. By afternoon, both grass and reporters covered the courthouse lawn.

The court, recognizing Corona's inability to pay for his own defense, provided him with counsel at public expense. Even in the early 1970s, defense counsel on a crime of that type would have run into many thousands of dollars. The first thing Corona's attorney did was to request and obtain a delay of one week before the entry of a plea on the charges. He justified that by saying so much time was needed to study the complaint and the available police evidence. Corona was returned to jail.

The judge, aware of the increasing media pressure for information, interviews, and comments about the matter, issued the first of four gag orders forbidding all parties from discussing any aspect of the case not already public record. All parties would basically ignore the gag orders. What they said, didn't say, or implied in response to media questions gave reporters the impression their queries had merit.

Sheriff Whiteaker, who obviously had no experience in dealing with a matter of national interest, made numerous statements including "We are sure he committed the murders." That may not have been in direct violation of the gag order, but it certainly gave it a close shave.

Meanwhile, the ever-helpful Ray Duron located a thirteenth grave. He also prepared a map of the Sullivan property showing where Juan Corona allegedly had been seen in the previous weeks. The map quickly came to the attention of the news reporters. It was incorrectly attributed to Juan and referred to in numerous stories as the "death map." Juan Corona did not draw the map and was unaware of its existence. Ray Duron, the close friend and former business partner of Nat, seemed particularly determined to make certain law enforcement investigators became aware of the relationship between Juan and the Sullivan ranch.

The search and digging resumed on 27 May. From then on, the Sullivan ranch took on aspects of a side show. Many reporters from television, radio, and newspapers appeared on the scene. Virtually everyone with an interest in the matter arrived at the orchard. The only exception was Corona's lawyer, who had been specifically forbidden by law enforcement agencies to go there. As searching and digging continued, the decision was made to use a backhoe in excavating further suspected graves.

It is interesting to compare the difference between the forensic techniques used on the Corona case with the Gacy case several years later. In the Gacy case, the bodies of the victims were uncovered with a care and precision matching that of a professional archaeologist on an excavation. In the Corona case, the bodies were dug hurriedly, in the dark, in the rain, and eventually, with a backhoe.

The thirteenth body was Clarence Hocking, a fiftythree-year-old transient from Illinois. In the grave with him was half a bottle of wine and a Friskies dog food bag. Number fourteen, James Howard, had been seen alive on 11 May. Number fifteen, "Jack" Smallwood, and number sixteen, Elbert Riley, had both disappeared on 12 May. One witness later said he saw them getting into a truck with the name Juan V. Corona painted on the side.

The next four bodies were excavated in quick succession using the backhoe. The last victim found that night was a local Native American, one of two non-Caucasians found. The digging went on until well after dark. For the second day in a row, a heavy rain was falling. The dark and wet were mitigated only slightly by using floodlights. That necessitated even more tampering with the site. Power cables now ran in all directions.

After the night of 27 May, five more bodies were uncovered. Of those, the twenty-first was a black man, the second nonwhite. Two bodies were found on 29 May and the last two around 5 June. The last victim recovered had two bank deposit slips with the name Juan Corona in his pocket. The total, counting the body taken from the Kagehiro property, was twenty-five. On 2 June, Juan Corona pled not guilty to all charges. Bail was denied.

Juan's attorney, Public Defender Roy Van den Heuval, began the process of preparing a defense. He proposed the use of the so-called "insanity defense." He was stymied in his effort by the Corona family. None of them were willing to authorize psychiatric examinations because of their absolute conviction Juan was both innocent and sane.

On 13 June, by mutual agreement, Van den Heuval withdrew as counsel for Juan Corona. Appointed in his place was Richard Hawk. Hawk, an experienced criminal attorney, almost immediately signed a contract with Juan for the literary rights on the case in lieu of other payment. From the moment of his entry into the case to the trial nearly two years later, Hawk left a trail of grandstanding and confusion, some of which has never been sorted out or understood. The Hispanics involved with the case nicknamed him "El Gavilan," which means "The Hawk" in Spanish. Some court watchers thought the name should have been "The Vulture."

Hawk's first action was to file a $350 million lawsuit against Sutter County, the location of the crimes, for slander and false arrest. Hawk would later say the ploy was designed to bring media attention to his client and to raise the morale of the Corona family. It is undoubtedly only coincidental the move also brought considerable media attention to Richard Hawk.

The background investigation into the crimes continued. The California Department of Criminal Investigation determined the bullet removed from the one victim who had been shot was a 9mm slug. That was consistent with the caliber of a gun, alleged to be Corona's, recovered during the search of the Sullivan ranch bunkhouse. Ballistics tests could not positively identify the bullet as having come from Juan's gun. The blood found on the machete recovered in Corona's garage did not match any of the victims tested.

The last of the victims was exhumed in early June. The autopsies now completed gave a consistent victim profile: all adult males over the age of forty, only two—a black and a Native American—were nonwhites. The victims are interesting considering the fact subsequent profiling and research has indicated serial killers normally kill within their own racial group. None of the victims was Hispanic. All the victims were itinerant farm workers.

The autopsies conducted on the first group of bodies revealed consistency in wound types and gave a rough estimate of the time span of the murders. The actual cause of death for all the victims, except for one, was hacking and stabbing wounds concentrated on the head and upper chest. One victim was shot in the head. Most of the victims were buried face up, and several had their shirts raised covering their heads. It is possible that was done to absorb blood loss as the victims were transported from the places where they were killed to their burial sites. There was no genital mutilation, although six had no trousers and one was nude from the waist down. None of the bodies had been in the ground more than six weeks, and some had been interred within the previous few days. That indicated the killings were still going on after the discovery of the body on the Kagehiro property.

One of the items seized from the Corona home on the night of his arrest was a ledger. It contained the names of several hundred men who had worked for Juan. Police authorities discovered the names of eight of the victims in the ledger. When that information was released to the media, it was subsequently referred to as "Corona's death list." That type of overblown and misinterpreted publicity became common.

In mid-June, Corona, still in the Sutter County jail, began to complain of chest pains. He was hospitalized with a suspected heart attack. A medical exam determined Corona either had had a heart attack or had come very close to having one. The physician in charge was concerned Juan might not survive preliminary hearings. Medications including Thorazine, a potent tranquilizer, were prescribed. Corona remained in the hospital for three weeks.

His illness gave the prosecution additional time to prepare their case against Corona. The authorities became very concerned he would die in custody, thereby opening the door to a wrongful death action against Sutter County.

On 1 July 1971, a Grand Jury convened in Sutter County to examine the evidence against Juan Vallejo Corona and to determine whether sufficient cause existed to bind him over for trial. They remained in session for twelve days, examined documents and forensic evidence, and questioned fifty-seven witnesses. At the conclusion, the vote was taken, and Corona was indicted on twenty-five counts of first-degree murder.

The formal indictments were handed down on 27 July. No one knew it would be well over a year before trial would commence. The intervening months were filled with the legal maneuvering, posturing, and manipulating common with cases of this type. Among issues raised were the question of venue and whether Corona could get a fair trial in Sutter County, the admissibility of certain items of evidence, allegations that evidence had been withheld from the defense, and the question of Corona's competence to stand trial. In the meantime, Juan was in and out of the hospital with recurring chest pains and other ailments.

In defiance of a court order, the Sutter County sheriff had personally hired a psychiatrist and placed him in the jail with Corona. Neither Corona, the prosecution, nor the defense knew about the move. The psychiatrist talked to Juan for an hour, then gave a report saying he had found no evidence of psychosis, but Corona was a hazard to himself and should be hospitalized for observation. Why the sheriff was not cited for contempt and jailed for his flagrant defiance of the rights of Corona and the order of the court is unknown.

In February 1972, the California Supreme Court voided the state's death penalty. The court said it constituted cruel and unusual punishment. However, they also took the position that individuals charged with death penalty crimes prior to their decision still would not be eligible for bail. Juan Corona remained in custody.

As the months went by, Juan Corona's status in the Hispanic community became almost that of a folk hero. Many saw him as the innocent pawn of the police who were desperately trying to cover up their own bungling and poor investigation. It was commonly thought the real killer was Natividad Corona. Nat was believed to be living in Mexico.

Also, attorney Hawk won his argument for a change of venue from Suter County to Slolano County. At last, on 11 September 1972, jury selection began for the trial in Fairfield, California, over sixty miles from Yuba City. The trial proper started on the twenty-ninth. By then, Juan Corona had already been in jail for 473 days.

The prosecution began the laborious task of presenting its case in an understandable way to the jury. From the first day, it was obvious they were facing an uphill battle. In the year and a half since the first body was uncovered, the initial confusion had been compounded many times. The jury faced conflicting information at three levels: the police investigation, the forensics of the case, and the implications of the rules of criminal procedure.

The police investigation, as discussed above, had been seriously mismanaged. Evidence taken from the graves was handled barehanded by many people. The use of a backhoe demolished the gravesites and made thorough investigation of the area impossible. Evidence was mislabeled, the bodies were mislabeled, and, in some cases, incorrectly identified, and some evidence was simply missing. Even the judge was outraged by the mess police and the prosecution had made of the evidence.

The police records in the case were filled with errors. One of the most glaring was a map showing the graves of the twenty-five victims. It was seven feet high, and each grave was shown by a blinking light. When questioned, however, one investigator was forced to concede the map conflicted with the police reports in five instances, with one grave being located in the middle of the Feather River.

Forensic tests failed to include extensive blood and fluid workups that are indicated in cases of this type. No testing was done for sexual activity on any of the victims, including the most recent who had been dead only a matter of hours. The completed blood tests proved rudimentary and inconclusive. No solid link to Corona was obtained from any of the physical evidence except the receipts found on two victims. Even with that evidence, questions arose about the possibility they might have been planted. The inadequate chain of custody beginning in the peach orchard made such accusations impossible to completely refute. The prosecution was forced to concede, because of the confusion in linking items of evidence to specific victims, they no longer could be certain even of the validity of the receipts.

The prosecution relied on a chain of circumstantial evidence and conjecture in making their case against Corona. The foundations of their case included some tire tracks that were similar to those left by Corona's vehicle and statements from several of Sullivan's field hands about seeing Corona in odd places around the ranch at varying times. Two out of three handwriting experts testified they were certain at least some of the names in the so-called "death ledger" had been written by Corona. Juan owned a 9mm pistol matching the caliber of weapon used to kill the one victim who died by gunshot. Jose Raya was also brought to the stand, allegedly to testify Juan had offered him a job. Courthouse cynics speculated Raya's testimony was to actually give the jury a look at his face and the scars of the attack three years before.

On 10 October, the prosecution admitted publicly they had doubts about Corona's guilt and the outcome of the trial.

Suddenly, new physical evidence in the form of tire tracks appeared. Those tracks matched Corona's vehicle. The tracks allegedly had been obtained sixteen months before and mislaid. A total of 1,650 pages of evidence, previously unknown to the defense despite the discovery process, also appeared during the course of the trial. The trial ended with four times as much evidence as had been available to the defense at the beginning.

The question of blood proved troublesome. Where had the victims been killed? Wounds of the type they suffered would have produced copious bleeding. Yet only flecks of blood were found any place where Corona was known to have been. That blood was also inconclusively typed. Juan's own blood type brought confusion when he was determined to be type A by police when he was, in fact, type O.

The weeks dragged on. Defense attorney Hawk, cited for contempt nearly twenty times, faced two and a half months in jail when the trial concluded. The prosecution was also cited numerous times. The judge had long since passed the point where he was willing to tolerate the courtroom shenanigans of the trial attorneys. He, however, refused to allow the defense to raise the possibility the crimes might have been committed by someone else. Certainly, if the jury had been aware of the behavior of Natividad Corona, they might have looked at the matter differently.

On the last day of 1972, defense counsel Richard Hawk made the decision not to call any witnesses on behalf of his client. The decision was a calculated risk Hawk decided to take. He was subsequently subjected to considerable criticism. Some of the criticism appeared to be legitimate. However, his decision was understandable. Hawk proceeded from the assumption the prosecution's case was so weak and riddled with error they had failed even to begin to prove Corona's guilt, let alone prove it beyond a reasonable doubt. On the other hand, his was a surprisingly naive approach for a trial lawyer to take. Juries will almost always assume it is as much the responsibility of the defendant to prove his innocence as it is for the prosecution to prove his guilt. The lack of witnesses to substantiate Corona's private explanations for various statements and items of evidence did nothing to ease that attitude as he did not testify.

Corona had explained the blood flecks in his vehicle by pointing out one of his daughters was subject to chronic nosebleeds. The jury never knew that. He also claimed to have carried an injured and bleeding worker to the hospital in his van. The jury never knew that information. He had suffered an infection in his leg and groin that would have made it nearly impossible for him to lift and move the bodies buried in April of 1971. The jury never learned those details. He also had a substantial alibi for the afternoon of 19 May when Kenneth Whitacre had been killed. The jury never heard that. The entire trial was flawed by a lack of rebuttal from the defense.

Final arguments lasted through 11 January 1973. Juan Corona now had been in jail for 590 days. As the trial ended after nearly four months, an aura of confusion about the entire matter still surrounded the case. The press repeatedly speculated the case would not end with conviction.

The courtroom battle continued and raged in the deliberations of the jury. Beginning with a seven-to-five vote for acquittal, the jury struggled for several days. On two separate occasions, they reported to the judge they were unable to reach a decision. On each occasion, the judge read them the jury instruction, sometimes called the "Allen" or "dynamite charge." This instruction calls for the jury speedily to resolve their differences and to reach a verdict to avoid a mistrial.

On 18 January, after forty-six hours and sixteen ballots, the jury found Juan Corona guilty on all counts.

Jurors later said the reasons for the verdict were Corona's failure to prove his innocence and a conviction that the matter would be re-examined through the avenue of appeal and retrial. One juror stated she still harbored serious doubts as to his guilt and felt he deserved a retrial. Several others commented Corona failed to prove he didn't commit the murders. Another said even with no evidence to show Corona's machete killed Whitacre, the defense failed to prove it "had not been used to kill the other twenty-four."

The United States Constitution states a defendant is innocent until proven guilty. In reality, the burden on the defendant to prove his innocence is often heavier in the eyes of the jury than the state's burden of proving his guilt. If juries were composed of lawyers rather than ordinary citizens, this concern would probably not exist. However, average jurors want to hear both sides of the story. Failing that, they'll usually go with what they have heard.

Corona's motions for a retrial were denied in early February 1973. He was sentenced to twenty-five consecutive life terms in prison. The laborious appeal process began with Corona in prison.

The years and the subsequent legal maneuvering went by. Juan, not a troublesome inmate, was the target of harassment by other prisoners. On one occasion, he was attacked and stabbed thirty-two times. He was blinded in one eye, and a piece of knife blade was permanently embedded in his skull.

The appellate issues were finally decided in May 1978. Juan, represented by two new attorneys, Alan Exelrod and Michael Mendelson, still maintained his innocence. His conviction was overturned and a new trial ordered. The state of California, however, spent four more years appealing that reversal.

The facts used to reverse the original conviction are indicative of the confused mess the entire case had become. The court said basically three reasons applied for overturning the conviction. The first was the fact Corona had been convicted entirely on circumstantial evidence without any hard facts or witnesses to link him to the crimes. Circumstantial evidence plays a major role in most criminal cases that go to trial. Yet American courts have always harbored an instinctive distrust of purely circumstantial cases. The feeling is, as it well should be, that additional evidence should be brought forward to link the defendant and the crime together.

The second reason for the reversal was the fact the defense attorney, Richard Hawk, had signed an exclusive literary and film contract with Juan Corona before the trial even began. In its opinion, the court said the act resulted in "an outrageous abrogation" of Corona's rights and "rendered the trial a farce and a mockery." The issue of literary rights arose again and again in the decades after the Corona trial. The matter finally came to a head in 1980 when several states, because of the Gacy case, passed what are called "profit from crime" laws. Those statutes make it illegal for a defendant, and by derivation his attorney, to profit in any way from criminal acts. That includes monies gained from selling book or movie rights.

The very concept of making a buck from human suffering is anathema to Americans. The fact Richard Hawk stood to gain financially from the Corona case, win or lose, stands as an indictment of his ethics and skill as an attorney and leaves an unavoidable taint on the entire 1973 trial.

The third reason was Hawk's failure to raise the issue of insanity as a potential defense. Hawk said that was not done so the defense could avoid giving the prosecution a potential motive. Given the nature of the insanity defense, it was a logical, if somewhat flawed, move. As it was, motive was never established.

The second trial began in on 22 February 1982, in Hayward, California. Under California law, a life sentence prisoner is eligible for parole after seven years. Juan had been eligible for release since 1980.

Imagine the same case tried with even less evidence than was available the first time. The intervening years had taken their toll. Four of the witnesses were dead, the blood samples had deteriorated to dust, and the fingertips used to identify the victims had been eaten by rats. Over fifty defense witnesses testified, including Juan. He was only asked two questions, answering "yes" he understood the state accused him of killing twenty-five men and "no" he did not kill the men.

Corona, now represented by four lawyers, sat through a second examination of the events from that lost spring eleven years before. The same judge, Richard Patton, presided. Some of the issues not raised in the first trial, however, were now brought forward. The question of Natividad Corona was made public at last. Nat, now thought to have died of syphilis in 1973, was presented to the jury as an alternate suspect. Still, when it was over, Juan was convicted and sentenced a second time.

Corona never received a parole, being denied eight times. On 4 March 2019, he died of dementia at age eighty-five in the California State Prison in Corcoran. Gloria Moreno, his wife, had divorced him in 1974 citing irreconcilable differences.

The final irony of the Corona case is inherent in the second trial. Most Americans believe the appellate system is designed to correct injustices that occur during an initial trial. The concept is valid. However, a second trial conducted more than a decade after the first is an injustice in its own right regardless of the outcome.

After a seven-month second trial, Juan Corona had been tried and convicted twice on each of twenty-five homicides. Despite the decision of the jury, the unanswered questions remain. This case, more than any other we will examine, demonstrates the need for the highest possible levels of skill, professionalism, and integrity by the legal authorities in dealing with serial murder cases.

John Wayne Gacy: Killer Clown

John Wayne Gacy Jr. was born on 17 March 1942 in Chicago, Illinois. His parents were of Polish and Danish descent and had been married in 1938. At the time of John's birth, his father was well into middle age. His mother, a native of Wisconsin, was a thirty-three-year-old housewife. John had two sisters, one older and one younger.

It is tempting to speculate along Freudian lines when examining John's nature and early life. His father, John Gacy Sr., was almost a stereotype of the hardworking, hard-drinking immigrant. Gacy Sr. was a perfectionist at home and on the job. A machinist, he could make his own tools and could literally build or repair anything in the house. He was, however, never satisfied with anything and especially not with young John. A good provider, Gacy Sr. was also an abusive parent and an alcoholic given to fits of rage. Unable to express affection, he was expert at expressing anger. John Jr. referred to his father as "the Old Man" and, even later in life, spoke of him in hushed, almost fearful tones. The Old Man went heavy on the razor strop and believed in pain as a way to teach his son—"I'll teach you to...."

John's mother, a neat, almost obsessive housekeeper, appeared to be a model parent. Only close examination reveals the cracks in that facade. Trapped between her affection for her husband and her natural desire to protect her children, she sometimes took drastic steps to defend them from their father. The images, words, and pain of some of those incidents surfaced years later in the negative aspects of John's life.

John said his mother told him he had been born with a serious heart condition known as "an enlarged bottleneck heart." Years later, a physician would say he had never heard of the term and could find no heart trouble at all in Gacy. It appeared John's mother invented the ploy to protect him from his father's outbursts and to keep him close and dependent on her. The Old Man hated all weakness, such as trust, emotion, and physical illness.

An incident occurred in 1944 that reflected the tension and fear in the Gacy household. Mrs. Gacy had just come home from the hospital after giving birth to her youngest daughter Karen. John was about two-and-a-half years old and his older sister Jo-anne nearly five. They were sitting at the dinner table when Gacy Sr. exploded in an outburst of rage. He began to brutally beat his wife. She ran screaming into the street. Neighbors, hearing the commotion, called the police. Joanne and John were scream-ing, and the Old Man grabbed his gun and left. Mrs. Gacy took the children and fled the house. The court refused to intervene. Finally, she and the children returned home. Gacy Sr. acted as if nothing had happened.

John's room was always immaculate. Those who remember him as a child say John was affectionate, hardworking, and eager to please. When he failed to meet his father's meticulous standards, it usually resulted in a beating and cruel verbal abuse. John said when he angered his father, the Old Man would call him "stupid" and a "dummy."

When he was four, the fifteen-year-old daughter of a neigh-bor took John out into the tall prairie grass. A mildly retarded girl, she took John's pants down and masturbated him. John re-membered that when he told his mother a lot of yelling went on in the house.

At age six, John stole his first item—a little toy truck. When she found it, his mother marched him back to the store to return it. John stole a lot over the years, usually small items. His mother would punish him, but then, for her, "it was over, and nobody had to talk about it again." Interestingly, it seems most serial killers are also thieves of one kind or another. Fortunately, the reverse is not often true, or the planet would soon be empty.

John had always been afraid of the dark, probably caused by the anxieties created by his father's behavior. Compounding those anxieties were a series of knife attacks on women in the neighborhood when John was in elementary school. Other chil-dren laughed and teased John when he expressed the fear that he might be hurt. Those actions may very well have been a contrib-uting factor to the false bravado and macho image so important to him as an adult.

When John was seven, another incident of sexual exploration occurred. John, a neighbor boy, and the boy's younger sister all took off their clothes and proceeded to play doctor. Anyone familiar with childhood development knows such incidents are normal and natural. More emotional damage can be caused by parental over-reaction than could possibly be caused by those mutual examinations. As usual, John's father beat him with the razor strop when the little girl told on them.

Later that year, an acquaintance of the Old Man began taking John for long rides in his pickup truck. John said those rides usually resulted in a wrestling match with John ending up with his face pressed against the man's crotch. Gacy said he never told his parents about the molestation. Early in his life, a firm correlation between force, pain, and sex had been established for John.

When John was ten, the family moved to a larger house with a basement. The Old Man's behavior deteriorated from then onward. He became more secretive and hostile. He kept the basement door padlocked, and he had the only key. John remembered one dresser drawer in the bedroom also was padlocked.

The Old Man began to do his drinking and raging in the basement. Those incidents usually occurred in the late afternoon, and the family could not have dinner until the Old Man calmed down and came upstairs to the table. Gacy Sr. always thought people were sneaking into his basement and stealing things. If he couldn't find something, he assumed young John had stolen it. Such occurrences always resulted in John having another close encounter with the razor strop. No one could ever defend himself or argue with the Old Man, because he simply never made mistakes.

John remembered his childhood as filled with anger and fear. He had a fear that something dark and evil in the basement would get him.

Mrs. Gacy defended her husband by saying he had a blood clot or tumor on the brain. Her idea was, when he drank, blood vessels would swell up and press on the tumor. Further, it was too dangerous to operate, and John should not argue with his father, or the tumor might burst and kill him. It is interesting, in her futile attempts to keep peace in the house, Mrs. Gacy defended family members by creating mysterious maladies that meant they were not responsible for their own behaviors. What is more amazing is Mrs. Gacy did not develop a real illness of her own from living in a household psychological pressure cooker.

By the age of ten, something was obviously wrong with young John. He sometimes had fainting spells, which lasted as long as a half hour. He spent nearly a year in the hospital between the ages of fourteen and eighteen. John began to think of himself as different. He was quiet, polite, somewhat sickly, and a loner. Gacy Sr. insisted John was faking his illnesses.

The Gacys were active in the Catholic Church. John attended parochial schools until age eleven. He was a fair student and got along well with others. At that point, at least on the surface, his life was typical of a Midwestern child growing up in the fifties. He carried papers, worked in a grocery store, and generally was friendly with people in the neighborhood. A Boy Scout, he had a dog and played street games with his friends. Four friends, according to John, protected him in case anyone tried to pick on him. The pattern of using others to protect himself showed up repeatedly in John's life.

Another aspect of his personality soon emerged. Once he stole all his mother's underwear and took them under the front porch. When the Old Man found out, the razor strop put in another appearance. John felt, thereafter, the Old Man never accepted him and thought of him as a "sissy" or a "fag." Other such incidents occurred when he was a teenager. His mother once disciplined him by making him wear women's panties. She never told the Old Man about the later incidents.

Gacy Sr. continued to pick on John. He constantly yelled at John because he was not perfect. The Old Man finally put away the razor strop. From then on, discipline came in the form of beating and punching. John swore he never hit back during those attacks.

In the summer of 1953, John went on a fishing trip with his father, an avid fisherman. In the Gacy family, going fishing with Gacy Sr. was a sign of growing up. It rained for two weeks, the fishing was terrible, and the Old Man got drunk and blamed John for the rain. He was never again allowed to fish with his father. Through no fault of his own, John had failed the rite of passage into manhood.

John's mother continued to encourage him in her uncritical way. He remembered her as naive, trusting, and limited in her ability to express her feelings.

Gacy, an indifferent student, daydreamed and showed passive resistance to his instructors. His grades were generally good but never outstanding, which brought him more criticism from his father. As John grew older, the family conflicts continued. When he attempted to come to his mother's aid, the Old Man referred to him as a "mama's boy" and a "sissy." The Gacy children were torn between love and fear for their father throughout his life.

John continued to have health problems. Once, after he developed a severe stomachache, his mother rushed him to the hospital. His appendix had burst. He felt the only way the Old Man would believe he was sick was by having an actual near-death illness.

John's sixteenth year proved especially troubled. He continued to have fainting spells and once spent nearly three weeks in the hospital. On another occasion, he had something that appeared to be an epileptic seizure. Struggling and kicking, he was placed in a straitjacket and hospitalized. A psychiatric evaluation was suggested by the attending physician, but the Old Man refused to consent.

Typical of most adolescents, John found himself in the grip of strange compulsions and thoughts. At sixteen, he thought constantly of death. Although he said he never considered suicide, he saw death as the ultimate gift from God.

Adolescence, sexual compulsion, and his constantly strained family life left Gacy a troubled, angry, and confused young man. His feelings of powerlessness began to emerge. He thought of becoming a priest. He saw the priesthood as clean, protected, and safe from temptation. He was fascinated by their power and saw priests as "God's cops." Gacy's fascination with police seemed locked into his desire for power and his feeling of personal powerlessness.

Constantly assailed by the Old Man's comments about "queers," John's masculinity was always doubted and threatened. He rarely dated and didn't have a steady girlfriend.

By age eighteen, John was five feet eight inches tall and weighed 200 pounds. He felt he had a body like a sack of flour and a face like the Potato Head toy. Instead of dating, he worked hard at part-time jobs. After public grammar school, he went to vocational school. He ran errands for teachers and was an assistant to the truant officer. In high school, he served as the Civil Defense captain and got a portable blue light for the dashboard of his car. He became fascinated by uniforms and played policeman, speeding off to a fire or accident with his blue light flashing.

John started his involvement in community affairs at this time. He joined several organizations for young adults, became active in local politics, and frequently volunteered for projects.

At age eighteen, John had his first adult sexual experience. He and a girl were parked and began petting. John became excited and began to undress her. She was a willing participant. True to form, at the magic moment, John passed out. When he came to, she had put on her clothes and insisted on going home.

During his high school years, Gacy attended several different schools in the Chicago area. At Carl Schuz High School, John was taken out of the building on several occasions in a straitjacket after flying into uncontrollable rages. As he approached maturity, John exhibited more and more of the Old Man's behavior.

As a student, John was average. He had better grades in English and science classes than in printing and auto shop. Business courses at Cooley Vocational High occupied John for a year. At his last high school, Charles A. Prosser Vocational, his attendance became erratic, and he dropped out after a couple of months.

By age nineteen, Gacy had attended four high schools in four years. He was unable to finish vocational high school because, according to him, the administration worried he might pass out and fall into the machinery.

In 1960, the local draft board examined his medical history and classified him as 4F: unsuitable for military service. His only sources of pride were his Civil Defense activities and his car with its flashing blue light.

The Old Man used money as a way of controlling John's behavior. He had purchased a new car for John, who agreed to pay him back in installments. Although it was supposed to be John's car, the Old Man would take the keys away at the slightest excuse. His own money, his own car, and freedom from the Old Man dominated John's thoughts.

In 1962, John and the car disappeared. He was found four months later in Nevada working for a mortuary. He had gotten a job driving an ambulance until they discovered he was not twenty-one years old as required by law. The mortuary continued to employ him as a night attendant. John often watched the morticians embalm bodies.

One night, the body of a teenage boy was brought in. The corpse, as is often the case, had a full erection. Alone with the body, John fantasized about feeling death in the dark. Summoning his courage, he climbed into the coffin with the body. At first, he lay on top the dead boy. Then sliding under the corpse, he cradled it in his arms. He never admitted to any overt sexual behavior.

John realized his experience with the corpse would have gotten him into trouble if he had been caught. He wanted to return to familiar and seemingly safer surroundings. A few days later, John called his mother and asked if she thought the Old Man would take him back.

Back in Chicago, John gravitated to sales work, an ideal area for him to use his talents at manipulating others. He talked his way into Northwestern Business College, did quite well, and graduated. His natural gregariousness and ingratiating manner usually hid the fact that what he said had little meaning or sense.

John became a management trainee for the Nunn-Bush Shoe Company in 1963 at the age of twenty-one. The following year as a reward for his hard work, John was promoted and transferred to a store in Springfield, Illinois. He joined the local Jaycee (Junior Chamber of Commerce) chapter and appeared to be well on his way to a normal life. However, he was still a police groupie and was obsessed with the idea of being in charge.

While in Springfield, he lived with his aunt and uncle. He dated frequently and said he preferred "normal sex." He did not like fellatio, because he could not bring himself to kiss the girl afterward. John proposed marriage to a steady girlfriend in 1963. She rejected him. The following year, at age twenty-two, John Gacy had his first sexual experience with a male. John's mother said if John's father had ever suspected any homosexual activity on John's part, he probably would have killed him.

On the night of his first experience, John and an older friend had gone out looking for girls to pick up. John said he and the friend had several drinks and then went to the friend's house. John passed out. When he awakened, he found he was nude, and the friend was sucking on his penis. John said it felt good. He said later, in addition to a hangover, he was severely depressed for several months because of the experience. He felt he had been outwitted by the older man and, once again, his father would consider him dumb and stupid, in addition to being a "queer."

Also in 1963, John met his first wife, Marilyn Myers. They dated for about nine months and were married in the fall of 1964. Marilyn, a protected only child, was vastly impressed by the aggressive, big spender from Chicago.

When her parents purchased three Kentucky Fried Chicken franchises in Waterloo, Iowa, the newlyweds moved into the parents' home in Springfield. John and Marilyn's son was born in 1966. Gacy appeared to be a loving and devoted husband and father.

In 1965, John Wayne Gacy Jr. was named third outstanding Jaycee for the State of Illinois. He had volunteered his time and energy for innumerable projects. John enjoyed being in the limelight and being seen with important people. He had now replaced the flashing blue light from his Civil Defense days with a similar red light. He carried the light on the dashboard of his car and told people it was for his Jaycee work in parades and other events.

John's in-laws never cared for him but wanted their only child Marilyn close to home. In 1966, his father-in-law offered John the management of the three Kentucky Fried Chicken stores in Waterloo at a very generous salary. Although his father-in-law considered him a braggart and a liar and most of his employees disliked him, there is no doubt Gacy was an extremely hard worker. He worked ten to fourteen hours a day, managed the stores efficiently, and substantially increased the profit margin of the three stores.

In the summer of 1966, an event occurred in Chicago that many think drew John's attention and further increased his urges to sexual violence. On the night of 13 July, Richard Speck, a drifter and sometime merchant seaman, entered a student nurses' dormitory. He raped and murdered eight young women. The brutal, sadistic murders gained worldwide attention. As a massive manhunt continued, Speck, still in Chicago, attempted suicide. He was quickly apprehended.

Later, while in prison in Iowa, Gacy said Speck was stupid, and if he had planned properly, could have gotten away with the murders.

John and Marilyn continued to look like an idyllic American family. His hobbies were woodworking and gardening, and he was an extremely avid home handyman.

The year 1967 was the high-water mark of John's life. His daughter was born, and John took great delight in showing off his children. The Old Man even came for a visit from Chicago and, surprisingly, treated John politely and as an adult. John had prominent friends in local business, politics, and even on the Waterloo police force.

Family life was not as rosy as it appeared on the surface. John, in typical grandiose fashion, gave the *Courier*, the Waterloo newspaper, an exaggerated biographical package on himself. People found him to be overbearing, arrogant, a braggart, and a liar. Sometimes his stories reached the point of absurdity, such as his statements that he had served in the US Marine Corps. His tireless manipulation of others, although sometimes successful, eventually alienated everyone who encountered him.

Gacy saw his activities with the Waterloo Jaycees as a way of obtaining social contacts and advancing his status in the community. Like any Jaycee chapter at that time, the Waterloo group was comprised of men under the age of thirty-five who were aggressive, business-oriented, and considered by most to be community leaders. Rumors of his involvement in wife swapping notwithstanding, John had many Jaycee friends and held the office of chaplain. He was thought of as a bright and dynamic individual.

Despite his big talk and his statements about having served in the armed forces, Gacy was a coward. He might confront a juvenile or someone much smaller than he. John, however, was never going to face off against anyone his size or larger. He was not inclined to test his will against anyone who might respond physically. Throughout his life, John's style had always been to shift blame to someone else or to deny any knowledge of whatever situation occurred. For example, when running for office in the Jaycees, his campaign consisted largely of playing other members against one another, rather than running on the issues.

By early 1967, John's efforts at creating a positive image were declining. His relationship with Marilyn had deteriorated to the point where, on more than one occasion, he was overheard saying, "If you want to, I'll let you fuck my wife."

The Gacys also began experiencing serious financial problems, largely because of John's indulgences in the seamier side of life in Waterloo. Marilyn's mother loaned them money to pay the household expenses after John spent his income on prostitutes and gambling.

John continued to indulge his fascination with law enforcement activities. A member of the Waterloo Merchant Patrol, he seized every excuse to prowl the streets at night in his car. He rarely, however, went out alone. He usually managed to convince one of the young male employees of the fried chicken stores to accompany him.

Several components of his later crimes now came into focus: establishing himself as a law enforcement/power figure, prowling the streets at night, and actively seeking the company of young males. In defiance of patrol regulations and Iowa law, John carried a handgun on those forays.

On the job, John socialized with and promoted only the male employees. Any young man who seemed inclined to reject his attempts at "friendship" was very likely to find himself "accidentally" burned with hot grease from the fryer. Always willing to give a good-looking boy a ride home, John had no time for his female workers.

By then, John was having sexual contact with young boys. The wheels had been set in motion that would shatter his ambitious dreams of a successful marriage, prominence in the community, and the presidency of the local Jaycee chapter. Prison loomed ominously in Gacy's future.

To guarantee himself a steady supply of young male companions, John spent considerable money and effort setting up the basement of his home as a sort of social club. He provided alcoholic beverages to minors despite the fact Iowa law considered it a serious misdemeanor punishable by a jail term.

Many of Gacy's attempts at seduction involved playing pool in his basement with those young men. Frequently, his comment would be they could play for money or "for a blow job." It didn't make much difference to him at the time whether he was the giver or the recipient of those sexual services.

The bizarre and nonsensical nature of his bragging stories reached the stage of absurdity. In his efforts to intimidate and manipulate teenage boys, John, at different times, said he had contacts with the Mafia in Chicago, he was doing research into human sexual behavior for the governor of Illinois, he was a scientist engaged in exhaustive research aimed at rewriting the sex laws, and as long as those young men cooperated with him, the sexual services of his wife Marilyn would be made available to them. It is very difficult to read statements such as those and conceive of anyone believing them. Anyone who ever encountered John Gacy or another of his ilk does not have that problem. These individuals, the pedophiles and serial killers, have an almost mesmerizing effect on their victims.

It is patently obvious only the young and naive or someone truly simple-minded would believe those stories. Yet combined with the aggressive nature and force of John's personality, many accepted his statements as gospel. In a society where children are raised to accept the pronouncements of adults as truth, it is not surprising John was believed. Beyond that, credibility was added by John's quasi-law enforcement status, his position as an employer, and the fact he was a well-known person in the community. Those aspects, combined with adolescent gullibility and hero worship, often gave Gacy free rein.

One employee of the Kentucky Fried Chicken shop, Richard Westphal, later told the Waterloo police that on several occasions John had suggested they play pool with a "blow job" as the stakes. Another time when he spent the night at the Gacy house, Marilyn Gacy entered the guest room and got into bed with him. After they had intercourse, Marilyn left the room and John entered. John had told Westphal several days before that if he ever caught him having sex with his wife, he would expect Westphal also to have sex with him. Westphal admitted performing fellatio on Gacy that night. He said he felt coerced and intimidated by Gacy. The event was the first provable incident involving John Wayne Gacy and a teenage boy.

Fifteen-year-old Donald Voorhees Jr., another employee of the fast-food restaurant, was told by Gacy that he could earn extra money assisting him with his "sex research." For several months during the summer and fall of 1967, they met in motels and John's recreation room. On those occasions, John would get the boy drunk, and the "experiments" would be conducted. They included oral and anal sex. Following the experiments, Gacy would closely question Voorhees about his feelings, reactions, and responses. On most occasions, John gave him a small amount of money. Gacy, using another of his standard intimidation ploys, also told the Voorhees boy that, if he ever discussed those experiments with anyone, it could place his life in jeopardy because of John's connections with organized crime in Chicago. It should be noted despite that assertion, which John made many times over the next fifteen years, there is no reason to believe John Wayne Gacy had any connections with organized crime in Waterloo, Chicago, or any place else.

In the late summer of 1967, a third employee, James Tullery, was invited over to Gacy's house for a few drinks, to play pool, and to watch dirty movies. During the evening, Gacy raised the subject of sex and suggested he and Tullery have oral sex. Tullery rejected the suggestion. At first, Gacy seemed to accept the boy's answer in good graces. A little later in the evening, Gacy suddenly pulled out a knife and threatened Tullery. When the boy again refused Gacy's advances, John lunged at him with the knife and succeeded in cutting him slightly on the left arm. The boy let out a yell that seemed to bring Gacy to his senses. Then, unbelievably, after allowing Gacy to bandage his arm, the Tullery boy permitted Gacy to demonstrate bondage on him. Bondage is a sexual deviance involving physical restraint for the purpose of creating an enhanced state of sexual excitement. After the boy was securely tied to a chair, Gacy attempted to straddle him and choke him. After James resisted and knocked Gacy to the floor, Gacy proceeded to choke the boy into unconsciousness. Gacy then released him and, amazingly, James Tullery stayed around for a while, leaving later in the evening.

Don Voorhees and James Tullery were acquainted with each other because they both worked at Gacy's Kentucky Fried Chicken store. Quite by accident, each discovered the other had been a victim of an attack by Gacy. After discussing their situations for several days, the boys eventually worked up enough courage to tell their parents. Don Voorhees' father, a prominent member of the Waterloo business community, was then involved in a campaign for the state presidency of the Iowa Jaycees. He was acquainted with John Gacy, who had asked Voorhees Sr. to be his campaign manager when he ran for the presidency of the Waterloo Jaycees later in the year. When Don's father told him this, Voorhees Jr. became extremely upset. He pleaded with his father not to have anything to do with Gacy. When questioned, he quickly revealed everything about his relationship with Gacy.

Life appeared to quiet down during the fall and winter of 1967. It was just a temporary lull. In March of 1968, Don Voorhees and James Tullery went to the Waterloo police and gave complete statements about their sexual relationships with John Wayne Gacy Jr. When contacted by local police, Gacy denied everything and demanded a lie detector test. He took the test in early May, and not surprisingly, failed miserably. One writer suggested the only thing believable on the test was John's name. A second test was also a dismal failure.

On 10 May 1968, John Wayne Gacy Jr. was indicted by a Black Hawk County grand jury for the felony offense of sodomy. If convicted, Gacy faced a prison term of ten years. The police obtained a warrant and searched his home. A large quantity of pornographic films and literature was found and confiscated.

In June, the heat on Gacy continued to increase. John went around to friends and acquaintances who had heard about the situation and attempted to justify his behavior. According to him, he was just helping the Voorhees boy learn about sex and later had loaned him money. The sodomy charge was a setup by unnamed political enemies who did not want him to have the power and prestige of the presidency of the Waterloo Jaycee chapter. John, a believable liar, convinced many people he was completely innocent and a victim of circumstances.

Gacy, now out on bond, was faced with a wrecked marriage, the imminent possibility of losing his job, and a large amount of adverse publicity. He withdrew at the last moment from the Jaycee presidential race. As the wreckage of his life piled up around him, Gacy's behavior became more frantic and bizarre.

During that entire period, he continued his activities with the Merchant Patrol. On 30 August 1968, Gacy drove around the Waterloo business area with an eighteen-year-old employee named Russell Schroeder. During the night, Schroeder, at Gacy's behest, broke into a lumber company and later stole some hubcaps from a car lot. Gacy kept a lookout and listened to his police scanner.

A couple of weeks later, Gacy offered Schroeder money if he would beat up Donald Voorhees. He thought that might scare Voorhees enough so he would not testify against him on the sodomy charge. Schroeder at first was not interested, but when Gacy offered to pay off the balance on his automobile loan and give him a small amount of cash, Schroeder agreed. Gacy also gave him a can of mace, which was illegal at the time.

Donald Voorhees and Russell Schroeder attended the same high school. Schroeder befriended Voorhees and took him to a remote park in rural Black Hawk County. They were allegedly going after some stolen liquor. When they got to the park, Schroeder attacked Voorhees, sprayed him with mace, and attempted to beat him up. Voorhees fled and hid in a cornfield until Schroeder left. Schroeder was later identified from a high school yearbook picture. After he was arrested, Schroeder quickly broke down and related Gacy's role in the incident. He also implicated him in the lumberyard break-in.

Gacy again was arrested and jailed. He was charged with going armed with intent, malicious threats to extort, and attempting to suborn perjury. While in jail, he provided police with information about wife swapping, gambling, and prostitution in Waterloo.

A few days after his arrest, Gacy was transferred from the Black Hawk County Jail to the University of Iowa Psychopathic Hospital. The hospital, eighty miles away, had one of the highest reputations for evaluation of criminal personalities in the Midwest.

During his two-month stay, Gacy meddled in ward affairs, freely expressed his opinion on everything, and constantly manipulated ward attendants and other patients for his own gain.

For the first time, a physical examination was administered to detect the truth about John's alleged heart disease. Not surprisingly, no disease was found. After an EEG was administered, brain damage was eliminated as a possible defense. Other than being overweight, John was in excellent health. On IQ testing, he scored in the bright-normal range and was found to be quite aware of the difference between right and wrong.

The psychiatric evaluation found Gacy to be what in the parlance of the time was called a "sociopathic personality." In layman's terms, that is someone who understands the difference between right and wrong but doesn't give a damn, is totally unconcerned about the impact of his behavior on others, and attempts to manipulate, lie, and alibi his way through life. The evaluation described Gacy as an individual incapable of feeling guilt. He was almost totally oriented toward self-gratification, was sadistic and manipulative, and, according to the discharge summary, very likely to commit more crimes.

Further, the psychiatric review indicated John was probably bisexual and more inclined to "thrill-seeking behavior" than being a true "deviant." He was found competent to stand trial on the Black Hawk County charges.

In many ways, the psychiatric documents from that evaluation are the most frightening aspect of John's early life. The psychiatric staff at the University of Iowa literally identified every factor that would later go into John's bizarre string of crimes in Chicago. It is more than hindsight to say, if those documents had come into the hands of people who understood what they were reading, Gacy would have been imprisoned in Iowa far longer, and he might never have been in the position to kill thirty-three people in Chicago.

On 7 November as the result of a plea bargain, John Gacy pleaded guilty to the sodomy charge involving Donald Voorhees. All other charges against him were dismissed.

That is standard practice in most criminal jurisdictions. By allowing the defendant to plead guilty to the most serious offense in return for the dismissal of the other charges, prosecutors see themselves as saving the taxpayers the expense of a trial. The other side of the coin is that the criminal will inevitably be released from prison sooner. Information about the dismissed offenses is frequently not available to law enforcement or correctional authorities.

On 3 December 1968, Gacy was sentenced to a term of ten years in the Iowa prison system. The term was the maximum sentence allowable under the law. He was immediately transferred from the Black Hawk County Jail in Waterloo to the Iowa Men's Reformatory at Anamosa.

His father cried when John was sent to prison. It was the only emotion besides rage anyone had ever seen the Old Man display.

After being processed and assigned an inmate number, Gacy was transferred to the quarantine/orientation section of the prison. He adapted very quickly to the highly structured regimen of prison life. Once again, his chameleon-like ability to adjust to any situation and to make himself acceptable to others served him in good stead. Upon release from the Orientation Unit in early January 1969, John, with his experience in food service, was assigned to the prison kitchen. He worked there during his entire incarceration.

John tried to head off any rumors that might be sent on the prison grapevine. He quickly began telling people, although he was in jail for sodomy, the charge grew out of his having shown pornographic movies to teenage girls. He also stated repeatedly he had been framed by his political enemies in Waterloo. He hinted his ex-wife was the daughter of Harlan Sanders, the founder of the Kentucky Fried Chicken empire. In fact, he and Marilyn were still married, and their divorce would not be final until August 1969. He also said he had been in the Marine Corps and suffered from heart trouble. His nonexistent malady put in another appearance.

John was active in the Reformatory Jaycee chapter. As a result of his activities in the Jaycees, he met the three people with whom he would be most closely associated in prison. They were three amateurish burglars from central Iowa: Larry Polsley, Duane Fulton, and myself, Raymond Cornell. During the next eighteen months, we would be his friends, protectors, and nearly constant companions.

His Jaycee activities also provided him with a cover for illicit activities. For example, his participation in the Toys for Tots program was really a cover for his sideline of manufacturing homemade booze in the kitchen basement.

To the staff, Gacy was a model prisoner who worked hard and appeared to be trying to improve himself in order to gain early release. Within six months, he was trying to coerce his counselor into recommending him for an early parole. At the same time, his exhaustive knowledge of food service and kitchen management got him quickly promoted to lead cook in the prison kitchen. He then used his position to build a power base that allowed him to dominate inmates and guards, steal food, and generally control one of the most important areas of prison life.

In the late summer of 1969, his appeal before the Iowa Supreme Court was dismissed. A few weeks later, Marilyn was granted a final decree of divorce from John and moved back to Springfield to live with her parents. Little by little, John's antagonism toward women began to emerge. At first, he made almost irrational threats against Marilyn. He said she was part of the great "get John Gacy" conspiracy. Later, he boasted he had enough power with the mob in Chicago that, if he should choose to give the word, her life would be forfeit. John began telling other prisoners as far as he was concerned, his ex-wife and children were dead.

The following months were filled with almost unceasing rhetoric against women, signs of what was to come.

At that time, John began actively to abuse prison homosexuals. On one occasion, Gacy poured boiling chili over an individual's hands in the prison dining hall. Another time, he had to be restrained from using a horseshoe to beat a particularly obnoxious homosexual. The homosexual inmates quickly figured out Gacy's antagonism could be used against him to create behavior bordering on the absurd. Cat calls and name calling would send him into a rage. That led to a war of words lasting for the remaining nine months of his incarceration.

Throwing himself into his Jaycee activities, his educational efforts, and his kitchen job, John attempted to fill every hour of the day with some sort of work. Those who celled next to him frequently commented it seemed as if he only slept an hour or two a night. He finished high school, earned college credits in psychology, became active in various group therapy sessions, and seemed to be constantly on the move. He also renewed his interest in the Catholic Church. The prison priest frequently allowed Gacy to serve as a lector at the Mass.

Before Christmas 1969, John hired another inmate to paint a portrait of his father from a photograph. The painting was not done on time, and the Old Man never saw it. John Wayne Gacy Sr. died on Christmas Day. John was unaware his father was ill and did not know he had died until 27 December. He was devastated by his father's death. Weeping and blaming himself, he spent the entire day with his prison counselor. The Old Man had died from cirrhosis of the liver, not from shame as John felt or from his nonexistent brain tumor.

Gacy became moody and withdrawn. He no longer seemed interested in his previous activities. In March 1970, a psychological evaluation called him a passive-aggressive personality and said it seemed unlikely he would commit further criminal acts. After his review by the Iowa Board of Parole in June 1970, he was granted parole to Illinois, transferred to a release facility, and left for Chicago in mid-July. He never returned to Iowa.

Despite the fact that the grimly pessimistic report from the

University of Iowa hospital was in his prison file, John's winning ways had lulled the staff into believing he was a model inmate and would be a model citizen. During his incarceration, no serious attempt was ever made to detect, identify, or treat sexual aberrations or deviance.

That fall, John, now living with his mother in an apartment, found a job at a restaurant in Chicago. Bruno's was a favorite hangout for the Chicago Black Hawks hockey team. Gacy soon wormed his way into their circle, began telling people he was the official chef for the team, and handed out free tickets to their games.

At Bruno's, John became acquainted with James Hanley, a Chicago police officer assigned to the hit and run unit. Years later, John would use the name Jack Hanley when cruising the streets of Chicago looking for sex and victims.

John attempted on several occasions to contact his ex-wife. His letters and phone calls went unanswered. Finally, he made his mother destroy all pictures of his ex-wife and children. Now they really were dead to him.

By November 1970, Gacy was openly associating with gay men. He also was paying for sex with other men. In February 1971, he was arrested for attempted rape of a nineteen-year-old boy. The case was dismissed when the boy, an avowed homosexual, failed to appear in court. John had been out of prison only eight months.

Back in Iowa, the parole board continued in blissful ignorance of Gacy's behavior. In October 1971, they discharged him from parole and recommended his citizenship rights be restored. In less than two months, his first victim would die.

A few months earlier, John, his mother, and sisters had pooled their resources and purchased a house at 8213 West Summerdale Avenue, Norwood Park Township, in Des Plaines, a suburb of Chicago. At first, John lived there by himself. The Summerdale area is a quiet, family-oriented neighborhood. John's house was no better or worse than those of his neighbors. A ranch-style home, it had two bedrooms and a detached garage. A formal dining room and a recreation room were added later. Built without a basement, the house had a crawlspace underneath about three feet high with a dirt floor. The hatchway to the crawlspace was in the bedroom closet. A previous tenant had had problems with seepage and kept a sump pump running most of the time.

John also had begun to realize his dream of owning his own business. Primarily using his mother's money, he started PDM Contractors. The PDM stood for painting, decorating, and maintenance. The house on Summerdale provided sufficient room for the quantity of construction and painting supplies necessary for John to run his business.

John began living with a twenty-year-old Army veteran named Mickel Ried. Gacy and Ried had been sexually involved with each other since the previous winter. Later, Ried would give some insight into the period leading up to the first killing. He said in the fall of 1971, Gacy had struck him on the head with a hammer. When asked why he had done it, John replied he had had a sudden urge to kill.

Gacy's business slowly grew, and he spent a lot of time puttering around the house with projects of his own. He allowed the bushes in the back half of the property to grow so the neighbors could not see any activity in his house or garage. Although not a particularly good craftsman, John always seemed more than willing to help his neighbors and soon became quite friendly with most of them.

John had begun dating a woman named Carole Hoff. She had been a close friend of his sisters and had dated him once in high school. Recently divorced, she and John talked and talked. He told her he was bisexual, but she chose to ignore that. She saw him as a perfect catch: bright, talented, industrious, and on the way up the ladder of success. In spite of his erratic behavior, he got along quite well with Carole and her two young daughters.

On Christmas day 1971, John completely lost control of himself. He began weeping and saying he had let the Old Man down when he was in prison and could not come to the funeral. On New Year's Eve, he suffered another blow with the death of his father's sister, Aunt Pearl. A few days later, he let the Old Man down again when he murdered his first victim.

On 3 January 1972, John Gacy, as he did every year, went to downtown Chicago to view the ice sculptures at the Civic Center. Across the street, seventeen-year-old Timothy Jack McCoy stepped down from the Greyhound bus, which was taking him home to Glenwood, Iowa. The Chicago Greyhound depot, like bus stations in most major cities, was a regular hunting ground for pimps, hustlers, and con artists.

Gacy walked up to McCoy and struck up a conversation. He later related that when he found out the young man had a twelve-hour layover, he suggested they go cruising for girls. Arriving at his house in the wee hours of the morning, they had drinks and mutual oral sex. According to Gacy, he awoke the next morning to find McCoy coming at him with a knife. They struggled, Gacy wrested the knife away, and stabbed McCoy several times in the chest. On 4 January 1972, McCoy's body became the first buried in the crawlspace. His remains would not be identified until May 1986, fourteen years after his death.

Gacy also described killing three other young men who have never been identified or their deaths dated. He had brought one young man home for sex for pay. The youth pulled a knife on Gacy and tried to rob him. Gacy calmed the youth, showed him some magic tricks, then strangled him. Another time, Gacy brought home two young men at once. Taking one into a separate room, John told the man he would tighten a rope around his neck three times so the boy would get an erection. Then Gacy would give him a blow job. The boy agreed, but John Gacy strangled him instead. When told his friend was dead, the second youth couldn't believe it. Gacy handcuffed him, led him into the room, and strangled him in front of his friend's body.

John and Carole Hoff had begun a sexual relationship in early January. She became pregnant almost immediately. Although John appeared to be happy about the baby, he was not terribly upset when Carole miscarried within a few weeks. Shortly after, in March, she moved into the house on Summerdale Avenue with John.

By early summer 1972, John was routinely cruising the streets of Chicago late at night looking for sexual partners. On 22 June, he was arrested and charged with forcing a young man into his car by identifying himself as a police officer. Gacy was also accused of forcing the young man to perform oral sex on him and then trying to run him down with his car when he tried to escape. John defended himself by saying the victim, Jackie Dee, was attempting to extort money from him in return for dropping the charges. Once again, his combination of luck and bravado won out. Mysteriously, the case was never brought to trial, and the charges were stricken from the record.

On 1 July, nine days after he was arrested and charged with another sex offense, John Wayne Gacy Jr. and Carole Hoff were married in a large formal wedding.

At the time, John was night manager of a Chicago restaurant called Barnaby's. During the day, he continued his attempts to get PDM Contractors off the ground. He was also maintaining a more or less normal relationship with Carole Hoff and her two children. In addition, he routinely cruised the streets for several hours after midnight. A schedule so demanding would probably have most people hospitalized and suffering from exhaustion in a month. Gacy continued this pace for the next several years.

Carole liked the Summerdale house and did her best to make it a home for John and her two daughters. One problem was the persistent foul odor coming from the crawlspace under the house. John passed it off as seepage from sewer lines and began spreading lime under the house. Carole, thinking it might be dead mice, asked John several times to call an exterminator. John refused. By then, at least one body lay buried under the house.

Although now too old to be a Jaycee, John continued to make contacts with people he saw as prominent in the community or who could be useful to him. He began throwing large theme parties and was considered by many to be an extremely good host.

For the first few months of the marriage, the relationship appeared to be going well. By the end of 1972, problems began to develop. Carole was concerned about John's frequent absences from the home at night, often from midnight until dawn. Their sex life began to deteriorate. During most of the marriage, John was impotent with Carole. On one occasion, she found him masturbating with a pair of women's silk bikini panties.

Gacy also had built a complete replica of the rec room of his house in Iowa. He was spending a great deal of time alone there. The similarity between John's seclusion in the recreation room and his father's seclusion in the basement is striking. Each of them had created a lair for himself.

Carole's parents were divorced in 1973. Carole's mother, an alert and suspicious woman, moved in with John and Carole. She and John were not compatible. Toward the end of the year, John faked a stroke and blamed it on Carole's mother. He subsequently obtained a court order and had her removed from the house in early 1974. John later said no killings happened during the time

51

his mother-in-law lived with them.

Although John was now working fulltime for PDM and making a good living, his marriage to Carole was rapidly failing. His constant fatigue, explosive temper, and violent outbursts became more frightening to her. Their sex life had become almost nonexistent. His criticisms of Carole became more strident and constant. He continually put her down as stupid and incompetent. It seems John was beginning to actively imitate his father. He complained constantly and criticized everything and everyone who did not suit him.

On several occasions, Carole found items in the house belonging to young men. John also began to bring home homosexual pornography. He was finally forced to admit to Carole that his preference was young males.

On Mother's Day 1974, John told Carole their sex life was over. Although their marriage lasted another twenty months, they never again slept together, and John lived in the front of the house while Carole lived in the back.

John did not kill with any regularity while Carole lived with him. Several reasons accounted for the absence of death. First, while his mother-in-law was with them, four females lived in the house, and privacy was at a premium. Gacy's type of crime requires privacy. Most of his victims were killed in the house. Secondly, the hatchway to John's crawlspace/cemetery was in the bedroom closet. After May 1974, Carole lived and slept in the bedroom. It is unlikely he could have carried a body through the room and down into the crawlspace in the wee hours of the morning without her noticing. However, her departure in February 1976 removed all restraint from John.

Through his construction company income, John had the money to indulge one of his other little vices. Like most serial murderers, John Gacy was a police freak. It is no coincidence that his vanity license plate "PDM" bore a striking resemblance to the "PD" license plates used by Cook County law enforcement officers. He had soon managed to obtain the paraphernalia of police work: handcuffs, phony badges, red flashing lights, spotlights, a gun, a long black car, a black leather jacket, and police scanners. This equipment helped validate his disguise as a policeman that would become central to his crimes.

One exception occurred to John's lack of murders during his

marriage to Carole. In August 1975, John Butkovich, an employee of PDM Contractors, disappeared. John later said he came across Butkovich while cruising in downtown Chicago. Carole was out of town that weekend. Butkovich had been in a fight earlier in the evening and was bruised and bleeding. John took him home to Summerdale Avenue and cleaned his injuries.

An argument had been brewing for several days between Gacy and Butkovich over pay. Gacy had many disagreements with his employees concerning pay and other matters. He constantly looked for ways to withhold money from them. Butkovich, who Carole Gacy had called Little John, argued once too often. They struggled and Butkovich hit Gacy several times. Gacy calmed him down and showed him the "rope trick."

In 1975, Gacy, being too old for the Jaycees, joined a Moose Lodge. He became very interested in their clown unit.

Except for a few family photographs, virtually every wall decoration and painting in John's house was of a clown. One can imagine his victims coming into the house, looking around, and being automatically put at ease by these pictures of joy. In the minds of most people, there is no more benign or pleasurable character than a clown. The idea that this pudgy Harlequin named John had hands bloody to his elbows would simply be beyond the realm of reason.

Gacy's clown repertoire included magic tricks. His magic had a darker purpose than the laughter of children.

His victims usually saw two tricks. The "handcuff trick" came first. To allay any possible fears his victims might have, John would place the cuffs on his own wrists, turn his back, and release himself. He would then invite his victims to try the trick. Once they were securely cuffed, he would reveal the solution, "You have to have the key." An extended period of sexual sadism and torture usually followed.

The last trick they ever saw was what John called the "rope trick," also known as the Spanish Windlass. It involves placing a knotted rope around the neck. A small stick or board is then inserted in the rope and slowly turned. Slow strangulation results. Strangulation of this type usually produces an involuntary erection.

Although John swore in his statements that his victims died quickly and painlessly, it is extremely unlikely. It is much more probable that by tightening and loosening the noose, John was able to enjoy repeated gratification over a period of hours before his victims died. When he got bored, they died.

Butkovich's body lay in the garage for several days. John, because of Carole's early return, had no access to the crawlspace. Finally, frustrated, he stripped the corpse and buried it in a trench under the garage. Gacy, enraged because the youth's body would not fit in the small hole he had dug, placed the corpse in a sitting position, then jumped up and down on it until it fit. He then sealed the makeshift tomb with concrete.

After the final divorce decree in March 1976, John and Carole continued to be friendly and to date occasionally. However, after the divorce, John began drinking and using drugs more heavily. During that time period, John's mother left Illinois and moved to Arkansas.

Between 6 April and the end of the year, he killed again and again, each time burying the victims in the crawlspace. Also, he committed a number of rapes that did not result in deaths.

Darrell Sampson, an eighteen-year-old boy, disappeared in Chicago on 6 April. His body was identified nearly a year after Gacy's arrest. He had been placed in the crawl space with his underpants stuffed down his throat.

Five weeks later, Randall Reffert and Samuel Stapleton, who were close friends, disappeared. They both died on the night of May 14 after being raped and brutalized. Their bodies were found in a common grave in the crawlspace. Reffert was identified by dental records and Stapleton by a silver bracelet he had had permanently welded around his wrist.

In May 1976, John Gacy hired a young man by the name of Michael Rossi to work for PDM Contractors. Rossi would become John's lover and one of the most mysterious figures in the Gacy case. Although he consistently denied any knowledge of the murders, Rossi also admitted to having lived in the house and to having supervised the digging of several trenches in the crawlspace. His long and close association with Gacy leads to a suspicion he knew more than he ever said. Gacy referred to Rossi as his "right-hand man."

On 3 June 1976, Gacy struck again. The victim was a well-liked young man named Michael Bonnin. His corpse, also in the crawlspace, would eventually be identified by dental records.

A week later, Billy Carroll Jr., a streetwise sixteen-year-old who made a living procuring other young boys for adult homosexuals, dropped out of sight. At the time of his disappearance, he was living in the Uptown area of Chicago. That slum area was a traditional hunting ground for street hustlers and criminals of all varieties. Later, Billy Carroll's girlfriend said she had had dreams about Billy filled with images of bright lights and concrete. His skeleton would be found in March 1979 in the crawlspace. He would later be identified by dental records.

Jimmy Haakenson, sixteen years old, left St. Paul, Minnesota, on 5 August 1976. He called his mother later that day to say he had arrived in Chicago. He wanted to have an adventure and explore the city by himself. His sunny smile disappeared after Gacy made Jimmy his twenty-fourth victim and buried the youth in the crawlspace. In July 2017, nearly forty years after his disappearance, Jimmy's DNA was matched to samples supplied by his brother and sister.

The Aragon Ballroom on the North Side of Chicago was a popular entertainment spot. On 6 August, Rick Johnston asked his mother to drop him off so he could attend a rock concert. The Johnston family was extremely upset when Rick had not returned the next morning. They notified police immediately. Rick, a popular, intelligent youth, was slender and attractive.

His closely knit family feared he had been abducted by a religious cult. They hired a private detective who found nothing. Police dismissed their concerns by saying Rick was a runaway. Time after time, that would be the response worried families received from law enforcement agencies.

An amateur psychic who was acquainted with Rick said he was under a house where it was very dark and cold. She said his feet were cold because he had no shoes. When the body of Rick Johnston was found, it was barefooted.

The Johnston family had to deal with one more package of grief. Due to a clerical error by the police, the missing person's report was dated 08-06-76 instead of 06-08-76. On paper, it appeared the Johnstons had waited nearly two months to report their son missing. For a long time to come, they would be criticized and unfairly accused of delaying their report.

William George Bundy loved to dive and was a gymnast. After dropping out of Chicago's Senn High School, he worked construction jobs, but it has never been confirmed that he ever worked for Gacy. Nineteen-year-old Bill headed to a party in October 1976 and disappeared. Later, after Gacy's arrest, Bill's family suspected Bill was one of Gacy's victims. Bill's mother tried to provide the police with his dental x-rays, but the dentist had retired and destroyed all his records. Thirty-five years later in November 2011, DNA samples from his sister and brother proved Bill was one of the crawlspace bodies.

Michael Marino, fourteen years old, and Kenneth Parker, sixteen years old, were longtime friends. They were last seen on 24 October 1976 at Clark Street and Diversey Parkway, a corner where Gacy often sought victims. Gacy would bury them in a common crawlspace grave.

Gregory Godzik was an employee of Gacy's PDM Contractors. After a date with his girlfriend on the night of 11 December, Greg disappeared. His remains were identified on New Year's Day 1979. He was in the crawlspace. It is probable Godzik dug the hole in which he was buried.

The Godzik family, like the Johnstons, responded immediately with a police report. They also were told their son was probably a runaway. Even when Greg's car was found abandoned and unlocked in Niles, a northern suburb of Chicago, police were not terribly concerned. When the Godzik family contacted Gacy, he replied Greg had simply failed to show up for work. Godzik's mother mentioned Gacy in her report to the police. Police failed to check Gacy for a prior criminal record. They did not interview him for over three months. If the authorities had run a check on John Gacy during that investigation, it is highly probable Gregory Godzik would have been the last victim.

By late 1976, John Wayne Gacy Jr. had hit full stride as a serial murderer. He was routinely abducting and murdering young men. The similarities between the victims were easily seen. They were usually of the physical type John himself described as being homosexuals: slight of build, usually blond, and typically under the age of twenty. It is interesting to note, although he raped a number of men over the age of twenty, the oldest of his known murder victims was barely twenty years old. Contrary to popular opinion, his victims were not all homosexuals. Many were normal healthy teenagers who were nothing more than targets of opportunity, often through PDM Contractors or John's cruising the streets.

His favorite hunting ground was the area around Washington Park. The location had been nicknamed Bughouse Square in the 1920s and 1930s when it was a favorite locale for radicals of various kinds and street speakers who would bring their soap boxes, stand on them, and lecture passers-by on the evils of contemporary society. By the mid-1960s, the area and its numerous small hotels and bars had become a favorite hangout for prostitutes of both sexes. By the time John returned to Chicago, it was known nationwide as a place for picking up homosexuals.

The most common method John used was to cruise up and down the streets until he saw someone who attracted him sexually, pull to the curb, and, after a brief conversation, offer them money or drugs in return for sex. On occasion, he posed as a police officer, although as time went on, both he and his vehicle became well known to the local street people. The transient lifestyle of the area's denizens made it easy for Gacy to take people away and not return them despite the fact both he and his vehicle were easily recognized.

Once he had gotten them back to the house on Summerdale Avenue, his behavior assumed an almost ritualistic mode. He invited them in and gave them food and drinks, and drugs if they requested them. Then came the magic tricks and death.

According to some sources, John may also have been involved in necrophilia. This is a term defining sexual activity with corpses. John admitted on one occasion that he spent an entire night with a corpse in bed with him. Some of his other habits included Russian roulette, torture of various kinds such as partial drowning, and an entire range of sadistic activities. After John was satiated, the victims would die. They were then taken into the crawlspace and buried in graves that had been dug unknowingly by some previous victims. Finally, exhausted, he would sleep for a few hours before resuming the trappings of his "normal" life.

John Szyc was a friend of Greg Godzik and John Butkovich. He knew Gacy but had never worked for him. Gacy picked up Szyc while cruising in Bughouse Square on the night of 20 January 1977. Gacy later said he killed Szyc because he asked for too much money in return for sex. Michael Rossi was in the house the night of the murder but allegedly slept through the entire incident.

Gacy also stole Szyc's belongings: his car, television, and radio, and some wigs and costume jewelry. Many of those items were found in the Gacy house after John was arrested. Szyc was found buried in the crawlspace.

The family of John Prestidge, a nursing student from Kalamazoo, Michigan, reported him missing on March 24. He had vanished in Chicago nine days before. Police listed him as a runaway. A psychic hired by his family insisted he was dead. His was the first of the bodies exhumed from Gacy's crawlspace.

Three more victims vanished into the crawlspace in quick succession: Matthew Bownan on 5 July, Robert Gilroy on 15 September, and John Mowery on 25 September. Each would later be identified through personal belongings or dental records.

Russell Nelson, an honors student from Minnesota, wanted to be an architect. On 19 October 1977, he disappeared while in a bar in Chicago. The friends with whom he was traveling were mystified. Police were notified, as was Nelson's family. He was later identified by his dental records as one of the skeletons in the crawlspace.

The following month, Gacy took two victims in one week. Robert Winch was a sixteen-year-old runaway who disappeared on 11 November. On the eighteenth, Tommy Boling, a trim, attractive young man of twenty, vanished from a North Side bar. Boling was married and the father of a baby boy. Winch was identified by his dental records and Boling by his wedding ring.

As 1977 drew to a close, the murders stopped, at least temporarily. In December, however, John committed at least two violent rapes. Although the victims escaped with their lives, police were less than responsive when complaints were filed. Law enforcement agencies in major urban areas often had to deal with individuals attempting to file questionable charges. The cynicism by police from dealing with bogus claims could have created an attitude that made it very possible to overlook serious crimes.

David Talsma and Robert Donnelly both went to the police after they had been abducted, beaten, and savagely raped. Because the crimes were men against men, the assumption was made that the victims were homosexuals. In the Talsma case, police refused to file charges altogether. In the Donnelly case, a charge of suspicion of deviant sexual conduct was filed but never prosecuted.

Robert Donnelly came as close to joining those buried in the crawlspace as anyone who survived. On New Year's Eve 1977, he was abducted at gun point from a bus stop in Northwest Chicago. A dark-colored car pulled up with its spotlight aimed on Donnelly. The driver demanded some identification and, when Robert leaned in to show it, he found a gun in his face. He assumed the man was a policeman and let Gacy handcuff him. Robert then was driven to Gacy's house.

The next seven hours were filled with brutal rape and torture. The violent story told by Donnelly illustrated vividly what the victims endured before they died.

Donnelly was shoved onto the couch in the recreation room. After three drinks for himself, Gacy forced a drink down Donnelly's throat. Turning him over, Gacy sat on Robert's back, pulling his head back by the hair until he screamed. Next, Gacy pulled Donnelly's jeans down, forced his knees apart, and sodomized him until he passed out.

For Donnelly, that was not the end of his suffering, but the beginning. Donnelly regained consciousness and was told to pull up his pants. Gacy grabbed the handcuffs and jerked him into the bathroom. Slipping a rope around Donnelly's neck, Gacy alternated twisting the rope and slamming Donnelly's head against the wall. Finally, Gacy held Donnelly's head under water in the bathtub until he passed out. Gacy allowed Donnelly to regain consciousness, only to perform the water torture on him two more times.

Next, Gacy urinated on him, savaged his rectum with a huge dildo, and began to play Russian roulette with a pistol pointed at Donnelly's face. Gacy told Donnelly that one live bullet was waiting for him. Gacy pulled the trigger over a dozen times until, finally, a loud report blasted into the room. Luckily, the shell was a blank cartridge. Five times more, Gacy choked the boy into unconsciousness.

Coming to, Donnelly found himself naked and gagged. Gacy, also naked, was fondling him. Punching him, Gacy forcibly turned Donnelly over and anally raped him with a dildo until he fainted. Donnelly awoke, and the dildo was again shoved up his rectum.

In agony, the nineteen-year-old begged Gacy to end it and kill him. John replied, "I'm getting around to that."

Finally, bored and satiated, Gacy forced Donnelly to shower

and clean himself up. Gacy drove him back to Marshall Field's in downtown Chicago, where Donnelly worked. As the young man got out of the car, Gacy told him no one would believe him if he reported what had happened.

Donnelly did bring in the police, and Gacy was arrested on 6 January 1978. Gacy, however, claimed the slave-sex routine was by mutual consent. It was the word of a respected businessman against a young man who spoke with a stutter. John was right; no one believed Donnelly.

Billy "Shotgun" Kindred was a tough street kid who thought he knew all the moves. On 16 February, he met John Gacy, and all the moves ended.

On 22 March, Gacy perpetrated another rape. Jeffrey Rignall was walking on the Near North Side at one-thirty a.m. when a sleek, black Oldsmobile with spotlights pulled alongside him. The heavyset driver with the genial features and engaging smile asked him if he wanted to share a joint of marijuana. After Rignall was in the car and relaxed from a few puffs, the man suddenly covered his face with a rag, and Rignall passed out.

At the Summerdale house, John carried Rignall inside. Largely a replay of the two rapes he carried out in December, John added a few refinements. He had built a replica of a medieval pillory and attached chains to the ceiling. Gacy later said he had gotten the idea for the board "From Elmer Wayne Henley. The guy in Texas." Henley was accused of over twenty homosexual rape/ murders before being killed by an accomplice.

Rignall found himself naked with his neck and wrists locked in the rack. His feet were locked into another device attached to the floor. Gacy stood naked and masturbated. On the floor were several long leather whips with wood and leather handles, some fireplace tools, and several plastic and rubber dildos. Gacy announced that he had total control over Rignall and explained how each item would be used.

Rignall endured hours of Gacy's torture. At four-thirty a.m., he awoke in a park near the lake. He was clothed, and only his driver's license was missing from his billfold. He spent a week in the hospital. The chloroform Gacy used to subdue Rignall caused permanent liver damage.

When Rignall went to the police, he openly told them he was a homosexual. Police cooperation and interest ended. Rignall, angered by their attitude, decided to investigate on his own. He had flashes of memory of the route his abductor had taken. He rented a car and staked out an exit on the Kennedy Expressway. Two weeks went by before he spotted Gacy and followed him to his house. When he returned to the police with a name and address, they still refused to cooperate. Several months went by before Gacy was finally arrested on a misdemeanor charge of assault against Rignall.

Rignall's life was in chaos because of the attack. He had incurred over $25,000 in medical bills and couldn't work because of his injuries. When the matter came to court in September 1978, he settled out of court for a mere $3,000. His driver's license was later found in Gacy's house.

An ironic problem arose for Gacy. His crawlspace cemetery was full. He had buried victims under his driveway, his garage, and his barbecue pit. His final four victims (or five, according to Gacy) were discarded into the Des Plaines River like so much trash.

As with every other serial murderer case, the Gacy case holds discrepancies. One is that John's total for the number of victims was thirty-four, rather than the thirty-three with which he was charged and convicted. The missing victim, according to him, was thrown into the Des Plaines River and the body was never recovered. This is not surprising as river bodies are often never found. The Des Plaines River is a tributary of the Illinois River, which is a tributary of the Mississippi River. The body could have been anywhere.

Timothy O'Rourke was a tough twenty-year-old who was interested in martial arts. He mentioned to a friend that a man named Gacy had promised him a job but had been giving him the runaround. In mid-June, O'Rourke went out for cigarettes and never returned. On 30 June, a badly decomposed, nude body washed ashore in the Illinois River six miles downstream from the I-55 bridge. Tattoos on the upper left arm led to identification as O'Rourke.

That July, John Gacy held his fifth and last theme party. It was the biggest one yet with hundreds of guests. John was dressed in an American Revolution costume to depict the central theme. These parties were not John Gacy having a sudden spasm of decency, but opportunities for him to continue his masquerade and to expand his base of influence.

Gacy's inner monster was under control until early November. He learned that Carole was planning to remarry.

Frank W. Landingin Jr., age nineteen, was a homosexual and would accept cash or gifts for promises of sex, then slip away before he performed sex with the buyer. He also dealt drugs, pimped, and was connected to the fringes of North Side gang activities.

After a drink in a North Side bar with his father at two a.m. on 4 November, Landingin left to find his girlfriend to make up after beating her the day before. He was next seen nine days later when duck hunters found his bloated body in the river. The autopsy showed Frank's bikini underpants had been jammed down his throat with vicious force. He had had sexual relations before death.

James Mazzara, known as Mo Jo, had dinner with his parents on Thanksgiving Day. The twenty-on-year-old was last seen walking alone toward Bughouse Square on 23 November.

Gacy later claimed that Mazzara was involved in sadism and bondage. After picking him up and driving him home, Gacy brought out his sexual paraphernalia. He fastened the young man in the medieval pillory. When Mazzara wanted twenty dollars more for each sex act and threatened to tell the neighbors he had been raped if Gacy did not pay, Gacy performed the rope trick. As Gacy said, "Since he liked pain, I did the ultimate number on him." In December, Mazzara's swollen body was found near where Frank Landingin's corpse had been located. Mo Jo's underwear had also been jammed down his throat.

Gacy continued to kill. However, his five-year reign of terror was nearly over. On 11 December 1978, John Gacy abducted his final victim. Fifteen-year-old Robert Jerome Piest was far from being a typical Gacy victim. He was taken from a drugstore parking lot in Des Plaines only blocks from Gacy's house. John was known by name at the drugstore where the Piest boy worked. Piest was a highly regarded, decent young man who had absolutely no contact with the gay lifestyle.

It is one of the many ironies of the Gacy case that young Piest, two merit badges short of Eagle Scout status, intended to obtain those badges by cleaning up the banks of the Des Plaines River. His body would be found in the river nearly four months later.

The eleventh of December was Rob's mother's birthday. When he did not return home that night, even though he was supposed to participate in a family celebration for his mother, his parents became extremely upset and called police. John Gacy's name quickly surfaced. Despite his criminal record in Iowa and his numerous arrests for sex offenses in Illinois, John was not initially considered a serious suspect in the Piest boy's disappearance.

When the Des Plaines police went to Gacy's house, they spoke with him at his front door. He admitted talking to the Piest boy the night before but denied knowing his whereabouts. John said if he heard anything he would contact the police immediately. John later admitted that during the interview, Rob Piest's body was still in the house. John had not had time to toss him into the river and would not do so until the night of 12 December.

As the days before Christmas passed, Gacy's name came up frequently. Finally, the law enforcement agencies in Cook County began to put together a speculative picture of John. At last, his name was connected with disappearances and rapes. Round-the-clock surveillance was ordered. John, feeling the momentum that would lead to his arrest, became increasingly erratic. Although he did not kill again, he did go to all his friends, make various self-serving excuses for his behavior, and, in effect, say his good-byes.

The surveillance began to take its toll. John was alternately grandiose, arrogant, humble, outraged, and depressed. Like Ted Bundy, John took a peculiar delight in leading the surveillance officers on high-speed chases. True to type, he could not resist the temptation occasionally to taunt the police. They would not forget his behavior in the months to come.

Convinced Gacy knew something about the Piest boy's disappearance, Cook County authorities obtained their first search warrant 13 December for the house and car at 8213 Summerdale Avenue. Although a large amount of incriminating evidence was obtained as the result of the search, Gacy was still not arrested.

On 19 December, Gacy invited two detectives into his home. While one officer searched the bathroom, he immediately noticed the unmistakable smell of rotting bodies coming from air blowing from a heating duct. A second search warrant was obtained on 21 December 1978.

It is interesting to note that also on 21 December, one day before he was arrested, John had signed a contract to have six inches of prestressed concrete pumped into the crawlspace. Had he done so, it is unlikely any judge, based on the evidence available at the time, would have authorized a warrant to cut through the concrete.

Finally, on 22 December, Gacy was arrested. He was charged not with murder, but with a marijuana offense. Police had already found Gacy's outstanding battery charge in Chicago and his Iowa prison sentence for sodomy. They had interviewed survivors of Gacy's torture.

During the following days and then weeks, Gacy's house was thoroughly searched and the crawlspace closely examined. Rotting corpses were quickly discovered. Investigators and evidence technicians were faced with logistical problems in exhuming the bodies. They ran sump pumps to remove the standing water. Then, as they shone flashlights around the crawlspace, they could see slight depressions in the ground. They feared the depressions were the graves of the numerous missing young men.

They decided they would have to remove the house floorboards to have maneuvering room. The excavation required the same careful techniques as an archeological dig. Unlike the recovery of bodies in the Corona case, the location of each bone and personal possession was precisely recorded. Photographs were taken of the progress and of each body site. The clinical procedures went smoothly.

Yet this was not a neat, tidy investigation. The crawlspace contained oozing mud over which Gacy had spread layers of lime through the years to try to control the sickly sweet smell of rotting flesh. As the corpses were uncovered, that smell made even the most hardened evidence technician wretch. Hundreds of red grave worms that feed on decaying flesh wriggled through the standing water. The body tissues immersed in water had decayed to a soap-like appearance called adipocere flesh. Even wearing protective clothing, the workers were in constant danger of infection from even the slightest scratch.

Law enforcement authorities had intended to restore the house to its original condition after the excavation was completed. However, a building inspector ruled the structure was unsafe due to the removal of so many boards to facilitate the work. The house was razed in April 1979. An entrepreneur bought the house's bricks and sold them through various detective magazines for twenty-five dollars each. He sold every brick. The lot remained vacant for many years. No one wanted to build on the site of so much death.

Even after the dead were later buried by their families, nameless victims remained. No more tragic fate can be imagined than to come into life, exist, and then go out, denied of everything including one's name.

As the house was excavated and then demolished, the murder charges began to pile up. By early 1979, John Wayne Gacy Jr. was charged with more individual counts of homicide than any individual in American history up to that time: thirty-three. Horror had come to the suburbs.

Although he would not go to trial for more than two years, one of the most exhaustive and expensive pretrial investigations ever conducted began. Dozens of officers from various law enforcement agencies would eventually become involved. Many items of physical evidence removed from Gacy's house were identified, evaluated, and followed up. Hundreds of friends and acquaintances from all over America were located and interviewed. The families of identified victims were notified.

Meanwhile, John called himself "Duke" after his first and middle names in reference to the actor John Wayne. Gacy languished in the Cook County Jail and, one suspects, enjoyed his new celebrity status.

Time passed and pretrial motions fluttered through the air like falling leaves. After numerous delays, the case of The People of the *State of Illinois v. John Wayne Gacy* was set for trial on 6 February 1980.

Because of worldwide publicity, jury selection was a major issue. Judge Louis Garippo who, coincidentally, had been a defense attorney for Richard Speck a decade before, was assigned to the case. The judge granted a change of venue for the purpose of jury selection to Rockford, Illinois, a small community nearly a hundred miles west of Chicago. The voir dire documents in the Gacy case would eventually come to be known as the "Rockford Files," nicknamed after the television show.

From the very beginning, all the parties involved in the Gacy trial were aware their every move over the next few weeks would be closely scrutinized by the world press. Probably no criminal trial had received so much media attention since the Manson followers were prosecuted for the Tate-La Bianca murders ten years before.

On Wednesday, 6 February 1980, opening statements were made in the trial. Prosecutor Robert Egan began the laborious process of laying out the State's case against John. The defense, headed by Robert Motta, began its task of convincing the jury that John was not evil but insane, a task made no easier by John's calm demeanor in the courtroom.

The opening days of the trial were consumed by the exhausting process of establishing the existence, the lives, and the deaths of John's victims. At that time, only twenty-two of the thirty-three victims had been identified. The other eleven were tried as John Doe cases.

The unidentified victims were buried in 1981 in separate Chicago-area cemeteries with stones marked "We Are Remembered." As of 2021, six of the victims have still not been identified and probably never will be. Gacy's genetic profile was entered into a law enforcement database for use in matching future newly recovered remains that might hold a killer's DNA.

The second phase of the trial was taken up by psychiatric testimony. This testimony took nearly a week and was extremely important to understanding the issues. Anyone familiar with the psychiatric aspects of the American criminal justice system is quite aware that there are as many differing psychiatric opinions as there are available psychiatrists. Certainly, John's case was no different.

To understand the context in which the psychiatric testimony was given, it is necessary to look briefly at the so-called insanity plea. The insanity plea is used in approximately one-half of one percent of all criminal trials in America. It works in roughly one-half of one percent of those attempts. The results in successful insanity pleas number only a few hundred nationwide annually. Contrary to the portrayal given at the time of the Hinckley assassination attempt against President Reagan in 1982, defense lawyers rarely use the insanity approach and only in cases of the most outrageous, visible mental illness.

Historically, the American version of the insanity plea rose out of a principle of British Common Law called the M'Naughten Rule. This principle requires a two-part test. The first part of the test speaks to the question of whether the defendant has the ability to understand the difference between right and wrong. The second aspect speaks to the question of whether that defendant has the ability to understand the consequences of his or her actions.

To the ordinary person, the crimes of John Gacy—ritualistic serial murders, sexual sadism and mutilation, burying his victims in his basement and yard, then tossing a few others in a nearby river for good measure—appear to be the acts of a true madman.

Psychiatric testimony speaking to that question went on for days. The crowded, hot courtroom saw tempers shorten as rapidly as attention spans while the war of the psychiatrists raged on. The court finally concluded John was sane. If one looks past the superficial aspects of his crimes, bizarre though they may be, one finds a logical, methodical, and calculating criminal at work.

The trial dragged into its third week. A long line of law enforcement officials from various police agencies were called to testify concerning their roles in John's apprehension. They often brought forensic material, and their testimony was frequently gruesome in the extreme. The forensic aspects of the Gacy case, and indeed those of any serial murderer with many victims, come to resemble the aftermath of a war. Parts of bodies jumbled together must be separated and identified, survivors located and notified, and an attempt made to reconstruct some aspect of the dignity lost by the nature of the victims' deaths.

After the prosecution and defense laid out their main cases, the complex process of rebuttal commenced. My own [Raymond Cornell's] direct involvement in the trial began then. On Monday, 25 February 1980, I flew to Chicago and spent the next three days reviewing the documents relevant to my testimony. During that time, I also encountered several of the other Iowa witnesses: Gacy's Waterloo friends and victims and staff members from the Iowa Men's Reformatory at Anamosa who had known John while he was in prison.

On Friday morning, 29 February, the Iowa witnesses were scheduled to testify in rebuttal. After a harrowing drive through a raging blizzard from downtown Chicago to the Cook County Courthouse at 26th and California Streets, the witnesses were individually sequestered in preparation for their testimony. Tragically, the first Iowa witness on the stand was Donald Voorhees

Jr., a slight, blond-headed young man who had been heavily drinking the night before. Riding to the courthouse, I sat next to him, and the aroma of alcohol was quite noticeable. He had been one of John's earliest victims and was now apparently caught in an emotional bind between what had happened then and his reason for being in Chicago. Soon after being placed on the stand and being sworn in, it was obvious he was not capable of giving good testimony. He mumbled, slurred his speech, and finally began weeping. After several attempts to elicit coherent responses, Judge Garippo was finally forced to dismiss the witness and order his testimony stricken. All Gacy's victims did not die. Indeed, the living ones suffered more and longer.

When we arrived that morning, it was discovered not enough holding rooms were available to sequester the witnesses. I was asked by a Cook County deputy if I would mind waiting in a holding cell until my turn to testify. What was to have been a twenty-minute wait lasted nearly four hours. As I sat alone, I realized the cell also contained some of the physical evidence used earlier in the trial. In one corner was the hatchway, which had been taken up and mounted vertically on casters, to the infamous crawlspace. In another corner on a library cart were the thirty-three body books. Each of those, a black eight-and-a-half-by-fourteen-inch binder, contained the in situ photographs of one victim.

As the minutes extended into hours, I finally succumbed to the temptation and looked at each body book. The memory of those photographs will be with me forever.

Just before noon, I was led into the courtroom and sworn in. As I walked to the witness chair, I glanced over at John. He nodded and gave a slight smirk. He seemed to be enjoying the trial more than anyone else in the courtroom. It was almost as if by hearing the details of his crimes he was reliving the pleasure they had brought him.

As I looked back at him, superimposed on his face were the pictures of gaping skulls, rotting flesh, and bloated corpses. My testimony was mercifully brief and confined to the facts of our lives in prison together more than a decade before. Noon recess was called when I finished my testimony.

When I walked into the hallway, I was met by the parents of Robert Piest, who both shook my hand and thanked me for what

I had done. I had nothing I could say to them. Their tragedy and those of the other families could no longer be encompassed by words.

As I rode the elevator down, I began to realize my life had also been changed forever. Never again could I ever assume anything or anyone was what he seemed to be. Evil could hide behind a mask of friendship. I would have nightmares for years following the trial. However, if someone as peripherally involved as I could pay a price that high, it is frightening to speculate what the cost must have been for the victims' families and the law enforcement officers who had been living with the case for over two years.

The trial extended two more weeks. Finally, on 11 March, closing arguments were made. The prosecution pointed out the facts of the case and their contention that John was indisputably sane and indisputably guilty. The defense attempted to convince the jury that Gacy had suffered from thirty-three instances of temporary insanity. The jury began its deliberations later in the day. In less than two hours, they announced a verdict: guilty on all counts.

On Thursday, 13 March 1980, at one-thirty p.m., John Wayne Gacy Jr. was sentenced to death for each of his thirty-three murders. After hearing the sentence pronounced, John gave a rare insight into himself. He said, "It's God's will. The jury just did to me what I've been trying to do to myself for so many years."

With that many crimes and convictions, the number of available appeals was nearly infinite. The jury decided that John Gacy should die. The courts would decide when.

Transferred to the Menard Correctional Center, John remained on death row for fourteen years. After reading numerous law books, he filed many motions and appeals. All failed.

The US Supreme Court denied Gacy's final appeal in October 1993. On 9 May 1994, John was moved to Stateville Correctional Center in Crest Hill to be executed by lethal injection. Before the injections started, the chemicals unexpectedly solidified and clogged the IV tube. Procedures were halted, the tube was replaced, and the execution resumed. John was pronounced dead after eighteen minutes at 12:59 a.m. on 10 May 1994. William Kunkle, a Gacy trial prosecutor commented, "He got a much easier death than any of his victims."

Ted Bundy: Evil Wears a Smile

Theodore Robert Colwell Nelson Bundy was born on 24 November 1946. He has been convicted of three murders in Florida and is suspected of murders and rapes in at least five other states. Ted may have killed when he was as young as sixteen, and he is believed to have committed at least forty murders. What is certain is Bundy left a trail of bloody bodies and skeletons throughout the northwest United States. His fondness for caving in the heads of young women made him one of the most feared and hated killers this country has ever known.

Bundy's life had been under a dark star literally from the day he was born. His birth was not the happy event the arrival of a first child is usually considered. Ted was conceived out of wedlock at a time when illegitimacy still carried a heavy social stigma. However, his mother was determined to keep her child and made many sacrifices to do so.

Eleanor Louise Colwell was the prim and proper daughter of a Philadelphia nurseryman. She had been seduced by a man named Jack Worthington, who claimed to be a World War II veteran and hinted of an old-money pedigree. When Eleanor became pregnant, Worthington disappeared. She never saw him again and was never completely certain Worthington was even his real name.

Twenty-two years old and seven months pregnant, Eleanor entered a home for unwed mothers in Vermont. Sixty-three days later, Ted was born.

Eleanor returned to Philadelphia, where she and her infant son began living a charade. Ted heard his mother referred to as his older sister and his grandparents as his mother and father. Undersized and slight of build, he sensed he was living a lie. However, he adored his grandfather/father Colwell. Ted identified with him, respected him, and clung to him in times of trouble. That probably was the most emotionally intense relationship of his life.

In Philadelphia, however, too many relatives knew the real story of his birth. His mother dreaded what Ted's growing up years would be like and never wanted him to hear the word "bastard." About the time Ted turned four, his mother went to court and had his name legally changed to Theodore Robert Nelson. Her choice of the name Nelson remains a mystery.

Shortly afterward, Ted and his mother moved west. Joining an aunt and uncle in Tacoma, Washington, they began a new life. Eleanor began referring to herself as Louise.

At first, Ted hated Tacoma. It was tremendously difficult for him to leave his grandfather behind. Angry and confused, Ted missed his grandfather and the comfortable old house in which he had lived. He did not know why his last name had been changed or why his mother had uprooted his life.

As time passed, he developed a deep contempt for anything he regarded as common. His attitude became linked to his self-image, self-doubt, and later conviction that he was a man wronged by life. He seems to have seen himself in the role of a prince forced to live with paupers. His uncle, Jack Colwell, was only a few years older than Ted's mother. Ted always called Jack his uncle even though he was, in fact, a granduncle. Colwell was a music professor at Tacoma's College of Puget Sound and a man of some considerable refinement. Later, Ted began to consciously model himself after his uncle.

Ted later grew to like Tacoma. A quiet, classic American town, the city, however, possessed another side. The downtown area had more than its share of honky-tonk bars, peep shows, porno parlors, and prostitutes. The seamier side of life catered primarily to soldiers from nearby Fort Lewis.

Louise's personal life finally began to improve. An active Methodist, she met John Culpepper Bundy at a young adults' social. Johnny Bundy, a North Carolinian, was shy, kind, and reliable. Also, both he and Louise were under five feet tall, a fact that could have attracted them to each other immediately. Uneducated and with few prospects for advancement in life, Johnny worked as a cook at the local VA hospital. John Bundy accepted Louise and her son completely. He considered her to be a gentle, God-fearing woman whose life history began the night they met. He did not question her past or judge her deeds. On 19 May 1951,

Louise Colwell and John Culpepper Bundy were married.

By the time Ted turned five years old, he had a third name. He was now Theodore Robert Bundy. That was a serious trauma for a child his age. Ted tried his best to block Johnny, the outsider, from his mind. Bundy's very presence upset Ted. Johnny's slow deliberate ways and Southern drawl registered as serious defects as far as Ted was concerned. Seen in the light of classic Freudian psychoanalysis, Ted Bundy was well on his way to significant emotional troubles by the time he was five.

Young Ted considered himself to be a Colwell. Other than being slightly darker in coloration, Ted most strongly resembled his mother and his grandfather: alert-looking eyes, high forehead, slender aquiline nose, and a ready smile. Unlike his mother, Ted was not physically small or possessed of her delicate mannerisms. By the time he was completely grown, Ted Bundy, at nearly six feet, would tower over his mother and stepfather.

The new family moved several times before finally settling into a house on 20th Avenue South in Tacoma. The carefully maintained, two-story home sat in the middle of an orderly, quiet neighborhood. The middle-class neighbors with their small yards and home handyman projects seemed very unappealing to Ted.

In keeping with the times, Louise did most of the actual parenting. A reticent, private person, she had difficulty discussing intimate or personal matters. Sex was not discussed in the home. Her childhood became also a closed chapter. Although his mother's favorite child, Ted found out she had been an extremely successful child in high school only when he happened to read her yearbook years later.

Ted spent time with his stepfather only grudgingly. Johnny tried his best to get through to Ted. Unfortunately, a positive relationship between the two never developed. In matters of discipline, Louise always had the final say. Although Johnny sometimes administered punishment, Louise always made the decision to do so. Without doubt, she formed the dominant force in their household.

Most of Ted's educational records are missing. However, he is remembered as an unexceptional student. When his first-grade teacher, of whom he was very fond, left to have a baby, Ted became extremely upset. Then, to add insult to injury, Ted found himself in the hands of a second-grade teacher who he considered to be menacing and inclined to discriminate against him. One biographer implied Ted attributed her attitude to the fact she was a rigid, doctrinaire Catholic and he was a Protestant.

By age seven, Ted began to sense he had a flaw. Escaping more and more into fantasy, he, like many others of his generation, dreamed of being adopted by Roy Rogers and Dale Evans. They were seen by the children of the day as the ideal parents: loving, kind, and attentive yet living lives filled with excitement and adventure.

Still fascinated by his Uncle Jack's flamboyant lifestyle, Ted felt deprived at home. He felt deeply contemptuous of his own family's modest way of life. A preoccupation with material wealth that began to develop at the time would stay with him and intensify in his later life.

Ted's first apparent gesture of defiance against Johnny was a passive one. Aware of his stepfather's white Southern background, he went out of his way to make friends with the only black family in the neighborhood.

Two childhood friends, with whom he remained close all the way through high school, later said he provided great company but at times seemed aloof and temperamental. They also said his eyes turned deep black when he was angry. Those eyes would be the most memorable and frightening sight his victims would ever see. Going from bright blue to deepest obsidian, they were the eyes of Death.

One of Ted's pet peeves was Boy Scouts, primarily because his stepfather was the Scoutmaster. Ted disliked Scout camp because of the sweat and dirtiness. He avoided the camping trips that other boys his age enjoyed so much.

Johnny continued his dogged efforts to develop a relationship with his stepson. He helped him with his morning paper route, and the two of them earned extra money picking beans in the local truck gardens.

Throughout high school, Ted's relationship with Johnny continued to deteriorate. Ted derived considerable pleasure from provoking his stepfather by playing mind games on him. He knew he could quickly irritate Johnny. Then, he would simply browbeat him until Johnny lost his temper and reacted physically. There is no indication his stepfather ever initiated an argument with Ted.

At that time in his life, the loner pattern, so common with serial murderers, first began to develop. Solitude provided a way to cope with his insecurities and fears. He developed a rich fantasy life, mostly built around the late-night talk radio shows of which he was fond. Alone in the dark, he could be part of a special and secret world in which he was equal to or better than anyone else. Sitting in the wee hours of the morning, he listened to, memorized, and imitated the various accents he heard. Later, he used an almost perfect English accent in several of his crimes. Being alone also allowed him to hide his habits of nail biting and compulsive nose-picking.

Handsome and a good athlete, Ted, however, lacked mental maturity. Feeling very self-conscious about being skinny, he turned to solitary sports. He was a minor success in track. Also, Ted liked skiing, although he probably stole his costly gear. Ted and several boys devised a crude ski-lift ticket forgery scheme and were never caught.

When he was not in class or on the slopes, Ted Bundy must have felt like a stranger in a strange land. Those who knew him in high school remembered him as being uninterested and uninvolved. Although a B average student, he never accomplished anything exceptional. He presented the picture of the classic teenage loner—attractive, well dressed, polite, but always on the outside.

Away from the teachers, Ted became the butt of cruel high school humor. His obsessive desire for privacy, even in the boys' shower room, led to merciless teasing on more than one occasion. The other boys knew eventually Ted would become angry and chase them away. His reactions provided a source of great amusement to his classmates but widened the gulf between Ted and others his age.

Bitterness and hostility grew in the shadow of his solitary life. As adolescence began the process of changing him into a man, Ted must have been frustrated and confused almost constantly. A friend who knew him at the time recalled Ted would head in the other direction at high speed whenever sex was mentioned.

He showed a lack of sensitivity to the feelings of women even deeper than that of a normal teenage boy. Females were attracted to him, yet his sexual naivete made their behavior incomprehensible to him. No indication exists that he had a significant relationship with any girl in high school.

Police research cited in Robert Larsen's book, *The Deliberate Stranger,* summed up Ted's childhood in the following way:

> Up through the fifth grade he was constantly displaying babyish activities. He was rather a loner, didn't want to get involved with too many people at the time. He liked to do superior work when he did it. That doesn't mean that he did superior work. He just liked to pass this off in school—this impression he did do superior work. His character was such that he was too good for any sort of discipline. I don't know whether this led from his mother's emphasis or what.

Family members also recalled Ted was picked up twice for suspicion of auto theft and burglary. He was never confined or found guilty of anything. In compliance with standard operating procedure in dealing with juvenile cases, all his records were shredded when he turned eighteen. Therefore, it is impossible to be more specific.

Even after many years, Louise never confirmed or denied to Ted that she was his mother and not his older sister. At home, he sometimes called her Louise, and other times called her Mother.

She, on the other hand, felt Ted had the most potential of all her five children and should go to college. By the time he was in his early teens, she was already encouraging him to save his money for tuition. The pressures of impending adulthood combined with his feelings of inadequacy to make Ted an unhappy, confused, lonely teenager.

It also was around that time Ted found out he was an illegitimate child. The recollections of those who knew him differed as to whether he was particularly upset about the information. Some said he had suspected for a long time and was not particularly ruffled when it became common knowledge. Others said he was furious with his mother for leaving him open to such humiliation. Ted never showed any open anger toward his mother. He kept everything bottled up inside.

He later stated the knowledge brought his normal social development to a halt. His prior progress had been less than exceptional. He matured little in high school and now felt cut off and alienated from his old friends. He lacked an understanding of appropriate social behavior and frequently found himself tongue-tied in social situations. His sense of insecurity deepened.

After graduating from high school, Ted attended the University of Puget Sound in Tacoma for the 1965–66 school year. He had earlier received a scholarship to the university. The student body at the university was comprised largely of high achievers, most of whom came from well-to-do families. Ted, with his lower middle-class background and insecurities, felt out of place from the very beginning. After he finished one semester, he never returned.

In the fall, he attended classes at the University of Washington in Seattle and declared a major in their Chinese studies program. His reasoning was China was the nation to contend with in the future. One suspects he also enjoyed the opportunity to wrap himself in a program most would consider exotic and difficult. As a student in the classroom, Ted continued to be mediocre at best. All during his academic career, there is little reason to believe he was ever a serious student or a profound thinker.

Possibly one of the most important moments for Ted came in late 1966 when he bought his first car. Like any other American youth of his generation, a car meant the ultimate freedom. He had the mobility to come and go as he pleased, and possibly for the first time, could be alone whenever he chose. The two vehicles Ted owned in his life were both Volkswagen sedans. The VW Beetle, nicknamed the "Bug," was a common sight on American highways during the 1960s and 1970s. The tough, durable, little car allowed him to scout out the secluded areas where he would later dump the bodies of his victims. On the other hand, no one would think of a murderer using a Bug as a getaway car.

Now nearly twenty, Ted still had not developed a serious relationship with a woman. His shyness, discomfort in social situations, and shame about his social background held him back. His negative self-image made it impossible for him to develop a relationship with the kind of woman he felt he should be able to obtain.

However, he began an elaborate construction of a public persona. He cultivated an air of scholarly wisdom and wholesome, serious intellectuality. His persona proved a key element in his ability to successfully approach his victims on college campuses and wherever students gathered. He developed an alter ego that was everything he was not, and most of all, was irresistible to women. That was the first of the many masks behind which Ted Bundy would live.

That phase of his life also saw an increasing distance between Ted and his family. His parents stated later they did not even know how to get in touch with him.

In early 1967, Ted met a young woman on campus named Stephanie Brooks. The daughter of a wealthy California family, Brooks was Ted's fantasy ideal: tall, darkhaired, bright, beautiful, and sophisticated. He quickly fell for her. She does not seem to have responded nearly as strongly. Little by little, he managed to overcome her reservations. They began spending more and more time together. For Ted, it must have seemed like a dream come true. Yet people who knew the two of them saw his attitude toward her as that of a cherished possession rather than a developing emotional relationship.

That attitude and behavior is typical of the so-called "psychopathic" personality. People are managed as if they are objects to be used and discarded at will. People as objects and the inability to feel guilt are fundamental to such individuals.

Ted and Stephanie's relationship would continue in some form for nearly six years. The most intense part of it came and went in 1967. A sexual aspect had developed rather quickly with Stephanie taking the initiative. Ted, prior to that time, seems to have been totally inexperienced.

By the time she graduated in June 1967, Stephanie was making attempts to bring their relationship to a painless close. She sensed Ted was adrift and had no real plans for his life. She knew he was manipulative and dishonest. She also was quite aware of his feelings of insecurity. Those were not attributes she wanted in a future husband.

Stephanie went home to San Francisco hoping that would end the relationship. Ted was right behind her. He attended a summer session at Stanford. In the fall, she insisted he return to Seattle, and she terminated the romantic aspect of their relationship. Ted was devastated. His alternate persona had let him down, and he could not understand why.

Retreating into isolation, he began the construction of a "new" Ted Bundy. He literally discarded all the failed aspects of his personality. Abandoning his interest in Chinese, at which he had failed during the summer session, he took up the study of urban planning. He withdrew from the social contacts he had previously maintained and, at the end of the year, he quit school and left town.

Ted followed a pattern he had used time after time. Faced with frustration, he withdrew into physical and emotional isolation. Later, a new and improved version of Ted Bundy appeared.

After dropping out of school, Ted traveled around the Northwest before returning to Seattle in the spring of 1968. Soon after, he met and befriended a drug user and petty thief who polished his talents in crime. He learned to practice the invisibility all successful thieves acquire: nice clothes, an amiable smile, and a forgettable face. Bundy became a sophisticated shoplifter. It is impossible to tell whether he stole for the item or for the thrill. Certainly, each would have had its rewards. He was never apprehended.

Another part of Ted's new facade was politics. Through a friend from high school, he became involved with the Republican party. A political campaign provided an ideal forum for Ted to utilize his talents as an organizer and manipulator. Like a chameleon, Ted adapted his mannerisms to move through the various levels of Seattle society. He obtained the necessary social graces to be accepted almost everywhere.

Bundy, despite his newly acquired social skills, continued to be as naive and ignorant of human behavior as ever. For example, while attending a party at the home of a prominent GOP official, Ted got drunk and found himself in bed with the hostess. His role was of seducee rather than seducer. The incredible faux pas occurred because of Ted's inability to translate the most basic human signals.

For the next several years, Ted became known not only for his charming personality but for his meticulously groomed and correct appearance. Ted was finally coming into his own. After the devastating blow dealt by Stephanie, his newest self-creation helped him to develop more of a conscious awareness of his own abilities and powers than ever before. The revised Ted Bundy appeared charming, sophisticated, droll, and charismatic.

In order to pay his way through college, Ted took a series of menial jobs. He served as a bus boy at a yacht club and a hotel, a stock boy at a surgical supply house, and a shoe salesman. At the hotel, he continued to be a petty thief. Items taken from the surgical supply house would be evidence in his later crimes. Most importantly, the sales job gave him the opportunity to develop his ability to charm women into almost anything. He never stayed at any job long and usually left under questionable circumstances.

A coworker at the yacht club, Beatrice Sloan, became well acquainted with Ted while he worked there. She suspected him of being dishonest and a schemer, but she allowed him to borrow money and to use her car. Sloan also indicated Ted stole money from drunken patrons of the club while driving them home. Ted boasted his father was a famous chef and his uncle was a power in Philadelphia politics. Like many others, Beatrice was charmed into ignoring Ted's faults.

By the end of November, Ted's carefully built life was falling apart. He received failing grades in his new major of urban planning at school. His political candidates had lost, and his personal life, as usual, proved void of contacts.

Shortly after the first of the year, Ted left Washington to visit relatives in Arkansas. From there, he seems to have gone to Vermont to resolve the question of his birth. In Burlington, Ted confirmed he was, indeed, illegitimate. His birth certificate indicated his father was a man named Jack Worthington, who allegedly was educated at Pennsylvania State University and had served in the US Army Air Corps. There is no indication Ted ever tried to locate his father, and no one named Jack Worthington ever came forward.

Ted now knew for sure that Louise was his mother and not his sister. Neither of the two father-figures he had known, John Bundy and Ted's grandfather, was his father. Although he later denied it, he must have had significant feelings of loss, confusion, and anger.

Ted spent the spring of 1969 in Philadelphia. He took classes at Temple University in the Theatrical Arts curriculum. He discovered he had one of those forgettable faces that, with a minimum of effort, can be made to look like almost anyone. The ability would stand him in good stead in the years to come. He was able to present many different appearances, confusing victims and witnesses and allowing him to live as a fugitive.

In May, Ted returned to the West Coast. His obsession with Stephanie Brooks had not abated. He showed up unexpectedly on her doorstep one day. She was not thrilled to see him. For a second time, Ted experienced rejection.

Ted again went into physical and emotional isolation. He became obsessed with the need to transform into someone else. He wanted to be the kind of man Stephanie would admire and see as a successful person.

Back in Seattle, Ted resumed his old haunts in the University area. In the fall, he met Meg Anders. For the next several years, Meg served as his primary relationship. She had already been married and divorced, and she had a three-year-old daughter. Meg was an insecure and somewhat jealous woman who distrusted men.

A petite woman, she wore her dark brown hair long and was usually well dressed. When she met Ted, Meg was working as a secretary at one of the Seattle colleges. Their friendship quickly turned into an affair, and Meg soon found herself deeply in love with Ted. Although she wanted to get married, Ted always had some reason why they should wait. Simultaneously, Ted was very attentive and was good to her and her daughter. Meg sometimes feared Ted was as interested in her family's social position and wealth—her father was a prominent Utah doctor—as he was in her. Meg's jealousy enhanced her suspicions that Ted saw other women.

Meg seems to have dealt with his dishonesty and occasional cruelties by rationalizing them away. She believed totally in his ability to succeed and often loaned him money to help him pay for his schooling.

Unknown to Meg, Ted still maintained a relationship of sorts with Stephanie. Stephanie now worked at a job that brought her through Seattle occasionally. When she was in the area, she always got in touch with Ted, and they spent time together.

In the fall of 1969, Ted enrolled as a student at the University of Washington as a psychology major. His grades improved dramatically from the previous year, and he became an honors student. Considered by his professors to be extremely bright, Ted finally seemed to have stabilized a bit. For the next year, he excelled at everything. He renewed his activity in Republican politics. His education was paying off with a greater degree of sophistication and social grace than he ever before possessed. In 1970, he saved a small child from drowning and captured a purse snatcher. On the outside, he appeared to be an ideal citizen.

Yet Ted continued to steal and to manipulate everyone around him. He made many plans but lacked the self-discipline to carry them out. His slender physique concealed a much greater strength than was apparent. A handsome man, he attracted women with his wavy brown hair, dark eyes, and pleasant features. He also developed an almost courtly approach toward them, which served to increase their vulnerability even further.

Meanwhile, more and more people who knew them assumed Ted and Meg would soon marry. Everyone noticed her visible affection and devotion to him.

By 1970, Ted developed an interest in hard-core, violent pornography. He also began lurking around the University District and peering into windows. Later, one of Meg's girlfriends identified him as the man she had caught in her yard late at night. Periodically, he proved very moody and depressed.

In the fall of 1971, Ted began a job at the Seattle Crisis Clinic. Part of his pre-employment screening was a test to determine his level of maturity and balance. Ted passed. He worked nights responding to telephone requests for help and advice. One person who knew him felt he became very good at the work and may, in fact, have saved the lives of several people. He continued in this position for several months.

Now in his senior year of college, Ted continued to do well. He finally graduated in June 1972 with a bachelor's degree in psychology. He became the first in his family to graduate from college.

His aim then seemed to have been to enter law school. While on the surface he appeared to be a prime candidate, his aptitude scores were unimpressive. His professors saw him as stable, responsible, and brilliant. Interestingly, one of his former professors remembered Bundy developed an interest in the psychological variables affecting jury selection. The topic would hold a great interest for him in the years to come.

In June, he was awarded an eight-week internship at the Harbor View Hospital Psychiatric Clinic. Unlike the faceless, disembodied voices he had helped at the Crisis Clinic, Ted was remembered at Harbor View as cold, detached, and almost abusive in his dealings with patients.

During the summer of 1972, Ted added a third woman to

his collection. Clair Forest was another slim brunette with long, straight hair parted in the middle. They spent considerable time together that summer but had sex only once. Her memory of the event revealed harshness almost to the point of brutality. She recalled him choking her with his forearm during the sex act. As she struggled to breathe, Ted continued to hold her down until he climaxed. Afterward, he acted as if nothing had happened.

In the fall of 1972, having failed in his attempt to gain admission to law school, Ted returned to another of his favorite arenas—politics. He worked as a monitor for the incumbent governor. His duties required he attend the speeches and public appearances of the Democratic opposition and report back to the Governor on what was said and done. He used fake mustaches and otherwise altered his appearance to avoid rousing the suspicions of his counterparts in the Democratic party. One suspects Ted truly enjoyed the opportunity to disguise himself and to function as a "secret agent."

From October 1972 to January 1973, Ted served as assistant director of the Seattle Crime Commission. Such crime commissions formed a common aspect of local government during the 1970s. The massive influx of law enforcement assistance monies enabled many local jurisdictions to dramatically improve and expand their law enforcement agencies. During his tenure, Ted worked on studies involving white collar crime and rape prevention. At the same time, his interests in pornography and window peeking continued.

In January 1973, he was employed by the King County Office of Law and Justice Planning. Criminal justice planning agencies usually received funding by law enforcement assistance monies. During his employment, Ted was involved in studies of recidivism for minor offenders. The position also gave him access to large amounts of raw law enforcement data. He had the opportunity to study the inadequate levels of communication between law enforcement agencies and the actual records of convicted felons. Once again, his fascination with rape victims was noted. Ted also attempted to start a law enforcement consulting firm called T.R.B. Associates, another of his grandiose schemes that resulted in nothing.

In April 1973, Ted received an appointment as the assistant to the chairman of the Washington State Republican party. Among the many benefits, including an excellent salary, came the use of a select credit card, a car, expense-paid travel, and the opportunity to rub shoulders with the heavyweights in Washington State politics. Ted, the handsome, personable, young party stalwart, drew recognition as a man on the way up. He was being carefully groomed for future political office.

In July, Ted flew to San Francisco to visit Stephanie Brooks. The new and improved Ted Bundy was now unveiled to her. He had changed his appearance, his mannerisms, his speech, and his lifestyle. The Ted who returned from Philadelphia in 1969 had disappeared. The current Ted was a power in Washington State politics and an imposing figure with an almost limitless future. Needless to say, neither Meg nor Stephanie knew about the other, or about Clair Forest. Underneath the imposing figure, the liar, manipulator, and thief remained.

Earlier that summer, Ted got accepted as a night student at the University of Puget Sound Law School. He also bought a tan 1968 Volkswagen sedan. The innocuous little hearse would carry more than twenty young women to their graves.

After his rejection by the University of Utah Law School the year before, Meg had urged Ted to reapply. His application for admission for the fall 1973 term was accepted. However, prior to the start of the term, Ted, now admitted to two law schools, wrote the dean of Admissions and indicated he had been severely injured in an automobile accident and would be unable to attend. The excuse was an out-and-out lie. Later, after his arrest in Salt Lake City, the authorities discovered his entire application proved nothing more than an elaborate fabrication.

Ted began classes at the University of Puget Sound Law School in the fall of 1973. He saw Puget Sound as a second-rate school. Yet, he was the one who had decided not to attend the far more prestigious University of Utah. From the beginning, his performance as a law student left a great deal to be desired. By the end of the semester, he became a clear-cut failure.

Soon after the beginning of the semester, Stephanie Brooks flew up from San Francisco to be with Ted. During her stay, Ted introduced her to one of his friends as his fiancé. He had finally convinced Stephanie to take him seriously. It had taken years to win her over, but he had done it. They made plans for her to return to Seattle during the Christmas holidays. She understood they would discuss marriage plans then.

When she returned to visit him in December, his manner became increasingly cold and distant. When she attempted to discuss plans for the future, Ted was unresponsive. After she returned home, Ted broke off all connections with her. She later said she felt his high-powered courtship and subsequent rejection was the culmination of a drawn-out and carefully planned revenge for the way she treated him nearly five years earlier. Later during police interrogation in Florida, Ted said, "I just wanted to prove to myself that I could have married her." Ted Bundy proved to be an individual capable of careful and subtle planning over a long period of time to achieve his goals.

On 25 November 1973, a fifteen-year-old girl named Katherine Merry Devine left home and started hitchhiking to Oregon. She was never seen alive again. On 6 December, her rotting corpse was found fully clothed in McKenny Park near Olympia, Washington. She lay face down in the damp forest. Most of her internal organs had been torn away by predators. The back of her jeans and panties had been slit with a sharp knife from waist to crotch. Investigators believed she had been raped, probably sodomized, then strangled. Although he was never charged, police officials later believed the crime to be the work of Theodore Robert Bundy. He had been in the area at the time.

On 4 January 1974, two days after Stephanie returned to San Francisco, a young woman named Joni Lenz was attacked only four blocks from where Ted lived. She was raped, sexually mutilated with a vaginal speculum, and battered about the head with a metal rod so severely that she was comatose for months and suffered permanent brain damage. It is quite possible the assailant thought she was dead when he left. From then on, the crimes increased in frequency. They averaged from two to seven per month after the Lenz attack.

Sometime after midnight on 31 January 1974, Lynda Healy, the weather reporter for a local radio station, disappeared from her basement apartment. She'd gone to bed around midnight. Later someone entered her apartment and clubbed her as she lay sleeping. A few feet away, her roommate slept undisturbed. The killer then removed her nightgown, dressed her body, made the bed, hung up the bloody nightgown, and carried her away. More than a year later, her crushed skull was discovered on Taylor Mountain a few miles east of Seattle. Her identification came through dental records.

On 12 March, Donna Manson, a nineteen-year-old hippie-type, brushed out her long straight dark hair and parted it in the middle. Her hair matched the style of the previous dead women. Ted was beginning to reveal his stereotypical victim. She left her dorm room to attend a jazz concert on campus at Evergreen State College near Olympia. She vanished from the college parking lot. Her body has never been positively identified. Ted Bundy had skipped class that night.

On 7 April, Susan Elaine Rancourt, an exceptionally bright young woman with a history of extreme caution, left her dormitory to attend a meeting on campus. After the meeting, she headed home and disappeared. Susan was very nearsighted and had left her glasses behind. Her path took her under a dark railroad trestle, and she might not have seen someone in the shadows. Her shattered skull would be recovered on Taylor Mountain nearly a year later. A Volkswagen Bug had been seen on Taylor Mountain around the time of her disappearance.

In April, a series of events occurred on campuses around Washington that would later demonstrate Ted Bundy's more polished, carefully thought-out modus operandi. Four young women were individually approached by a man who had his arm in a sling and asked for assistance with a load of books. On each occasion, the women complied and carried his books to a VW Bug parked in a darkened lot. At the last moment, all instinctively shied away, but Bundy had proved to himself that the "broken wing" technique would work more often than not. He would sometimes vary the technique by using crutches rather than a sling. It is impossible to say how many times their natural sympathies would cost women their lives.

Ted continued in law school although his attendance was erratic at best. Finally, on 10 April 1974, he withdrew from classes. He had not been working that spring and had been living on unemployment.

By now, Ted's killings and approaches to women reached the point where they occurred regularly, primarily the second and third weeks of each month. However, due to the number of jurisdictions involved, the authorities were as yet unaware they were dealing with a serial murderer. Ted used the advantage as long as he could.

On the evening of 6 May, Bundy again expanded his field of operations. Roberta Kathleen Parks, a student at Oregon State University in Corvallis, disappeared without a trace from the campus student union. Kathy Parks had had a violent argument with her father two days before on 4 May. On the morning of the sixth, she learned he had had a massive coronary. Connecting the health issue to the argument, she became extremely upset. A tall, attractive woman, Parks had a history of dramatic mood swings. Her disappearance was initially thought to be voluntary, possibly suicide.

Years later while in jail in Florida, Bundy, without confessing to the crime, gave an insight into the occurrences of that day. He said he had decided to commit another assault but to do it in a way that would not connect it to the other crimes. His earlier work as a researcher for the Crime Commission taught him that by crossing police jurisdictions and varying his modus operandi, he could throw police off the track.

Ted implied he struck up a conversation with Parks in the student cafeteria. Her visible distress and obvious need for comforting attracted his attention. When the charming man with blue eyes and dark hair sat down at her table, he must have seemed like a godsend. Within minutes, Ted convinced her that he was a student, a great guy, and sincerely interested in her. She willingly followed him to his car. Before she knew what was happening, she found herself in the remote countryside, miles from any help.

Pulling to the side of the road, Bundy ordered her to remove all her clothes. He raped her, then, tying her up and tossing her into the back seat of the VW, he set out for Seattle. He later said he was undecided whether to kill her at that point. By the time he got to Seattle, it was after midnight. Tired and probably irritated by her pleas for mercy, he raped her again. Shortly after, her body was placed in his "cemetery" on Taylor Mountain.

Her skull was found ten months later. She was one of the earliest victims to be positively identified. The elongated shape of her skull from her premature birth made the identification relatively simple. Even though her skull was the only skeletal part ever found, the injuries reflected the terrible beating she suffered. Most of her upper teeth had been broken out by multiple blows. Her skull had been fractured in several places and crushed by some sort of blunt instrument, possibly a tire iron.

On 23 May 1974, Ted started a job at the Washington State Department of Energy Services. He considered it a temporary position since he finally had decided to attend law school in Salt Lake City in the fall. While working there, Ted met Carole Boone. She would later become his wife and the mother of his child. At their starting point, however, they were merely friends.

Two days later, Ted picked up a hitchhiker, fifteen-year-old Brenda Baker. Four weeks later, her battered, decomposed corpse was found at the edge of Millersylvania State Park.

Ted struck again in only six days. By an odd coincidence, the next victim's name was Brenda Ball. A streetwise, uninhibited young woman, she also was picked up while hitchhiking. Ted talked her into coming to his apartment. They had sex, voluntarily for once. She had been drinking and soon passed out. Ted strangled her in her sleep. His busy schedule did not allow him to immediately dispose of her body. The corpse remained in his closet for several days. Finally, she was dumped on Taylor Mountain. Her skull was discovered along with the skulls three other women the following year. She was identified from dental records. Weather and the wildlife had carried away the rest of her body.

Ted's next victim died on 11 June. Georgeann Hawkins, a straight A student at the University of Washington, left her boyfriend's fraternity house to walk home to her sorority. She had less than a hundred feet to go. Hawkins, at five feet two inches, an attractive, lively brunette, rarely went out at night because she was afraid of the dark. Like Susan Rancourt, she was very nearsighted but had left her glasses at home. The brightly lit alleyway between the fraternity and her own back door seemed safe. Within the last forty feet, she disappeared.

The body of Georgeann Hawkins has never been identified. One of the miscellaneous human bones found near Issaquah, the second of Ted's "cemeteries,'" was a female femur that probably belonged to Georgeann Hawkins. Georgeann, however, as of 2021 is still listed officially as a missing person.

Four sets of human remains were found on Taylor Mountain. Four more would be found near Issaquah, a small community a few miles from Lake Sammamish.

The murders continued all summer, reaching a high point

with a double abduction/homicide at Lake Sammamish in July. The Lake Sammamish area is a popular recreational spot for young people in the Seattle area.

On Saturday, 14 July, Ted Bundy separately approached six young women at Lake Sammamish. He again used the sling ploy. Of the six, two would be abducted, raped, and murdered. Their bodies would not be found for several months. Those were Ted's ninth and tenth victims. That time, Ted left clues. He let his face be seen, and he gave his true first name to the women he approached.

Ted left his apartment in Seattle and arrived at Lake Sammamish by noon. It was one of those warm, sunny days so rare to the Seattle area. Thousands of people swam, sunbathed, and sailed that afternoon. Serial killers seem to sense that the two best times to take a victim are when a person is alone or in the middle of a crowd. Bundy was comfortable in either situation.

The first person approached was an attractive, petite brunette named Jennifer Rutledge. A few minutes after noon, a handsome, smiling young man with his arm in a sling came up to her and politely asked if she would help him load a small sailboat onto the top of his car. Rutledge went to the car with the man, but, seeing no sailboat and noticing an odd look in his eye, she made an excuse and hastily left.

Janice Ott, twenty-three and married, encountered Ted next. A student at Eastern Washington State College at Cheney, she also seemed sympathetic to the man with the sling. Ott had ridden her bicycle to the lake, parking it next to where she lay sunbathing. When the man asked for her help, she got up, gathered her belongings, and wheeled her bike into the parking lot. Ted, however, got a little too eager. Several people, including Jennifer Rutledge, saw him talking to Ott and heard him say his name was "Ted." When Ott and Bundy left the area, it was twelve-thirty. He returned later; she did not.

Later in the afternoon around four, the mysterious "Ted" returned to the lake. He approached a sixteen-year-old girl coming out of a public restroom. He asked her for help launching his sailboat, and when she said no, he pulled on her arm and attempted to walk her away. Frightened, she pulled loose and rapidly walked off. Quickly forgetting the incident, she little knew she'd had a brush with death.

Moments later, another woman was also approached. The man with the sling needed help with his sailboat. She also refused, saying she was on her way home.

Shortly before five, Ted tried again. The target was a twenty-three-year-old whose suspicions were aroused by the strange look in Bundy's eyes. She told the stranger with his arm in a sling that she was in a hurry to meet someone, and she wasn't strong enough to help. He turned away and disappeared into the crowd.

By five, the crowd was beginning to thin out. Ted, still unsatisfied, tried one more time. Eighteen-year-old Denise Nasland had had an argument with her boyfriend. A strikingly attractive young woman, she had taken four Valium tablets and had been drinking beer. When the man with the sling asked for her help, she never hesitated. Her friends remembered her as the type who would always help someone less fortunate than she.

After talking Nasland into the car, Bundy drove her to the farmhouse where he had earlier taken Janice Ott. Ott had been raped and left tied but was still alive. He raped Denise while the bound Janice Ott watched. When he was finished, Ted strangled and bludgeoned the two young women to death. Stripping their bodies of any possible identification, he tossed them into the back of the car and drove a few miles away. Parking near Issaquah, he dumped their nude bodies into the underbrush.

Six weeks later, the torn skeletal remains of the Sammamish victims were recovered in the Issaquah area. They had continued to suffer indignities even after death. Wild animals had scattered their flesh and bones over the hillside.

Bundy later recounted the sequence of events to police investigators in Florida. He never showed the slightest trace of remorse or guilt.

After Lake Sammamish, events began to move quickly. The deaths and disappearances finally began to assume a pattern. Moreover, the police had witnesses, a name, a vehicle, and a composite sketch. They knew they were dealing with a killer whose trademark until now had been a lack of evidence.

Forced to grope blindly in the dark, police prayed, somehow, they could apprehend the faceless monster before he killed again. Those prayers were not answered. Bundy was not apprehended for any of the ten murders he had committed in the previous eight months.

Slowly, a net of suspicion began to appear around the private life of Theodore Robert Bundy. His sometime girlfriend Meg Anders noticed Ted was never with her when any of the victims disappeared. She also wondered about the fact he drove a Volkswagen, which now had been identified as the suspect's vehicle type. Her suspicions were compounded by the discovery of medical supplies (plaster of paris and crutches), a sack of women's clothing, and a lug wrench that had apparently been converted to a weapon.

The composite drawing released by police after the Lake Sammamish incident closely resembled Ted Bundy. One of Meg's friends also questioned whether Bundy and "Ted" the killer were the same. Yet in the face of what to most of us would be overwhelming suspicions, Meg continued to cling to her dream of a future as Mrs. Theodore Robert Bundy, Attorney at Law.

Even his coworkers became aware of the resemblance between Ted Bundy and the mysterious killer "Ted." When he returned to work on Wednesday, 18 July, after a six-day absence, people in the office kidded him about the similarity. Bundy passed off those comments by saying he had been home with a bout of the flu.

By late summer 1974, Ted's activities began to take a toll on his health. He noticeably lost weight, and his behavior became bizarre and erratic. Added to the pressure of having committed several murders, he worked a full-time job, maintained at least one relationship, and prowled the streets all night long.

Meg Anders found Ted had gone from being a considerate lover, to an interest in bondage and anal sex, to other types of bizarre sexual behavior, finally, to no sexual contact at all. Her long, straight hair parted in the middle became a point of contention. When she said she was going to get it cut and restyled, Ted became very upset and insisted she not do so. Meg knew Ted, on occasion, was prone to wearing fake beards and mustaches, using techniques he had learned at the Temple University drama department. She also noticed a pattern of fatigue that directly coincided with dates of the attacks by the mysterious "Ted."

A Seattle psychiatrist specializing in aberrations of the criminal mind gave a remarkably accurate "Ted" profile. The killer would be between twenty-five to thirty-five years old, mentally ill, but not the type who would draw attention to himself as a potential criminal. He feared women and their power over him.

The man would also evince at times "socially isolative" behavior.

Evergreen State College, a beautiful campus situated near Olympia, Washington, proved the scene of "Ted's" next appearance. On the night of 1 August, a young woman was surprised and frightened in a dorm laundry by a mysterious man who suddenly appeared behind her. She later said he was "real wild looking." Three months later, she tentatively identified the man as Bundy. That was the same campus from which Donna Manson had vanished five months earlier.

The next day, Ted surfaced again. Carol Valenzuela, a fresh-faced eighteen-year-old, occasionally hitchhiked. Although married, she exhibited a free spirit. During the daylight hours of 2 August, she disappeared from the downtown area of Vancouver, Washington.

In October 1974, the remains of Carol Valenzuela and an unidentified woman who had been murdered about the same time were discovered in a high valley between Olympia and the Oregon border. The skeletal remains were nude and had been tossed into the underbrush. Forensics experts determined Valenzuela had probably been strangled.

Those women, Bundy's eleventh and twelfth victims, were the last of his known Washington/Oregon crimes. The next few weeks were occupied with far more mundane matters.

By the time Ted Bundy left Seattle for Salt Lake City on Labor Day weekend 1974, he had managed to fail law school but had become an efficient killing machine. He was known to have approached twenty-six women between November 1973 and the end of August 1974. Of those twenty-six, twelve were dead, their bodies dumped in remote locations; several others were brutally attacked and raped; and only a few evaded his clutches.

It might also be instructive to digress a moment and point out on several occasions prior to that period, Ted had been in close proximity to serious, unsolved crimes. As long ago as 1962, a mysterious disappearance occurred a few blocks from the Bundy home in Tacoma. In 1966 when Ted was living in Seattle, two women were bludgeoned with virtually the identical technique Ted later used. One died and the other barely survived. Further, unsolved homicides of women in Philadelphia while he was there fit his modus operandi. Also, beginning in the fall of 1969, a series of thirteen homicides occurred in Vancouver, British Columbia. Vancouver is less than two hundred miles from Seattle and easily accessible by car.

Most of those women fit the type—long, dark hair parted in the middle—of most of Ted's victims. If those crimes could be proven to be, indeed, the work of Theodore Robert Bundy, his total number of murders might be double or triple the number of which he was commonly suspected.

One of the great difficulties in understanding and solving the acts of Ted Bundy, or indeed any other serial murderer, is the logistics of figuring out what crimes are his handiwork. It is often easier to include those for which he was a good suspect than to exclude those that were merely similar. In a situation involving a serial killer, the temptation is strong to wipe out any unsolved homicides in the area with even the vaguest similarity by simply clearing them from the active case files using the police euphemism "cleared by arrest." This question will arise again in our examination of Wayne Williams, the so-called "Atlanta child killer."

When he arrived in Salt Lake City, Ted found himself in his favorite hunting ground—a college campus. In the dark recesses of his mind, he must have seen this situation as almost ideal. He was now older, more traveled, more sophisticated, and better looking than most of the other males on campus. Articulate and a law school student, he would seem an ideal match to many of the younger female students. Add to that his positions as a night dormitory manager and later as a security guard on campus, and one has a killer's nirvana. Short of giving him a license to kill co-eds, there is virtually nothing else Ted Bundy could have wished. He did not delay long in availing himself of the opportunities.

In quick succession, three young women disappeared in Utah, one approximately every two weeks during the month of October. Scattered throughout the murders were approaches to many other women. A few were attacked, but most merely brushed him off, never knowing how close to death they had come. Ted's gas credit card slips revealed he did an extraordinary amount of driving during the latter half of 1974. One FBI authority said it is not unusual for a serial murderer on the prowl to drive a quarter million miles a year.

Nancy Wilcox was a beautiful brunette cheerleader from Holloday, Utah, a small town south of Salt Lake City. She had quarreled with her parents and was thought to be a runaway.

Last seen on 2 October, she was described as riding in a VW Bug. Her body has never been found.

Melissa Smith was a police chief's daughter. A seventeen-year-old high school girl from Midvale, Utah, she is remembered as having a moody disposition. On Friday, 18 October, she left a local pizza parlor and headed home. Nine days later, her battered, nude, filthy corpse was found near a park east of Salt Lake.

Melissa had been unbelievably brutalized. A knee-length stocking had been tightly bound around her throat, shattering the hyoid bone. Her entire body was covered with bruises inflicted before death. Some authorities speculated she had been kept alive as long as a week. Some of her injuries were consistent with torture. That was based on the fact there was little decomposition, and her body had not been dismembered by wildlife. She had been repeatedly raped and sodomized, and twigs and dirt were found in her vagina. Although strangled, the actual cause of death was listed as massive head injuries. She had been beaten with a heavy metal object, possibly a crowbar or tire iron, and had suffered massive skull fractures. Difficult though it is to believe, the already savage killer was becoming even more violent with his victims.

On 27 November, another body was found close to the site where Melissa's body had been located. The nude, frozen corpse of a young female had been battered to the point where her face was unrecognizable. The body was subsequently identified as Laura Aime. Her father, with whom she maintained a close relationship although she no longer lived at home, was able to identify her only by some small scars on her arm.

Laura, a slim six-footer, had dropped out of school and was working in a cafe in her hometown of Lehi. Later, eyewitnesses identified a regular customer at the cafe as none other than Ted Bundy. That was the only case of which we are aware where Bundy made himself so visible to his intended victim. As the savagery of the killings increased, so did the killer's arrogance.

Laura had disappeared nearly four weeks before on Halloween. She had attended a party in Orem, a small town forty miles south of Salt Lake. Around midnight, although she was drunk, she left the party to walk to a restaurant and buy cigarettes. She was not reported missing for four days.

The body of Laura Aime was more severely battered than

any victim to date. Numerous skull fractures appeared on both the back and left sides of the head. Her jaw had been broken, and a deep cut inflicted on the back of her head. Once again, a nylon stocking had been tightly knotted around the victim's throat. The sexual injuries were equally brutal. She had been sodomized and raped. Sperm was found in both the vagina and anus. The wall of the vagina had been punctured by some foreign object. Investigators speculated the victim also had been kept alive and tortured for several days after her abduction.

Ted Bundy would later be positively identified as a suspect in the Aime killing. By then, police authorities had accidentally disposed of all the physical evidence in the case. Since hair samples were a significant clue, the Aime family was forced to endure the emotional trauma of an exhumation.

Lynn Banks, a childhood friend of Meg Anders, returned home to Ogden, Utah, in the fall of 1974. While home, she read about two of the Utah murders. Struck by their similarity to the Seattle crimes, Lynn urged Meg to contact the Seattle police. Nothing came of that contact. Finally, because of Lynn's constant suspicions, their lifelong friendship came to an end, one more casualty of Ted Bundy. Ted never knew that Meg had contacted the police.

Meanwhile back in Salt Lake City, Ted was getting his usual mediocre grades in law school. Drinking heavily, he attempted to work and go to school. That, plus the physical toll of his criminal activities, left him exhausted much of the time.

Ted continued to maintain frequent contact with Meg by telephone. Constantly sleeping with other women, not to mention raping and murdering them, Ted demanded absolute fidelity from Meg.

In every criminal career, a crucial turning point occurs. For Theodore Robert Bundy, the pivotal moment came on 8 November 1974, in the small town of Murray, Utah. That day, he allowed an intended victim to see him up close and then escape alive and uninjured. His long slide to the Florida electric chair had begun.

Between six-thirty and seven in the evening, Ted pulled into the parking lot of a Murray shopping mall, less than a mile from where Melissa Smith vanished the month before. Parking his car, he went inside a bookstore. Approaching an attractive young woman, he told her someone had attempted to break into her car in the parking lot. He asked her to accompany him back to the lot to determine whether anything had been stolen.

The young woman, Carol DaRonch, began following him toward the lot. Feeling somewhat apprehensive and noticing he had alcohol on his breath, she asked him to show her some identification. It is interesting that, like most of us when approached by someone with an air of authority, DaRonch did not at first suspect anything was amiss. Rather than immediately asking for identification in the safety of an openly public place, she followed him out of the brightly lit areas of the mall. Only after several factors aroused her suspicions did she become apprehensive. When asked to produce some official identification, the man chuckled and continued toward the parking lot. When they arrived at her vehicle, he asked her to open both sides of the car. After opening the driver's side and examining the interior, she refused to open the passenger side and allow the man into the vehicle.

The man then informed her they would have to return to the "police substation" in the mall. Returning to the mall, he came to a locked door. Turning to DaRonch, the man said his partner had apparently left and they would have to go downtown. That time, they proceeded, not to her car, but to his. As they went to the parking lot a second time, DaRonch asked a series of questions to which the man had no answers, evasive answers, or chuckles. Seeing his car was a slightly battered Volkswagen Bug, her suspicions were fully aroused. When she asked him to show her some identification, he flashed a badge quickly in front of her face so she could not examine it. Even then, she voluntarily got into his car.

As they pulled from the parking lot and onto the street, the man instructed her to fasten her seat belt. DaRonch refused. By now, fearful vibrations had begun. She again noticed the strong smell of alcohol on his breath and, examining their route of travel, realized they were headed away from the center part of town and the police station. At that moment, as they passed an elementary school playground, the man suddenly swerved off the street to the curb. Slamming on the brakes, he lunged for her and attempted to fasten a pair of handcuffs on her wrist. She panicked and a struggle began. He succeeded in getting one cuff on her right wrist. Then, as she continued to resist, screaming and attempting to exit the passenger door, he accidentally fastened the second cuff on the same wrist. Reaching between the seats, he produced a pistol. Pointing it at her head, he ordered her to keep silent or "I'll blow your brains out."

DaRonch, whose life was now in definite peril, continued to attempt escape. She finally succeeded in getting the door open and was halfway out of the vehicle. The gun disappeared and a tire iron replaced it. As he swung it toward her head, she managed to ward off the blow and tumble out onto the ground. Leaping to her feet, she fled away from Ted and toward an approaching car. The man who attacked her finally fled the scene, driving away into the night.

The incident, more than any other in Bundy's history, demonstrated his ability to play on the gullibility of others, his chameleon-like skill as a con man, and the instant and awesome ferocity of which he was capable. Given the circumstances and the threat of apprehension, the average criminal, even the average serial murderer, would have fled as far and rapidly as possible. Ted did not. Driving down the road a mere twenty miles to the small town of Bountiful, Utah, he returned to the hunt.

Noticing a crowd at the local high school, he pulled in and parked. Like most small towns in America, a crowd at a high school on a November night meant one of two things: a sporting event or a class play. That time, it was a class play. Bypassing the front door, Ted entered through the rear and went backstage. The first person he encountered was the high school drama teacher. He tried a similar ploy on her to the one he had used on Carol DaRonch minutes before. The drama teacher, like DaRonch, never questioned the authority figure. Noting later that he was a handsome man and well dressed, she recalled she would have been willing to accompany him to the parking lot except she was too busy.

Returning to the parking lot, he tried again, next approaching a sixteen-year-old girl and asking her to help him start his car. She refused. Unfortunately, she did not take the incident seriously or report it to authorities.

The curtain finally came up on the evening's performance. No one could say where Ted spent the hours during the performance. However, a little before ten-thirty, a student named Debby Kent, who attended the play with her parents, left to pick up her brother at the local roller rink. She was never seen again. Residents of a nearby apartment house heard screams and saw a vehicle exit the school parking lot at high speed. Shortly after, the drama teacher saw a man fitting Ted's description sitting in an aisle seat watching the end of the play. He was noticed because of his heavy, labored breathing and the distraction it caused some members of the audience. When the play ended, everyone left except the Kent family.

By midnight, Debby's parents discovered the family vehicle still in the parking lot. She was nowhere to be found. Ted had gotten his victim of the evening. What an act of supreme arrogance, after killing Kent, whose body was probably still in his car, to return to the audience and watch the end of the play! Like the supreme egoist Ted was, it did not seem to have occurred to him that was risky, stupid, and malevolent almost beyond belief.

Like any other predator that misses a kill, Ted had continued that night until he succeeded. It is quite possible, given the alcohol on his breath, the DaRonch abduction failed because Ted was intoxicated. Then as the evening wore on and he regained full use of his faculties, he attempted other attacks until he finally succeeded. The evening gives a frightening glimpse into the mind and behavior of a serial murderer. He was not to be deterred by adversity; his need was stronger than any risk. Like the inexorable killing machine he had become, he would not and could not stop until he had achieved his goal.

No known killings occurred in the next month.

In mid-December 1974, a highly publicized crime conference was held in the neighboring state of Nevada. A major topic of concern at the conference was the number of missing young women in the northwest quadrant of the United States. After the conference, some of the publicity resulted in Meg Anders' calling the sheriff's office in Salt Lake County, Utah, and giving the name of Ted Bundy as a possible suspect.

Another month went by before Ted's seventeenth victim disappeared. It is possible the pressure of semester finals, the holiday season, and the increased emphasis of law enforcement on those crimes was responsible for Ted's two-month hiatus. On the other hand, there is no way to tell whether hitchhikers or other transients might have disappeared during the timeframe.

The next five victims came from Colorado. It is unknown as to why Bundy chose to change his field of operations. Perhaps the increasing pressure from the aggressive response of Utah law enforcement convinced him it was time to alter his hunting ground.

On 12 January 1975, Ted's seventeenth victim disappeared. Caryn Campbell went to the Wildwood Inn in Snowmass, Colorado, with her fiancé, a doctor, to attend a medical conference. She suffered from a mild cold and was somewhat distressed after a disagreement with her fiancé over setting a wedding date. After dinner, she set out for her room to get a magazine. She chatted with some other doctors in the corridor outside her room. When they left, she turned toward her door less than twenty feet away and vanished.

Thirty-six days later, a park employee driving along a dirt road less than three miles from Snowmass saw birds circling in the sky. Suspicious, he parked his vehicle and walked into the underbrush. Less than twenty-five feet from the road was the nude, frozen body of Caryn Campbell. Semen residue was found in her vagina. Her skull had been crushed by a number of heavy blows. Because of the elapsed time and damage to the body by wild animals, it was impossible to gain much in the way of forensic evidence from her corpse. It was certain she had suffered at least three blows, any of which would have been sufficient to kill her. The contents of her stomach made it likely she had been killed within minutes of disappearing.

An eyewitness later picked Ted Bundy's photo as a man she had seen in the corridor of the hotel. By the time Bundy went to trial, she could no longer make a positive identification.

On 15 March, another young woman vanished, that time from Vail. Julie Cunningham, like most of Ted's victims, had long, dark hair parted in the middle. She left her apartment at night, headed for a bar, and disappeared forever.

Denise Oliverson disappeared on April 6. Following a fight with her husband, she mounted her bicycle and pedaled away. Her bicycle and sandals were found. She has never been seen again.

On 15 April, a month to the day after the disappearance of Cunningham, Melanie Cooley vanished. The high school student bore a striking resemblance to Debby Kent. Eight days later, her body was discovered partially clothed and battered. A blow from a large rock had fractured her skull. A filthy pillowcase was twisted around her neck.

All that spring and early summer of 1975, the pressure on law enforcement agencies to apprehend the killer of young women increased. Press coverage was extensive and new, more comprehensive, psychiatric profiles were made available to the public. The killer was portrayed as a man in the grip of a terrible homicidal compulsion. He was described as having other types of criminal behavior in his past and as a probable sexual psychopath.

Theodore Robert Bundy was one of two hundred suspects. Ted's history of petty crime would not have been readily apparent. He had not been before the court since he was a juvenile, and those records had long ago been destroyed. Several people who knew him, however, were aware of his continuing history of petty theft. Meanwhile, Ted was drinking more, and once again as had happened at the University of Puget Sound, his grades in law school were deteriorating.

After the end of the spring semester, Ted returned to Seattle for another visit. He spent time with Meg Anders, and they finally decided to marry at the end of the year. Meg did not tell him that on at least two occasions, she had turned in his name as a suspect in the long series of murders.

By the first of July, Ted was back in Utah. He took his twenty-first and twenty-second victims that day. The body of Shelley Robertson was found in August inside a mine shaft. Nancy Baird has never been found.

At two-thirty a.m. on the morning of 16 August 1975, Ted Bundy was arrested at last. A Utah highway patrolman, driving an unmarked car, happened to notice Ted's Volkswagen cruising around the officer's home neighborhood. Falling into line with Ted, the officer threw on his bright lights in order to read the license plate number. Bundy responded by shutting off his lights and speeding away into the dark. After a chase, Ted was finally stopped. When questioned, he said he had been to a movie and then gotten lost. The officer who stopped him noticed the passenger seat was missing and that, in addition to the fact the driver was garbed entirely in black, aroused the officer's suspicion. He requested permission to examine the interior of the vehicle. In the car, he saw a ski mask, crowbar, ice pick, rope, and wire. Also found were a pair of pantyhose with eyeholes cut in them, a pair of handcuffs, and some garbage bags. Ted was arrested on the scene but charged only with Evading an Officer.

For the first time, Ted was brought into direct contact with a law enforcement agency. What would have been a routine stop had turned into an arrest only because Ted had fled and attempted to lie to the officer. He was released on his own recognizance the following morning. A few days later, additional criminal charges of Possession of Burglary Tools were filed against Bundy. Ted, of course, protested his innocence and portrayed himself as enmeshed in a law enforcement conspiracy.

His phenomenal ability to lie to and manipulate women did not extend to law enforcement personnel. Each time he talked to police, he made lies, omissions, and succeeded in snaring himself further.

One thing Ted did that would cause him problems later was to sign a Consent to Search form. Under Utah law, since the car search was not conducted under the authority of a search warrant, the officers had no authority to remove any of Ted's belongings. However, many of the things they discovered in his apartment were felt to be relevant to some of the disappearances and certainly caused the investigation against Bundy to intensify. Among the items of interest were a map of Colorado with the Wildwood Inn in Snowmass marked; a brochure on the recreation center in Bountiful, Utah; Ted's long-distance phone bills; and a bill from Chevron for his gasoline credit card. The authorities were especially interested in the Colorado material as Ted had denied ever having been in the state. It was one of many almost pointless lies that would trip him up.

When they examined his tan VW, the police noted a large tear in the upholstery in the back seat. They photographed the tear, and it would become important in the identification of the kidnap vehicle by Carol DaRonch.

Like Charlie Manson, one of the most fascinating things about Ted was his ability to dramatically change his appearance from one day to the next. By changing the way he parted his hair, going without a shave for a few days, and even changing the way he walked and stood, Bundy could appear to be someone totally different. That time, his chameleon ability did not work. Both Carol DaRonch and the drama teacher from Bountiful were able to identify him as the man they saw on 8 November 1974.

When she was finally allowed to view Ted's VW, Carol

DaRonch found the car had been sanded, the dents pounded out, and repainted. He had also repaired the upholstery. The police who had him under surveillance recalled Ted seemed to take delight in cleaning, washing, and scrubbing the car inside and out while they watched. They had no legal grounds to stop him from destroying or altering what they felt was valuable evidence.

From the time of his arrest on 16 August, no further known killings occurred. The preliminary investigation against him continued. Records of all his gasoline credit card purchases were requested, all his educational records were subpoenaed, and his friends, including Meg Anders, were contacted and interviewed.

Finally, on 2 October 1975, Theodore Robert Bundy was arrested again in Salt Lake City, Utah. In addition to the charges previously brought against him, he was now charged with Aggravated Kidnapping and Attempted Criminal Assault. Bond was set at $100,000. Later in the day, a lineup was arranged. In rapid succession, Carol DaRonch, the drama teacher, and Tamra Tingy (a friend of the missing Debby Kent) identified Bundy in the lineup. Unable to raise the money for his release, Ted was remanded to jail in Salt Lake City.

Learning to survive in jail apparently presented a minimum of problems for Ted. His manipulative skills and his ability to be agreeable to almost everyone stood him in good stead. He does not seem to have encountered any serious problems during his eight-week stay in jail.

Bundy is said to have spent a great deal of time reading and studying the Bible. This is called the "convict Christian syndrome." It is a common phenomenon among the imprisoned. People who, when free, would never enter a church, suddenly develop an intense interest in religion and saving their souls. The sincerity of this behavior is always open to question. If all those conversions were sincere, every prison in America would be a center of religious piety. Certainly, we found no evidence Ted was of a particularly religious frame of mind before his first incarceration time.

Prior to trial in Salt Lake City, Theodore Robert Bundy became a member of the Church of Latter-day Saints. Meg Anders, a Mormon, had been urging him to join the church for some time. After his arrest in Utah, the Mormon missionary who sponsored Ted said, "I wouldn't hesitate to line him up with my sister." It is difficult for us to believe that shortly before he went to trial on a criminal charge in Salt Lake City, the center of the Mormon faith, he suddenly experienced a religious revelation, which, only coincidentally, would make him more palatable to a jury.

On 13 November 1975, another of the periodic meetings of major law enforcement agencies in the Northwest United States was held. Because of its location, it was called the Aspen Summit Meeting. Authorities from several states were convinced by now that Ted Bundy was the elusive "Ted" killer who had plagued the Northwest for so long. In spite of the fact they had what they felt were over forty points of connection between Ted Bundy and the Washington State murders, they still had no hard evidence. The lack of physical evidence prevented the filing of further charges against him.

On 20 November, a few days before his twenty-ninth birthday, bond was posted for Ted Bundy. The resources to accomplish the bond seem to have come from a group of friends and family who were convinced of his innocence.

While on bail, Ted returned to Seattle, where he was under surveillance twenty-four hours a day. That resulted in a game of hide and seek quite similar to the games played by two other serial murderers: John Gacy and Wayne Williams. The surveillance officers were taunted, teased, harassed, and sometimes evaded by Bundy. Ted's attitude, like that of many criminals of his caliber, was the police were a bunch of stumblebums barely above the level of the mentally challenged.

The circle of evidence around Bundy continued to tighten. Valid evidence from his credit card slips placed him in Colorado on the days of two of the murders in that state and within miles of the crime scenes. In Washington, Bundy's parents, who were convinced of his innocence, refused to cooperate with police or to allow their home in Tacoma or their vacation cabin to be searched. They would maintain their belief in his innocence throughout the criminal investigation.

One of the hidden tragedies of crime has always been that nearly everyone in one way or another who is connected with a person like Bundy is, in the final analysis, a victim. All of these murderers have friends and family who, through loyalty or a misguided belief in their innocence, will suffer irreparable damage to their lives. Often in the pursuit of criminals, it is easy to forget they, too, have loved ones. This does not mitigate the crime; it merely expands the tragedy.

Among Ted's belongings were a number of items that could be considered as either cooking utensils or weapons, such as knives and meat cleavers. Although some suspected one or two of the victims might have had their throats slit, no evidence of a significant departure from his bludgeoning modus operandi appeared. Links with the crimes continued to accumulate: the fact he had friends in and previous experience with many areas of the crimes; his fascination with exploring only country roads; and, most of all, his strange habit of calling Meg Anders shortly after each crime was committed.

Anders, true to form, quickly fell back under Ted's spell and was convinced the love of her life was an innocent man. Once again Ted's manipulative skills were running in high gear. Ted maintained the attitude he was an innocent man grievously wronged by the criminal justice system. He made a point of projecting the attitude that his upcoming trial was more of a test of the system than a determination of his guilt or innocence.

On 23 February 1976, trial was opened in the *State of Utah v. Theodore Robert Bundy.* The trial was conducted before a judge only. This is an option a criminal defendant can exercise in some states, including Utah. Another option Ted exercised was to represent himself in court. Despite his two years of law school experience, one cannot help but be reminded of the old adage that a man who is his own lawyer has a fool for a client.

As trial proceeded, it became obvious to all in the courtroom that Ted was lying on a number of major points. He had the ego to think his smooth articulation could overwhelm the truth. His strength and flexibility of ego was the main thing that made Bundy so fascinating and yet led to his downfall.

His testimony about the night he was arrested was a good case in point. Ted had his usual facile excuse for the entire incident. According to him, he had sped away into the night with his headlights off so he could roll down the windows and get rid of the smoke from a marijuana cigarette. At the time, he had told the arresting officer he was lost. Time after time, he would make nonsensical statements like that in such a way as to make them almost believable.

The most dramatic point in the four-day trial came with the

testimony of Carol DaRonch. Ms. DaRonch, at that point the only uninjured survivor of an attack by Bundy, was a shaky witness at best. She found herself in the position of being cross-examined by the person she had accused of having attempted to abduct her. While she was being examined by the prosecution, Bundy, sitting at the defense table, stared unblinkingly at her. Obviously shaken, she still identified Ted positively and repeatedly. The judge was impressed with the fact that in spite of Bundy's repeated changes of appearance, witness DaRonch continued to identify him each time.

Ted utilized his chameleon abilities during the trial. By changing the way he parted and wore his hair, by changing his body movements and his demeanor, he attempted to create confusion about his identity and the validity of identification by the witnesses.

Closing arguments were heard on 27 February 1976. On 1 March, Ted Bundy was found guilty by the court of the crime of Aggravated Kidnapping. Ted, true to form, immediately made a statement to the effect that the judge had found him guilty based on pretrial publicity and public opinion rather than on the substance of the evidence. He singled out for special attention the testimonies of Carol DaRonch, the investigating officer, and a prison psychologist. Sentencing, originally set for 22 March, was delayed for a period of ninety days so a presentence investigation could be conducted.

A presentence investigation or evaluation has become almost de rigueur in felony cases. This is a valuable working tool both for the judge in imposing sentence and for correctional authorities and parole boards in determining the length and nature of incarceration. These investigations are confidential and not available to the public. They include both a background investigation and a psychiatric or psychological investigation.

In his later statements, Ted said he found the psychological examinations to be "malicious, slanted, and infernal." At the time of the Utah investigation, he told people the evaluations found him to be normal with no psychosis or dissociative reactions. The statement was taken out of context. As one psychiatrist said, "I feel that Mr. Bundy is either a man who has no problems or is smart enough and clever enough to appear close to the edge of 'normal.'"

At the end of the ninety days, for unknown reasons, sentencing was delayed for an additional thirty days on the DaRonch kidnapping. Finally, on 30 June 1976, sentencing was iimposed. Witnesses recalled Ted entering the courtroom in a cocky, sarcastic, almost flippant manner. Then, for over an hour, he exhibited his entire range of emotionally manipulative tools. He argued, wept, disputed, and indulged in grandiose gestures with words and movements. All of that notwithstanding, Ted was sentenced to a term of not less than one or more than fifteen years in prison for the crime of second-degree kidnapping. The sentence would make parole available in approximately a year and a half.

Although his conviction was based on eyewitness testimony and circumstantial evidence, shortly after the trial was over, a significant piece of hard evidence surfaced. A successful matching of hair samples from Bundy's vehicle to the hair of Carol DaRonch was finally obtained. The evidence should have eliminated any lingering doubts about his guilt.

Shortly after sentencing, Ted was transported to the Utah State Prison at Point of the Mountain. The institution, also remembered as the site of Gary Gilmore's execution, is a maximum-security institution oriented primarily toward violent, dangerous offenders.

Ted's recent baptism into the Church of Latter-day Saints was now followed by a routine excommunication. As much as any Christian group, the Mormons deal harshly with those who violate the laws of society.

However, incarceration, plus the ever-present threat of additional charges, kept Bundy on edge and, in the eyes of some security officers, made him a constant escape threat. It was noticed that as he moved about inside the prison, his eyes were never still, and he seemed to be assessing everything in sight with an eye toward escape. Other inmates also noted he was frequently short-tempered and irritable and seemed to be under pressure even beyond that brought about by life in a maximum-security institution. Toward the end of the year, the Utah Court of Appeals denied Bundy's appeal on the DaRonch kidnapping conviction.

As summer progressed, the carefully woven net of evidence linking Ted Bundy to Caryn Campbell in Colorado began to tighten. Evidence began to accumulate from different sources. The search of Bundy's apartment had revealed the credit card receipts and brochures from various tourist attractions placing him in the area at the time of Campbell's death. An FBI lab expert, in examining various fibers found in Bundy's VW, found verifiable hair samples from not one but three of Bundy's victims: Carol DaRonch, Melissa Smith, and Caryn Campbell.

Hair and fiber evidence, often one of the few pieces of physical evidence available in serial murder cases, can be very questionable unless handled and analyzed properly. We will see this type of evidence used again and again in the cases this book examines.

Also, forensic examination determined the indentation in Campbell's skull perfectly matched Ted's crowbar. Further, the authorities found an eyewitness who said she saw Bundy in the corridor of the Wildwood Inn the night Campbell disappeared.

Back in Utah, the first few months of Bundy's incarceration went by with a minimum of fuss. Although overshadowed by the fate of Gary Gilmore, Ted used his "celebrity" status to gain a place in convict society. His easy casual style and his willingness to offer legal advice brought him quick acceptance from the other inmates. Although he does not appear to have made any close friends among the inmates, he gained the confidence of many. His polite, respectful manner also made him acceptable to the staff.

Moving about the prison, he very carefully gathered every bit of information that could help him in an escape attempt. It is impossible to say what the final focus of his escape plans were, but, once again, Ted the meticulous planner was setting in motion a carefully thought-out plot.

On 19 October, Bundy, in a routine shakedown, was found to have in his possession a number of items necessary for a successful escape. Those included a social security card, a fake driver's license, road maps, and airline schedules. It is probable some of those items were manufactured in the prison print shop where Ted had sought and gained employment. As the result of his misconduct, Bundy was placed in isolation for fourteen days and then ordered housed in a maximum-security detention block.

Three days after the incident, on 22 October 1976, Bundy was charged with the murder of Caryn Campbell in Pitkin County, Colorado. A few weeks after the charge, on the day he celebrated his thirtieth birthday, Ted Bundy was extradited to Colorado.

For the first time, Ted was beginning to draw the large crowds of reporters that would signify him as a criminal of national stature. However, at the time, the most famous criminal in America was another resident of the Utah State Prison, Gary Gilmore. Bundy later said he despised Gilmore for what he saw as Gilmore's amoral manipulation of his girlfriend, Nicole Barrett. It is ironic but Ted, like the rest of us, was certainly not immune from occasional spasms of hypocrisy.

Arriving in Aspen, Pitkin County, Colorado, in mid-winter, Ted again found himself upstaged by a more newsworthy criminal. When he arrived, movie star Claudine Longet was on trial in Aspen for the murder of her lover, Spider Sabich.

After his incarceration in Utah's penitentiary, Bundy became an outspoken critic of the jail administration. He repeatedly referred to the management of the Pitkin County Jail as a "Mickey Mouse operation." Ted, after a year and a half in jail, had no trouble adjusting to another secure environment.

That winter, he read the book *Papillion* several times. This provides a rare insight into Ted in the midst of one of his personality transformations. He had gone from Ted the law student, to Ted the accused criminal, to Ted the convict. The next logical step was Ted the escaped convict, whose indomitable desire to be free overcomes all obstacles.

The pretrial maneuvering on the Campbell case continued throughout the rest of the winter and into spring. Ted, exercising his options, fired his public defender lawyers and began to conduct his defense himself. The trial judge assigned to the case, in an effort to assure adequate legal representation, allowed Bundy to defend himself but appointed the public defenders as "legal advisors."

Against Ted's wishes, on 13 April, he was transferred from Aspen to the Garfield County Jail in Glenwood Springs, some sixty-five miles away. Ted later boasted he walked in the door of the jail and presented the authorities with a list of demands. His law school experience and his temporary status as his own defense attorney gave him standing that any other inmate would not have had. Those demands included a typewriter, a desk, access to an adequate law library, free and confidential use of the telephone, help from forensic labs and investigators, and, last but not least, three full meals a day. The three meals a day issue grew out of the long-term practice in the county of only providing a morning and an evening meal. Appearing before a judge and complaining about severe weight loss, Ted won his cause. As we will see later, he had no intention of eating the meals.

When questioned about the cost of those items to the tax-payers, Ted made a very valid point about the situation in which all criminal defendants find themselves. He said, and rightfully so, that the citizenry never questions the expenditure of resources available to the prosecution. The entire wealth and might of the state are focused against the defendant in a criminal case. If, indeed, there was to be a fair trial, surely the individual on trial should have equal access to such resources.

On 7 June 1977, he was transported back to Aspen for a hearing on the applicability of the death penalty in his trial. Arriving at the courthouse, he was remanded to the custody of a deputy who had had only one day's previous experience with Ted. During a midmorning break, Bundy asked to go to the law library. In accordance with previous rulings, he was not chained or handcuffed. Using the tall bookshelves to conceal his movements, Ted opened a second-floor window and leaped to the street below. A passerby, startled by seeing him jump, went into the sheriff's office and told them what she had seen.

After the usual law enforcement confusion, the hunt for Ted commenced with a mere forty-five-minute delay. Four hours after his escape, the bloodhounds arrived. Finding his trail quickly, they followed him to a nearby riverbank where they lost the scent. Ted already knew the riverbank and had included it in his escape plan after kindhearted deputies had earlier acquiesced to his requests for an occasional stroll in the fresh air. What appeared to be an impulsive escape attempt was, in fact, a carefully thought-out and executed plan.

Once again, humor and irony came together to rain on Ted's parade. While he wandered lost in the mountains, local entrepreneurs hawked T-shirts emblazoned with the logo, "Ted Bundy Is a One Night Stand." Even then, Ted was again robbed of top billing in the world of crime. By coincidence that same week, James Earl Ray, the convicted assassin of Martin Luther King, escaped from the Tennessee State Prison at Brushy Mountain.

Five days later, after an extended foot tour of the local countryside, Ted, exhausted, hungry, and freezing, wandered back into Aspen. About two in the morning of 13 June, two local deputies, seeing a car driving erratically, pulled the vehicle over and realized they had not another drunk driver, but Ted Bundy.

Three days later, on the morning of 16 June, additional charges of burglary, theft, and escape from custody were brought against Bundy. The judge rescinded his earlier order and, from then on, Ted was transported in leg irons and handcuffs. His other privileges were undisturbed.

After his return, Ted discovered the long-suffering Meg Anders had finally come to her senses and was involved with another man. Remarkably unruffled by the news, Bundy immediately began to gear up his relationship with Carole Boone. By the end of the year, Boone had become his primary relationship.

Ted, in the enforced idleness of incarceration, developed a strong interest in health and body building. It never seemed to have occurred to the jail authorities that Ted's interest in exercise might have been anything more than a newfound fascination with physical fitness.

On another front, Bundy's exhaustive pretrial motions continued through the long, drawn-out process of hearing, examination, and decision. On 2 November in response to one of Bundy's motions, the trial judge ruled that the Utah cases could not be addressed at the Colorado trial. The court, however, did allow the admissibility of the testimony of Carol DaRonch and some of the physical evidence found in Ted's apartment. On 23 December in response to another Bundy motion, a change of venue was granted in the case. The decision was one of those situations where one wins the battle and loses the war. Ted was nonplused to discover half of the inmates on Colorado's death row had been sentenced from Colorado Springs, the new site of his trial.

Ted was not enormously concerned about the turn of events because he had no intention of hanging around. After nearly a year in Colorado's jails, he had formulated and was ready to carry out a second escape. In early December, he began to change his behavior patterns little by little. Complaining of a weak stomach, he began to refuse breakfast and to work throughout the night. Sleeping late, his breakfast tray untouched outside his cell, Ted encouraged a relaxed level of surveillance by his guards. By mid-month, his cell went unchecked from suppertime until noon the next day.

Using a smuggled hacksaw blade, he cut a twelve-by-twelve-inch square through an old light fixture in the metal ceiling of his cell. By fasting, dieting, and exercising, he had slimmed down to a wiry, fit, 140 pounds. His ruse about jail food was about to pay off.

On 30 December 1977, while the live-in jailer and his wife were gone, Ted slithered through the hole in his ceiling, negotiated the ventilation system, and emerged into the jailer's closet. Changing clothes, he opened the door and calmly walked into the night.

His movements during the next few days took him by bus to Denver; by plane to Chicago; by train to Ann Arbor, Michigan; by stolen car to Atlanta; and then by bus to Tallahassee, Florida. The seventeen-hour head start he had gotten in Colorado would prove fatal for three more victims.

Once again, Ted Bundy's activities were overshadowed in the press by another criminal. At the time of his escape, the national news was dominated by the crimes of the Hillside Strangler in Los Angeles.

Arriving in Tallahassee on 8 January 1978 after nearly two and a half years of incarceration, Ted would cover an unbelievable amount of ground during the next few days. Drawn as if by a magnet, he went to the campus of Florida State University and began the process of creating another identity. Ted decided on the name of Kenneth Misner, a graduate and former track star. He obtained a university ID card and used it to accumulate other documents. During his stay in Florida, Bundy would go by that name and the name Chris Hagen.

Using the skills he had learned from other cons, Ted began the process of submerging himself into the community. He was wise enough to know he had to be very cautious about obtaining employment and making himself visible to authorities in any way. He once again began the process of changing his appearance. Going on an aggressive junk food diet, he began to gain weight. It also appears the consumption of alcohol began to play a greater role in his day-to-day life. He had sworn to himself that he would become a very law-abiding and upright citizen. It almost seems as if he had managed to erase the memories of how and why he had come to Florida.

Caught in the inflationary spiral of the Carter years, his money began to disappear far faster than he had planned. Within a few days, he was reduced to purse snatching and stealing to keep himself in funds. So much for his law-abiding intentions. Using classic criminal rationalization, Bundy told himself he would never steal from anyone who couldn't afford it, and, therefore, it was all right.

Ted cased a number of campus bars. On Saturday, 14 January 1978, six days after his arrival in Florida, Ted Bundy followed a young woman back toward the campus. She arrived home safely because Bundy had stopped at the Chi Omega house.

The Chi Omega sorority house was only five blocks from Ted's apartment. It was a top sorority housing the brightest and most beautiful women on campus. On that night, it also became the site of one of the most vicious, brutal, and senseless crimes in the annals of American criminal history. Like his spiritual cousin, Richard Speck, Bundy entered the Chi Omega house prepared to do murder. The exact details of what occurred in the predawn hours will never be known.

The bloody aftermath found by police when they arrived at three-thirty a.m., 15 January, reflected the accumulated rage, anger, and lust of a serial murderer suddenly unleashed after two and a half years of imprisonment. In one gigantic orgy of violence, Bundy bludgeoned four young women, raped and killed two of them, and left the survivors with permanent crippling and disfiguring injuries. One of the dead women, Lisa Levy, had her right nipple nearly bitten off. On her left buttock were two deep bite marks. She also had been sodomized with a Clairol hair spray bottle. The other corpse, Margaret Bowman, had a hole smashed in her skull large enough that one officer said he could have put his entire fist into her brain.

Still unsatiated, Bundy crept through the alleys to a duplex eight blocks away that he had apparently previously cased. Entering the home of Cheryl Thomas, he approached her sleeping form and, once again, bludgeoned his victim. Only the noise arousing her neighbors saved her life. Thomas, a talented dance student, suffered permanent brain damage and never danced again. A few minutes later, Bundy was at home in his own apartment house, calmly chatting with another tenant.

The next two weeks saw Tallahassee in the grip of terror. The faceless attacker had come and gone. Perhaps the most frightening aspect was that there had been no evidence of him since.

Meanwhile, Bundy, living under the name Chris Hagen, began an active campaign of theft. Stealing several purses and wallets, he used the credit cards and money he obtained to go on a wild spending spree in clothing stores, restaurants, and bars. Almost daily, the amount of alcohol Bundy consumed increased. It is as if the events of 15 January had acted as some sort of catharsis and, at least for a while, the dark side of Bundy's nature was resting.

On 5 February, a white Dodge van registered to the Audio-Visual Department of Florida State University was stolen. The next day, a fourteen-year-old junior high student in Jacksonville, Florida, nearly two hundred miles away, was approached by a man driving a white van. Only the timely appearance of her older brother saved Leslie Ann Parmenter from becoming another Bundy victim.

Three days later, on 9 February 1978, twelve-year-old Kimberly Diane Leach became the last of Bundy's victims. A petite, attractive girl who looked older than her age, she was taken from a Lake City, Florida, school yard.

Eight weeks later, her mummified remains, nude from the waist down, were found in a metal hog shed. Her mutilated body had been left in a sexually revealing position and rigor mortis had set in. Her neatly folded clothes were found next to the body. Investigators thought her throat had been slit at the moment of climax and a knife used to mutilate her genitals.

Back in Tallahassee, the heat was on. Police beefed up surveillance on the campus. General law enforcement coverage in the community increased dramatically.

On 10 February, Ted Bundy, at long last, finally made the big time. That day, the Federal Bureau of Investigation gave Ted a place on their Ten Most Wanted Fugitives list. He was described as an escapee from Colorado who was wanted for questioning in a series of sexual murders beginning in California in 1969. He was never charged with a crime in California or a crime that occurred in 1969. Our research leads us to believe, although he may have committed offenses in California that year, it is far more likely he was responsible for sex murders in Philadelphia, and possibly Vancouver, British Columbia, during that period.

Ted Bundy often said he considered the FBI as vastly overrated. That opinion is shared by many career criminals.

On the morning of 11 February 1978, the *Tallahassee Democrat* published excerpts from a psychological profile of what was now being called the Chi Omega Killer. He was described as a loner with deep emotional problems rooted in childhood who probably lived by himself. Psychological profiles can be a useful tool in law enforcement. However, they are usually very generalized and are often more valuable during the trial phase of a criminal case than the apprehension phase.

The following day, Ted packed his belongings at the Oak apartment and prepared to leave. Before departing, he scrubbed down every part of his room, even the walls, to erase any fingerprints. He also abandoned the stolen van nearby. The van would later be impounded by the police and processed as a stolen vehicle. After stealing another Volkswagen sedan, he left Tallahassee and headed west. The clock had begun ticking on the last forty-eight hours of freedom Bundy would ever know.

At one-thirty a.m. on 15 February, a police officer in West Pensacola, Florida, suspicious of an orange Volkswagen sedan, ran a routine plate check and discovered the car was stolen. Turning on his flashers, he attempted to pull the vehicle over, but the driver sped away. After a high-speed chase, the vehicle was stopped and the driver ordered out. The police officer then commanded the driver to lie face down on the pavement. As the officer attempted to handcuff his suspect, the man suddenly rolled over, kicking the officer's feet out from under him. Grappling for possession of his gun, the officer managed to fire one round. Breaking off the struggle, the suspect fled into the night. The officer fired another shot, and the suspect fell to the ground. As the officer approached the prone figure, the suspect once again came up fighting. After another struggle, he was subdued, handcuffed, and taken into custody.

After forty-six days, several thousand miles, and numerous felonies including three more murders, Theodore Robert Bundy had been apprehended for the third and final time. As the officer read him his rights under Miranda, Bundy repeatedly asked and then begged the officer to kill him. It is tempting to speculate that in some way his long series of atrocities had finally caught up with him. It is possible, at long last, the shadow of guilt was looming over the monster in human form.

On the other hand, Ted seemed to have recovered from any

temporary spasms of humanity very quickly. By three a.m. when his formal interrogation began, he was, as usual, lying adroitly. The arresting officers thought he was Kenneth Misner. He had in his possession three sets of identity cards, twenty-one credit cards, a bike, a television, and a car—all of which were not his. After being treated for his injuries, not surprisingly, Ted refused to give his correct name.

A day or so later, after he had been correctly identified, Ted Bundy gave the most frightening of his many interviews. Off the record, when told he was suspected of as many as thirty-six murders, Bundy smiled and said, "Add one digit to that and you'll have it." Did he mean thirty-seven, one hundred and thirty-six, or three hundred and sixty?

Some speculation by Bundy-watchers considered the period immediately following his arrest the closest Ted ever came to admitting his crimes. Those present recalled a Ted Bundy they had never seen before: weeping, visibly crushed, and apparently without hope. If, in fact, national cooperation between police agencies had been a reality and Ted had been interviewed by those familiar with his technique of lies and evasion, one must suspect many unanswered questions would have been put to rest.

By 17 February, Ted was giving another of his famous "off the record" interviews to the press. At one, he began by saying his fantasy life had taken over his real life. That was a patently obvious effort by a sophomoric law student to prepare the way for an insanity defense. It is no surprise Ted avidly devoured newspaper accounts of the trial and the insanity plea of David Berkowitz, the so-called Son of Sam killer. Brothers under the skin, perhaps he felt he had something to learn.

Ted remained in jail for several months, shuttled back and forth between Tallahassee and Pensacola. Finally, on 27 July 1978, the county sheriff at Tallahassee, betraying an ignorance of modern law enforcement that is nothing short of mind boggling, held a press conference so he could publicly read Ted's indictment for murder. This type of irresponsible grandstanding is always a threat to a fair trial and a proper conviction. The sheriff, in his lust for the public eye, did two things he had not planned on: one, he nearly cost the prosecution their case, and two, he gave Ted Bundy the thing nearest to his heart—a return to the limelight. The press conference would haunt the sheriff for years to come.

Ted, making the best of his enhanced stature, spent the next eleven months periodically making statements that seemed almost designed to chill the marrow. While one police investigator described Ted as "the kind of guy you'd want your daughter to bring home," Ted, on the other hand, was saying, "I'm the most coldhearted son-of-a-bitch you'll ever meet." On another occasion, when asked how many states might be interested in him, Ted said, "six states ... Some of them don't even know they're involved." The last statement is made even more striking if viewed in the light of our previous comments about the unsolved murders in Pennsylvania and British Columbia.

It would be nearly eleven months before Ted went to trial on the first of his Florida crimes. In the intervening time, Ted, once again acting as his own attorney, flooded the court with his various pretrial motions. Like other jailhouse lawyers, he seemed to have proceeded on the assumption that if he filed enough motions, he was bound to win one now and then. He was correct. He won another venue change and was enjoying fair success at representing himself, which was very much against the wishes of the court.

During that phase, Ted was submitted to the attentions of several psychiatrists and psychologists. Like major murder trials before and since, most of what those individuals produced was gobbledygook and the remainder often confusing. We are not attempting to discard psychiatric testimony as a tool for the court, merely to place it in perspective.

In the Bundy case, one exception was Dr. Al Carlisle from the Utah State Prison. His insights into Bundy's personality were more firmly grounded in reality than the comments of his colleagues. That probably was attributable to the fact he had seen Ted so many times while he was incarcerated at Point of the Mountain. As an experienced correctional professional, he was able to cut through Bundy's manipulative word games and accurately describe his dangerous, troubled personality.

During those months, Ted continued his practice of giving the occasional glimpse into his true nature. On one occasion, he said, "I don't fear death. I don't fear anyone or anything!"

On 31 May 1979, Ted was allowed to begin contact visits with Carole Boone. One result of the contact was the birth of a baby girl fathered by Theodore Robert Bundy. Another aspect was

Ted's ability to obtain alcohol and drugs through those visits. That same week, he was alleged to have given and then withdrawn a plea of guilty to second-degree murder. That was not surprising. Ted without a trial meant Ted without an audience.

In early June of 1979 as the result of one of Bundy's pretrial motions, a venue change was granted. Like the situation in Colorado, pretrial publicity was cited as a reason why Bundy could not receive a fair trial in the community where the crimes occurred. The trial was moved to Miami.

Finally, on 25 June, trial began. For the first time in American history, live television coverage of a criminal trial was carried. The long-held reservations of many jurists were now to be tested. Many concerns were raised. Would the judge and jury be distracted by having a camera and crew moving around the courtroom? Would the witnesses, especially in a lurid, sexual trial like that one, be less candid because of the television camera? Would the witnesses fear retaliation by friends of the defendant? If the defendant were acquitted, would his personal reputation not already have suffered damage by having his face seen by millions on the six o'clock news? Legal and social philosophers are still arguing the merits of such coverage. That debate will continue for years to come.

Voir dire was completed, and a jury was finally empaneled. The days to come would reveal the effectiveness of the long series of pretrial motions. Ted, for his part, had gained a great deal. He had received a venue change, had been allowed to represent himself, and was successful at excluding several pieces of important evidence.

The prosecution had been successful, however, in keeping the testimony of several eyewitnesses, fiber evidence, and, most importantly, the bite identification prepared by an odontologist who matched Ted's teeth to the marks on the buttock of Lisa Levy. Those bite marks were the first absolute physical evidence to link Ted Bundy to one of his victims since 1974. Their importance could not be overstated. Beyond that, the evidence was largely circumstantial.

During the trial, Ted was not granted his usual access to the law library or a typewriter. It seemed, at long last, law enforcement was beginning to view him as a security risk. Perhaps some compensation was the new cadre of Bundy followers who sat behind him during the trial.

Some women exhibit a morbid attraction in being close to one of these killers. This syndrome will be seen again and seems to have some relationship to a twisted perspective of the killer as a symbol of masculinity. Ladies love outlaws.

After four weeks, forty-nine witnesses, and endless motions and objections, the jury began deliberations at three p.m. on 23 July 1979. A little after nine the following night, they brought in a verdict. Theodore Robert Bundy was found guilty of two counts of first-degree murder and eight other connected charges.

Despite an emotional appeal from his mother four days later, the jury recommended Ted Bundy be put to death in Florida's electric chair. That sentence was imposed by the judge.

Immediately following sentencing, Ted was transported to the Florida State Prison at Raiford and assigned to death row. Ted Bundy was now a member of one of the most exclusive clubs in the world—the residents of death row. Ted would occupy a cell formerly held by a man named John Spenkelink, who had been executed only two months before.

Some of Ted's celebrity status still clung to him. He received many letters from women, religious groups, and the morbid.

The State of Florida still had unfinished business with Bundy. On 7 January 1980, he was brought to trial for the murder of twelve-year-old Kimberly Diane Leach. His iron self-discipline and composure seemed to have shattered. Overweight, on edge, and sometimes disinterested, Bundy sat through a woefully inadequate defense. Appearing drugged or intoxicated, he seemed to be merely going through the motions.

On 6 February 1980, Ted Bundy and Carole Boone applied for a marriage license. They were married on 9 February as Carole sat on the witness stand during the penalty phase of his trial. Their wedding date was also the second anniversary of the death of Kimberly Leach. One wonders what the family of the Leach girl thought as they witnessed the flaunting of the liberties our legal system gives us.

Three days later on 12 February, Ted was sentenced to death a third time.

Ted's schemes for escape continued at Raiford Prison. In July 1984, guards found two hacksaw blades hidden in his cell. He had sawed completely through a steel window bar, sealing the top and bottom in place with a homemade soap-based adhesive. Months later, guards found a hidden mirror. He also mailed unauthorized correspondence to John Hinkley Jr., the would-be assassin of President Ronald Reagan.

Always desiring to be the center of attention, Ted allowed interviews with writers and FBI agents. He divulged details of his crimes and thought processes. While at first killing to avoid being caught, Ted confirmed murder became part of the adventure. His ultimate possession was taking the life of his victims. He provided gruesome details of how and where he performed the murders and what he did to the bodies afterward.

Several execution dates came and passed due to legal wrangling. His interviews with writers and law enforcement agents continued, with Ted often withholding details to try to obtain another stay of execution. Also, Ted's supporters tried for the only option left, executive clemency. Several families of Ted's Colorado and Utah victims, however, refused to petition the Florida governor despite missing information in their relatives' cases. Even Carole Boone accepted his guilt and moved back to Washington with her and Ted's daughter.

Ted's charisma failed him in the end. After spending nearly nine years on death row, he was executed by electrocution at the Florida State Prison (Raiford) in Bradford County. He died at 7:16 a.m. on 24 January 1989. Large numbers of revelers danced, sang, and lit fireworks near the prison, cheering the hearse with Ted's corpse as it left the prison. As directed in his will, his body was cremated, and his ashes were scattered in secret in the Cascade Range of Washington State.

As Ted stood before the court getting married and awaiting sentencing, the citizens of Florida drew a sigh of relief because Bundy would no longer be a threat to women. Meanwhile, the people of Chicago were holding their breath. In Chicago, nearly fifteen hundred miles away, the same grisly dance with death had begun three days earlier with the opening statements in the case of the *State of Illinois v. John Wayne Gacy.*

TWO FOR ONE: THE HILLSIDE STRANGLERS

It has been said that in a moment of whimsy, God Almighty picked up the east coast of America, shook the continent, and all the nuts fell west to California. Certainly, many villains ended up in the Golden State: Charles Manson, Caryl Chessman, the Zodiac Killer, the Zebra Killer, and those two sterling examples of family loyalty—Angelo Buono and Kenneth Bianchi.

Angelo Anthony Buono II and Kenneth Alessio Bianchi, although not related by blood, were nominally cousins. Buono's mother and Bianchi's adoptive mother were sisters. Together, those men would become known as the Hillside Strangler. Although the media labeled ten killings in the fall of 1977 and winter of 1978 as the Hillside Strangler case, there were, in fact, two killers.

Angelo Anthony Buono Jr. was born in Rochester, New York, on 5 October 1934 of Sicilian parents. He had one sibling, a sister five years older than he. His parents were divorced when he was still a small boy. Jenny Buono and her two children relocated to Los Angeles, California. The shattered family settled in the Highland Park area south of the city proper. That area attracted many migrants to the West Coast. Angelo would remain in the area for years to come.

Although born into a Roman Catholic family, young Angelo had no formal religious training. He received his limited education in the Los Angeles public school system. His lack of adequate education would hamper him all his life and may have caused much of the hostility and distrust that defined his personality. Adding to that, he had a noticeable speech defect.

Sometime after the family arrived in Los Angeles, his remarried father, Angelo Sr., also relocated there. He would remain a remote figure, uninvolved in the lives of his children.

Although little is known about Angelo's day-to-day life as a young man, one feature that stood out was his almost maniacal loathing for his mother. Most of his life he referred to her as "that cunt" and called her a whore. Even though she dated, she never remarried, and there is no evidence Jenny Buono was promiscuous.

By age fourteen, Angelo was a fully developed street hood. Stealing expensive cars and cruising the streets of the city with his friends, Buono fantasized about picking up a hitchhiker, raping her, and then "fucking her in the ass."

In 1950 at the age of sixteen, Angelo quit school. Within months he was in serious trouble. He picked fights, ran with gangs, and earned a reputation as an all-around bad actor. He was arrested for car theft, committed to a juvenile institution, and escaped. Rearrested in December 1951, he was sent to a secure juvenile institution in central California. Released on parole at age seventeen, he returned to the streets and resumed his activities.

Every boy needs a hero. Angelo Buono picked Caryl Chessman, the Red Light Bandit, who was one of the most notorious rapist-robbers of his day. He would masquerade as a police officer and approach young couples parked in lovers' lanes. Flashing a gun and badge, he would kidnap the girl, take her to a secluded spot, and force her to perform fellatio. Chessman was arrested, tried, and convicted in 1948 of various offenses, including kidnapping with infliction of bodily harm. He was sentenced to death. For the next twelve years, Chessman fought in various courts to head off his date with California's gas chamber. He was finally executed in 1960. Chessman was widely respected in the judicial field for his intelligence and his ability to defend himself in various legal forums.

Although Buono admired Chessman very much, he criticized him for not killing his victims. No living witnesses meant no court testimony.

By the mid-1950s, Buono developed an image of himself as a sort of stereotypical movie gangster. He dressed like a hood, drove Cadillac convertibles, and perfected a technique of gaining sexual pleasure from women using fear and intimidation. His favorite place for taking girls was a secluded, eerie area called Landa Street.

While Angelo Buono was busy perfecting his techniques, the other half of the deadly duo was born a continent away. Like Buono, Kenneth Alessio Bianchi was born in Rochester, New York.

His mother, a teenage prostitute he would never know, gave birth on 22 May 1951 and surrendered him for adoption the same day.

Baby Kenneth, a full-term, breech-birth child, was placed in a foster home immediately. An elderly woman fed him, changed his diapers, and ignored him the rest of the time.

After a brief stay in a second foster home, young Kenneth, now about three months old, was adopted into the family of Nicholas Bianchi. Bianchi, a second-generation Italian Catholic, had married Frances Sciolino, sister of Jenny Buono. Ken Bianchi would grow up the adopted, overprotected, only child of a hypochondriacal, dominant mother.

Like John Gacy and Ted Bundy, Ken Bianchi grew up in a household fraught with emotional turmoil, confusion, and parental inconsistency. Frances Bianchi had suffered a hysterectomy while in her early twenties. Given the time and her ethnic background, the severe emotional blow of not being able to have children left her depressed and unstable. After ten years of childless marriage, the opportunity to adopt and raise young Ken seemed like a gift from God to the Bianchis. All the love and attention she had been unable to lavish on children of her own were focused on the infant. As is often the case, with those positive emotions came negative aspects as well. Her obsessive attention to the health of the child created tension in the home, which eventually spread to his school days and followed him throughout the course of his life.

Neighbors and teachers noticed the family situation was unusual and unhealthy for Ken. They, plus the doctors who frequently saw Ken, several times reported the Bianchis to the Rochester Society for the Prevention of Cruelty to Children, Inc. For all his growing up years, regular reports by the Society were made on the nervous state of the mother and the manipulative, hostile, and dependent characteristics of Ken. Psychiatric help was recommended for both, but Frances would have nothing of the sort.

Ken had constant problems retaining his urine. Frequent medical examinations by numerous doctors involved the probing of Ken's genitals. According to experts, children can come to feel raped by such examinations. Frances seldom agreed with the doctors' reports. She frequently kept Ken out of school because of the teasing by other children and his wetting his pants. Small children can be incredibly cruel, yet to hide a child away and not encourage him to stand up for himself is destructive in the long run.

The various ailments Ken suffered in his childhood seem to have been largely the result of Frances' concerns rather than legitimate health problems. Still, his asthma led the family to move to Los Angeles from Rochester in 1957.

The Bianchi family stayed in Los Angeles for some time. While there, the family often visited the home of Angelo Buono. Buono, sixteen years older, remembered Ken as an obnoxious pest who frequently wet his pants.

After returning to Rochester, Frances wanted a higher standard of living. At her urging, the family bought a home they could not afford in the suburbs. Both she and Nicholas worked, but they still lost the home in 1959 and moved to more modest surroundings. She was depressed, but Nicholas was glad to be rid of his financial worries. His health had suffered from the ordeal of trying to make ends meet. The strain had taken a toll on Ken, also.

For six years, Ken attended the Holy Family elementary school. Even the small tuition strained the family's resources. His tested IQ was 116, well into the bright-normal range. Yet, his teachers felt Ken worked far below his capacity. He was indifferent to schoolwork, but good at verbal tasks and creative writing.

When Ken was thirteen, he and his father had one glorious fishing trip together. They talked man-to-man and began a new relationship that Ken badly needed. Ken wanted to gain some independence from his mother. He, however, was confused about his own identity and so dependent on her that he had been unable to free himself. The fishing trip showed Ken a freedom he had never known.

The next week, tragedy struck. Nicholas died of a heart attack while at work. Mrs. Bianchi became hysterical when told. Ken fled to his room, devastated. For days, he hid in the darkened attic, sobbing out his broken heart in long talks with his dead father. For three years afterward, his nightly dreams were the time to talk with his father.

Frances had to work to support herself and Ken. Left alone, Ken became a frequent purchaser of hard-core pornography in Rochester's adult bookstores. Borrowing the family projector, he would show porno movies to his friends. His mother found his film collection, but even her angry lecture and tears could not stop him.

Ken always felt ordinary work was beneath him. Ahead lay some undefined greatness.

While Ken was still a young boy, Angelo had already sown many wild oats. In 1955, the twenty-one-year-old Angelo got his teenage girlfriend pregnant. Although he married Geraldine Vinal in June in a Protestant ceremony, Angelo fled one week later. His son Michael was born the following January. He had contact with Michael but would not permit his son to call him Dad. Around the Buono house, his wife was known as Aunt Gerry. It is unknown under what circumstances they parted. What is known is that the marriage was brief and painful for Vinal and her infant son.

In November 1955, Angelo served sixty days in the county jail for petty theft in connection with a stolen car.

In 1956, Mary Catherine Castillo, sometimes called Candy, became pregnant by Buono. His second son, Angelo Anthony Buono III, was born at the end of the year. Angelo and Candy were married on 15 April 1957 in a Catholic ceremony. Four other children followed in rapid succession.

They occupied seven homes in seven years, beginning with a cottage behind Jenny's house. Angelo made good wages as an auto upholsterer but stole whatever he could not afford. Once in 1962 and twice in 1964, he was back in jail for petty theft associated with cars.

Candy Buono was a battered wife before the term was invented. She was the object of all Angelo's perverse sexual urges. She endured marital rape, brutal intercourse, slapping, pinching, and any other form of abuse Angelo's fertile mind could devise. His favorite degradation was anal intercourse. Once when she tried to resist, he knocked her to the floor and violently anally raped her in front of her five small children.

Exhausted and fearful, Candy divorced him in 1964. The court awarded child support, which she never received. Angelo refused to pay a dime and began spelling his name Bono to avoid detection. When she tried for a reconciliation, Angelo handcuffed her, drove her into the hills, stuck a pistol in her stomach, and threatened to kill her. Like most battered women, she seemed to believe the failed marriage was her fault.

The next year, Angelo moved in with twenty-five-year-old Nanette Campina. She had two children, including a fourteen-year-old daughter, Annette, by a previous marriage. Angelo fathered Tony in 1967 and Sam in 1969. Following his pattern, Buono regularly beat Nanette. He told her he would have her killed if she ever considered leaving him.

In March of 1968, Angelo received probation for stealing a car. In September, the court discovered that Bono was Buono and ordered him either to pay child support to Candy or to spent weekends in jail. Angelo chose jail. By 1971, the jail time he had served reduced his felony auto theft conviction to a misdemeanor.

That same year, Nanette, taking advantage of Angelo's absence, fled to Florida with her four children. She never returned. Annette had told her that Angelo had fondled her and made obscene suggestions. Nanette also suspected Angelo had raped her daughter. Later, Buono would brag he had "banged" his stepdaughter and then turned her over to his sons for sex. It was later revealed he had also had intercourse with at least one of his sons.

Angelo was undaunted. Deborah Taylor became his third known wife in 1972 in a Las Vegas wedding. They never lived together.

Angelo changed residences often. Through an actor friend, Angelo managed to meet many Hollywood people who became his clients. He built a reputation as an excellent upholsterer of classic and antique cars.

Going into business for himself in 1975, he opened an upholstery shop in Glendale, a suburb of Los Angeles. He worked alone except for occasionally hiring a local boy.

Obsessed with neatness and privacy, Buono's behavior became increasingly bizarre. One of his favorite leisure activities was using binoculars to spy on girls in a local high school while he masturbated. He built a metal awning between his shop and the adjacent house to conceal his activities. His reputation as an upholsterer was only surpassed by his reputation as a stud. He used and discarded women frequently.

Despite his attitude, women were drawn to Angelo Buono. He seemed the stereotypical macho man who spoke little and had muscular arms, tattoos, and aggressive mannerisms. His swaggering walk and overt way of examining females gave them the impression he was a man who knew what he wanted and got it. He was openly fond of very young girls.

Dying his hair to look younger, Angelo began seducing his sons' girlfriends and any other young female with whom he could get close. His wallet was stuffed with high school pictures, often with erotic inscriptions. He did his best to conceal the fact he spoke with a lisp and had an ulcer. His one-story frame house next to the shop was immaculately clean and neat. He did his own cleaning as he trusted no one. Concealed in the house were five rifles, two .45 caliber semi-automatic pistols, and a Thompson submachine gun. Like most other serial killers, he had a great fondness for television police shows. His favorites were about tough-guy heroes who did as they pleased and took what they wanted.

Back in Rochester, Kenneth Bianchi was having problems of his own. Marrying shortly after his eighteenth birthday in 1969, he discovered his bride, Brenda, was also immature and under the thumb of a dominant mother. They had married to escape from home. Now they quarreled frequently. Afterward, Ken would woo her with flowers and romantic poetry. Ken's jealous belief that she cheated on him hurt the marriage.

Bianchi's childhood pattern of lying and manipulating continued. He set high standards for women and attempted to impose his values on them. He insisted on conservative female dress and absolute fidelity, but he cheated whenever the opportunity arose. Finally, he came home one day to discover Brenda had taken everything from the apartment and had moved out. He was confused and devastated.

In a 1972 letter to a girlfriend, Ken Bianchi, then twenty-one years old, said he had killed a man. He said he was not worried about being caught, because he had made it look like a heart attack. He also believed he was a suspect in the "Alphabet Murders." Those crimes, the killing of three young girls, aged ten and eleven, were linked by the fact that each victim's first and last initials were the same. He thought police were searching for a man driving a car similar to his. In reality, police had no suspects, and the crimes were never solved. The girlfriend dismissed the letter as another of Bianchi's boastful lies.

Bianchi's adroit lies continued. He told people he was going to become a police officer. He had been fascinated with police work since high school. Enrolling at a local community college, he took courses in psychology and police science. Psychology intrigued him. It allowed him to spend endless hours with his favorite subject: himself. Also, it provided an alternative to the Roman Catholic insistence on personal responsibility for behavior. He viewed Freudian psychology as an excuse for any behavior the community found unacceptable. After all, one cannot be held accountable if one is subject to impersonal controlling forces going all the way back to childhood.

Bianchi was an indifferent student. His class attendance was sporadic, and he often faked illnesses as excuses for his absence. He maintained a high C average for a while but, when his grades slipped, he dropped out.

Following school, Ken hopped from job to job. He applied with the local sheriff's department and, when rejected, he blamed the test rather than himself. Obtaining work as a security guard for a local firm, Bianchi followed his pattern as a petty thief. Often suspected, he was never caught. Working briefly as a bouncer in a bar, he hid his cowardice by saying he disliked violence. Next as an ambulance attendant, he gained experience with first aid, became inured to the sight of blood, and grew accustomed to death. He said he liked the idea of saving lives.

Ken's life became more complicated when his mother remarried. For the first time, she encouraged him to make a life of his own, rather than continue the long dependency relationship with her. She wrote to California and asked her sister, Jenny, to have Angelo take Kenny in and look after him until he got on his feet.

Angelo agreed to let Ken live with him temporarily. Angelo had not seen Ken for nearly twenty years. The pesky bedwetter, now twenty-five-years-old, was six feet tall, weighed 180 pounds, had permed his dark hair, and wore a mustache. Ken arrived in California filled with idealistic images of the California lifestyle. He felt all his sexual taboos had been left on the other side of the continent.

Ken saw Angelo as a real ladies' man. His CB handle was the "Italian Stallion," after a porno film starring future "Rocky," Sylvester Stallone. Ken perceived Angelo as a "real man" who didn't waste his time with the niceties; he knew what he wanted and simply took it. Bianchi quickly figured out that, to stay around his new ideal, he had to anticipate and fulfill Angelo's every need. He became an adept and willing slave to his stronger older cousin. Buono, on the other hand, saw Ken Bianchi as a wimp who didn't know how to handle women.

One thing they had in common was a mutual contempt and hatred for women. In the years to come, that hatred would flower and blossom in death. Their attitude was revealed in an incident that occurred soon after Bianchi's arrival in California.

It was Sunday, 2 January 1976. Angelo, Ken, and Angelo's son, Angelo III, were lying around the house with nothing to do. Inspired by hormones, they contacted an outcall prostitute. Two blow jobs and three lays later, she demanded her money. Angelo, pulling a fake badge from his wallet, ordered her from the house. That was the first time Ken saw the badge trick.

The example of the power of a badge inspired Ken to apply for jobs with the Glendale Police Department and the Los Angeles Police Department Reserves. He was turned down both places. He must have felt as if all the police departments in America were using the same unfair test.

Ken was next inspired to try his hand at human services. Lacking the necessary education, he purchased two bogus diplomas in psychology and would later open a counseling center. Like his cousin, Angelo, he was not deterred by minor matters such as laws, morality, and ethics in obtaining what he wanted in life.

Bianchi finally succeeded in getting a job with the California Land Title Company. He performed property title searches for Los Angeles County at the county Hall of Records. He was later promoted to title officer at the company's main office near Universal City.

Very pleased with his progress, his mother sent him enough money to make a down payment on a car. The vehicle, a dark blue 1972 Cadillac with a white vinyl top, was later used in several murders.

Bianchi had begun smoking marijuana on a regular basis. After having a severe hallucination, probably caused from smoking pot laced with angel dust (PCP), he cut back to a few puffs on an occasional basis.

It is difficult to imagine two more unlikely and incompatible roommates than these cousins. Angelo had a studied macho, silent man approach to life, and Ken chattered like a magpie, was financially irresponsible, and constantly complained. The only things they had in common were their gender and their sexual deviances.

Ken began to miss the structured life he had lived in New York. No regular meals, little sleep, and the constant comings and goings in the house left his nerves frayed. At Angelo's insistence, Ken finally got a residence of his own in July 1976. He moved into a small apartment at 809 East Garfield Avenue in Glendale, six blocks away from Angelo. He would live there until the end of the year.

Both Bianchi and Buono were sexually involved with many women at the time. Among others, Ken was attracted to his new next-door neighbor, Kristina Weckler. She was not interested in Ken Bianchi and let him know it.

It did not take Bianchi long to find solace with another woman. Twenty-one-year-old Kelli Boyd had been born and raised in Bellingham, Washington, a few miles below the Canadian border. A very traditional girl, she had married shortly after high school, but the marriage had failed. She was petite, five feet two inches, 125 pounds, with blond hair and hazel eyes. Her family had moved to the Los Angeles area in May 1976.

Kelli was employed briefly at Pier I Imports, then obtained a job at the California Land Title Company, for which Bianchi worked in a different branch. She did her job and went home, avoiding the Hollywood party scene. Kelli's sister worked in Ken Bianchi's office and introduced them in November. However, they did not date until New Year's Eve.

They made a striking couple. Kelli, blond and petite, and Ken, dark, tall, muscular, and mustached. He seemed gentle, friendly, and eager to please. Bianchi made it clear from the outset that his goal was marriage and a family. Kelli was drawn to him immediately, and a few weeks later moved into his tiny apartment on Garfield Avenue.

They both sincerely tried to make the relationship work. Kelli was quite aware of Ken's insecurities and jealousy. She did her best to reassure him and did not question his comings and goings. She felt uncomfortable around Angelo Buono, as if sensing his hatred and contempt for women.

Ken still worked when he chose and spent most of his leisure time watching television. Although not a reader, he did have a few psychology texts in the apartment that were used in his counseling scam.

Using his adept skills at lying, Bianchi convinced a real psychologist, Dr. Weingarten, to rent him office space in his building. Ken advertised on flyers as a weight reduction consultant for young women. He had few clients and always needed money.

Both cousins were chronically short of money. To help them with their financial situations, Angelo suggested they get girls to prostitute for them. Sometime before, Ken had met sixteen-year-old Sabra Hannan, a runaway from Phoenix. She had come to Hollywood to be a model. She was five feet four inches tall, with blond hair and blue eyes, and a pouty lower lip. Ken, posing as a talent scout, told her if there was ever anything he could do for her, to contact. him. Bianchi had stolen some letterhead stationery from Universal Studios and used it as part of his talent scout charade.

In June of 1977, Sabra called Ken and asked him to pay her airfare from Phoenix to Los Angeles. He did. He picked her up at the airport, drugged her into unconsciousness, and put her in a hotel near Buono's house. When she awoke, she found she was in captivity.

The next day Sabra met Angelo Buono, who told her she had to work for them for one year. A few days later, they moved her into Angelo's spare bedroom. Angelo got Sabra to pose nude for photographs, telling her it was for an artistic modeling job. He suggested prostitution on several occasions, but she declined. She was told not to leave the house without permission from either Ken or Angelo.

One day, Sabra broke the rules and went shopping without permission. When she got back, Angelo forced her to strip and proceeded to beat her with a wet towel. Ken also joined in the punishment. That was the first time Bianchi had ever hit a woman, and he liked it very much. Angelo told Sabra from now on she would be their whore. She then was forced to give each of them a blow job.

The next few weeks must have seemed to the two men as if all their adolescent fantasies had come true. An attractive young woman became their virtual slave. Customers at Angelo's upholstery shop next door were shown photographs of the young woman from Arizona and asked if they would like some of the action. A steady stream of men went from the shop to the house. They paid Angelo; Sabra was not given any money and was not always fed. However, the two had one more surprise for her.

Up to that point, neither Buono nor Bianchi had indulged their predilection for anal sex on Sabra. One night, Angelo came home with a large dildo, gave it to Sabra, and ordered her to insert it into her rectum to prepare herself for anal sex. When she tried but could not insert it, she was ordered to practice.

The two men organized an orgy for seven other men. One of those was a police chief in a local suburb and another an aide to a member of the Los Angeles County Board of Supervisors. The aide was so grateful for the enjoyable evening that he sent Bianchi a decal with the seal of the County of Los Angeles. With the seal on his Cadillac, Ken could park his car in spaces reserved for county officials.

The cousins seemed to have begun tiring of Sabra Hannan. She was told she would be freed if she could recruit a replacement for herself. Amazingly, Sabra went to Phoenix and brought another girl, Rebekah Gay Spears, age fifteen, back to Los Angeles with her.

Becky, the daughter of an outlaw motorcyclist, was a small girl with a large, sad-looking mouth. Frail and looking defenseless, she was an easy target for the now-experienced abusers. She was placed in Buono's spare bedroom. After being threatened with death, she agreed to have anal sex with the two men. Becky was anally raped so brutally and so frequently that her sphincter muscles were torn. She could no longer control her bowel movements. She was forced to wear a tampon to hold in her feces and was not given medical attention.

Sabra was placed in a nearby apartment. Although no longer living at Buono's house, she was still under their control psychologically. Angelo, of course, reneged on his promise to free her. He worked out a deal with a local outcall prostitution service. During the day, the two girls worked at Angelo's house and at night they worked for the outcall service.

In August of 1977, Ken Bianchi and Kelli Boyd moved to a larger apartment at 1150 North Tamarind in Hollywood. The longer the two lived together, the more convinced Kelli became that Ken was and would continue to be immature. His irresponsibility caused constant money problems. If he didn't feel like working, he would simply call in sick and spend the day at Angelo's playing cards.

That fall, Kelli and her girlfriend went on vacation together. While in Denver, Kelli was raped and, as a result, contracted venereal disease. She did not report the rape to the police and did not tell Ken about the incident until he, also, contracted VD. While being treated, Kelli discovered she had been pregnant since May. Because of Ken's insecurities and, undoubtedly, his continuing infidelity to her, Kelli had a difficult time convincing him that she had been raped and was not pregnant from having an affair.

During that time, Ken continued to propose marriage, but Kelli put him off by saying she wanted time to think. She wanted the baby but was quite uncertain about Ken's role as a husband. He was, at times, thoughtful, kind, and attentive, but other times saw him staying out late and manifesting his almost insane jealousy.

Bianchi told Kelli many lies during their relationship. The biggest lie was he had cancer, which was why he wasn't regular or punctual about work. The worry about his illness added further stress to the course of her pregnancy. Ken told her of his frequent treatments at a local hospital, but he would not let her accompany him, because he said he didn't want her to see the unpleasant effects.

He smoked marijuana at home and, on occasion, sold pot to others. He lost his title company job when his supervisor found marijuana in his desk and asked him to resign or be fired. He quickly found a similar job with the Stewart West Coast Title company in downtown Los Angeles.

Ken and Kelli moved again to an apartment at 1950 Tamarind Avenue just a few blocks from their first residence. Ken decorated the walls with his collection of framed phony degrees and certificates. Those included a Master of Science from Columbia University and a diploma as a certified "sex therapist."

The two men continued to supplement their income with the earnings of Sabra Hannan and Becky Spears. The two involuntary prostitutes were bringing in several hundred dollars a month. One night, however, Becky was sent on an outcall to the home of a Beverly Hills lawyer. She told the lawyer everything, including being beaten and being held prisoner and having her life threatened. The lawyer, disgusted with her physical frailty, still sympathized with her situation. He bought a ticket and put her on a plane back to Phoenix.

When the cousins found out, they were furious. Angelo attempted to threaten and intimidate the lawyer into either bringing her back or paying for the lost income. The lawyer, however, had a 300-pound bouncer friend go to Angelo's house and explain the realities of life to him. Buono was so frightened he left the lawyer alone. It seemed his courage did not extend to confrontations with other men.

In September of 1977, Sabra Hannan finally escaped and left the state. With the extra income gone, Ken Bianchi began missing his car payments and soon the fights with Kelli escalated. He and Angelo, angry and frustrated, began talking of raping and killing a prostitute.

Later in the month, the two men were out cruising and picked up two teenage girls. They flashed a badge and had sex with them in the car. They then pushed the girls out of the car and drove away. The two young women were naked but lucky to be alive.

The next night, they attempted to pull the same stunt again. Buono and Bianchi stopped in front of two young girls, one of whom fled. The other, holding her ground, was screen-legend Peter Lorre's daughter, Catherine. When they flashed a badge, she told them she was waiting for a ride from someone just down the street. The men were awed at her identity and were afraid they had been seen by the mysterious driver. They let her go. She had lied about the ride waiting, but at least she was alive, unlike others to come.

In early October of 1977, Angelo's mother, Jenny, had surgery for vaginal cancer. The prognosis was bad. With mixed emotions, Angelo visited her in the hospital. He was forty-three years old.

Buono and Bianchi, attempting to recover the lost income from Sabra and Becky, contacted a young woman named Jennifer Snyder, who had been a friend of Sabra's. Jennifer went to work for them as a prostitute.

In the meantime, Buono purchased what he thought was an outcall client list of 175 men. When a prostitute delivered the list, four other women, all prostitutes, came with her. One was a black woman named Yolanda Washington, who worked the north side of Sunset Boulevard near Highland Avenue. Since the early 1960s, Hollywood Boulevard and the Sunset Strip had been the sex-for-sale centers of southern California. Both male and female prostitutes were available at any time of the day or night.

The list turned out to be an incall list, rather than the desired outcall list. The men on the list wanted to go to the hooker's place for their sexual gratification.

The cousins were furious. Ken, outraged and angered at women in general, slapped Jennifer around. When he tried to force her to submit to sodomy, she threw him off, turned, and prepared to fight. Ken backed down and fled. Now afraid of the men, Jennifer, like her predecessors, fled for her life.

After working up through a scale of violence, the two men were now ready. At eleven p.m. on 17 October 1977, Kenneth Bianchi and Angelo Buono picked up Yolanda Washington, supposedly for a trick. They stripped her and raped her in the back of Ken's car, and then Ken strangled her. Unknown to Angelo, Ken also took and kept a large turquoise ring Yolanda always wore. The corpse was dumped on Forest Lawn Drive, south of the Ventura Freeway, near the Forest Lawn Cemetery where many movie stars are buried. The body was found the next day.

Yolanda Washington had become a prostitute so she would have enough money to raise her young son and to have more time with her child. Now her child was alone, and she was dead.

On an average day, the Los Angeles Police Department coroner's office received forty-five bodies, one approximately every thirty minutes. Of those, about one in six was the result of a homicide.

The coroner determined Yolanda Washington had been tossed from a car on the freeway and her body had rolled down the hill. She had been strangled from above by someone of great strength. The killer had used some sort of cloth ligature, such as a nylon stocking, to asphyxiate her. She had had sexual intercourse with two men, one a nonsecretor (someone whose bodily fluids do not contain antigens of the ABO blood group), before death. As was often the case with the death of a prostitute, her death went virtually unnoticed by the media and the public.

The next to encounter the deadly duo was fifteen-year-old Judith Ann Miller. Judith, a pale, thin young woman, stood only five feet two inches and weighed about ninety pounds. She dreamed of being a model or a movie star but already had a history of prostitution. One of her favorite hangouts was the area around Hollywood Boulevard and Wilcox. She disappeared the night of 30 October and, the next morning, was found next to the curb in a residential area in La Crescenta, north of Glendale.

Buono and Bianchi had gone out cruising the night of 30 October. As they drove slowly down Sunset Strip, they saw the small, reddish-haired girl sitting alone on the sidewalk by a diner. Bianchi got out of the car and walked past her. Meanwhile, Buono drove around the block and pulled into the driveway by her. He struck up a conversation with the girl, who got into the car. As Angelo drove past Ken, he stopped and Bianchi approached the car. Displaying a badge, he told Judy Miller that she was under arrest for prostitution. Her previous experiences told her what to expect. She was handcuffed and placed in the back seat. The men said they were part of a special police task force.

They drove to Buono's house, which the girl was told was a special satellite police station. Once inside, they began their attack. Stuffing an orange, garage-type work rag in the young girl's mouth, they fastened it in place with masking tape. They then took a section of the white polyester foam used to fill car seats and taped it over her eyes. Rifling her purse, they discovered she had only about two dollars to her name, but they took it anyway.

The handcuffs were removed, and she was ordered to take off her jacket, blouse, and brassiere. The men then handcuffed her again and stripped off the rest of her clothes. Placing her in the spare bedroom, they stood beside the bed and flipped a coin to see which of them would rape her first. Angelo Buono won. He ripped the tape off her mouth and removed the rag. Some said that was done to force her to commit fellatio. Others suspected it was done so they could savor her screams. Bianchi took Polaroid photographs of Buono as he raped the girl.

After Buono was sated, it was Ken's turn. He proceeded to rape her, both in the vagina and in the rectum. When he was finished, he put the rag back in her mouth and retaped it securely. Most of her clothes and belongings, plus the Polaroids, were placed in a green garbage bag. From his shop, Angelo brought in a large wooden spool containing the white nylon cord used to trim the edges of auto seat covers.

Bianchi then redressed her in her panties and slacks. Recalling his ambulance experiences and the circumstances of the first murder, he knew that when they killed her, her bowels and bladder would relax and she would foul herself. He was unconcerned about that but wasn't taking any chances Angelo might get angry at him if the victim made a mess.

They tied her ankles tightly together, and Ken sat on her legs while Angelo pressed her to the floor with his knees on her shoulders. Placing a plastic grocery sack over her head, Buono looped a section of the cord around her neck and began to pull. Frantic to survive, she bucked and resisted so strongly that, at one point, she succeeded in throwing Buono off. He immediately got back on her shoulders and began pulling again. Finally, the frail, young, street kid went limp, shuddered briefly, and died.

They removed and discarded all the accessories of their murder but kept the handcuffs. Placing her body in the trunk of Ken's Cadillac, they drove up to La Crescenta and stopped in front of 2844 Alta Terrace Drive. Angelo Buono had once had dinner with the woman who lived there. They removed Miller's body from the trunk and placed it face up on the curb. As is often the case with killers of this type, the degradation of the victim did not end with death. Sightless eyes staring up into the starry California night, Judith Ann was positioned with her arms wide, knees up, and legs spread. She would be found that way at six a.m.

The case was assigned to the Los Angeles County Sheriff's Office. In professional law enforcement circles, the homicide detectives of LACSO are considered to be among the finest in the United States, if not the world. The investigating officers on the scene quickly concluded the body had been placed by two men. Investigators found adhesive residue on her face. Ligature marks were noticeable at her neck, wrists, and ankles. The wrist and ankle bruises were irregular and splotchy. The coroner later determined correctly that the young woman had been both tied and handcuffed.

The killing, unlike that of Yolanda Washington, quickly drew media attention. The graphic details were reported in both the *Los Angeles Times* and the *Herald Examiner*.

Investigators received no response to their ad in the Times asking for help in identifying the body. Checking the Hollywood street scene, they learned she was Judith Miller. For over a week after her death, she had been the nameless contents of one of the coolers at the Los Angeles County morgue.

At that point began the long cat and mouse game between police and the killers. It is not enough to merely come up with suspects or even to make arrests. The killers must be identified irrefutably on the basis of their own actions.

After the Miller killing, Angelo concluded the police arrest ploy would work on any woman, not just a hooker. After a few days of sitting around the house, the cousins struck again.

On the night of 5 November 1977, they spotted an attractive woman driving a bright green VW convertible. Following the car to the parking lot of her apartment house, the two men approached twenty-one-year-old waitress Lissa Kastin. They identified themselves as police officers and informed her that her vehicle had been identified as being at the scene of a robbery. She was told she would have to come in for questioning. After arguing for several minutes, Kastin relented and agreed to go with the two men. She protested about being placed in handcuffs but gave in when convinced it was just standard police procedure.

Once again, they drove their victim, handcuffed in the back seat of the Cadillac, to the Buono house. Angelo had carefully laid out the tape and other accessories they had used before so successfully. They refined their technique somewhat. Rather than remove the handcuffs in order to strip the victim, Lissa's clothes were cut from her body with a large pair of upholstery scissors. When they saw her nude, both men were repulsed by the quantity of dark hair on her unshaven legs. Angelo was especially put off and did not bother to touch her. Ken, equally repulsed, responded by brutalizing her genitals with a soda pop bottle. Angelo became even more upset because Ken's actions caused her to bleed on his carpet.

The murder procedure itself was similar to the previous two times. However, Angelo added one cruel refinement. Strangling her to the point of death, he then released the ligature and allowed her to breathe. Several times, Lissa Kastin was brought back from the edge of death and allowed to live. Totally unsatisfied with the sexual aspect of the crime, they attempted to gratify themselves with the feelings of absolute power they obtained through the repeated strangulations. Finally, Lissa Kastin died.

By and large, the crime had been unsatisfactory. However,

ever willing to learn from their mistakes, they decided to select their future victims carefully to take only the choicest and most attractive women. Ken was fascinated by the almost endless variations to be had from the repeated strangulations approach.

Kastin's nude body was placed in the trunk of Bianchi's Cadillac and taken to the grounds of the Chevy Chase Golf and Country Club, where it was dumped. The next morning a woman jogger discovered her corpse.

At the coroner's office, the body of Kastin, then still unidentified, was placed alongside that of Judith Ann Miller for comparison. The similarities in the method of death were easily noticed: the same bruises at the neck, wrists, and ankles; the strangulation by ligature; and the manner in which the body had been discarded. The strangled body was located only a few miles from where Judith Ann Miller had been found.

All those commonalities led the authorities to believe they were the work of the same men. Also, they were certain it had taken two men to lift the body over the guard rail around the golf course and drop it.

Lissa's body was formally identified by her father the following day, 7 November, after he heard a radio report of the body description. It was determined Lissa Kastin had disappeared about nine-fifteen the previous evening. The restaurant manager where she worked had become concerned and called her family, who were unable to locate her.

Three days later under public pressure, police released some information to the press. The two girls were "strangled in the same fashion." Three different law enforcement agencies were now involved: the Los Angeles Police Department, the Glendale Police Department, and the Los Angeles County Sheriff's Office.

Around that time, the name "Hillside Strangler" was first used to describe those crimes. Police had referred to the dead women as the hillside victims. In a logical extension, the killer(s) came to be referred to as the Hillside Strangler. The name would generate terror in the months to come.

Police continued to allow the press to draw erroneous conclusions about the crimes and victims. This is often done so that, when someone comes forward to confess, the police have a method of determining if they are dealing with a murderer or just one more nut case. In the Hillside case, two young females who had disappeared on 10 and 17 November were initially included on the Hillside list, even though police knew from the MO those were unrelated crimes.

On 10 November, a detective succeeded in locating the family of victim Judith Ann Miller. Her parents and two younger brothers were living in a rundown hotel in a skid row area. Years of poverty had ground away their emotions until they were indifferent to her death. They merely said Judy ran away from home sometimes but had always returned. That time, she wouldn't be coming home. Detectives also located one witness, Markust Camden, who had seen Judy at the diner on Hollywood and Wilcox between nine and ten on the night she died.

Angelo told Ken to get a real police badge to use on future forays in the night. Bianchi obtained a California Highway Patrol badge at a swap meet. Slipping further into his fantasies, Ken Bianchi told his coworkers at the title company that he worked as an undercover policeman on the side. He carried an attaché case in which he kept the phony badge and identification, the handcuffs used in the crimes, and photographs of nude women.

On Wednesday evening, 9 November, twenty-eight-year-old Jane King finished her acting class and stood waiting at a bus stop at Mayfair Market. The two cousins, unimpressed by any of the hookers on Hollywood Boulevard, cruised by. They were immediately attracted by the slim girl in high heels and tight jeans. Pulling around the corner, Ken Bianchi got out and strode over to the bus stop as if he, too, were waiting for the bus. Using a calm and reassuring tone, Bianchi struck up a conversation with the young woman. He noticed her long, tapered, graceful hands; beautiful face; and lush body. She was definitely the kind of victim they wanted.

When Angelo pulled in front of the bus stop, Bianchi pretended he had just spotted a friend and began talking to him. Ken asked Angelo for a ride and then offered to take King along, also. At first, she refused, but finally accepted when Ken told her that he and Angelo were cousins and both were in the LA Police Reserves. To convince her, he flashed his badge.

Ken said Angelo really needed to go home first. Would she mind if they dropped Angelo and then Ken would take her home afterwards? Suspecting nothing, she agreed.

When they arrived at Buono's house, she became their fourth

doomed victim. Following their pattern, they cut her clothing away and discovered King had shaved her pubic hair. Her lithe body, beautiful face, and hairless genitals were the stuff of Angelo's fantasies. Angelo, to his enormous delight, won the coin toss. King resisted strongly until Angelo threatened to beat and mutilate her. After Angelo finished, she fought Bianchi as he raped her anally while Angelo sat watching and masturbating. Finally, Angelo put a plastic bag over her head, tightened and loosened the noose several times, and then strangled the woman to death. Later, her battered corpse was rolled into the bushes at the Los Feliz offramp of the Golden State Freeway.

King was reported missing almost immediately by both her boyfriend and her roommate. They described her as a quiet introvert who was fond of exercise and health food. A friend at her acting class had offered her a ride that night. She had refused, saying she would wait for the bus.

The cousins, weary and satisfied, made their way home. In discussing the crime, they both liked the idea of a victim too young to have pubic hair. They decided their future victims would be very young and preferably virgins.

Police continued to investigate the crimes. After several interviews, witness Markust Camden finally admitted he had had intercourse with Judy Miller the night she had vanished. He had taken her to the diner for coffee. Afterward, she left him to find a trick and make some money. Camden said he stood outside the diner until he saw her picked up by a "dark blue limousine." Camden said the driver of the car, whom he was certain he would recognize if he saw him again, had been Latin-looking with a large nose and dark curly hair. He had been alone in the vehicle.

The Hillside Strangler nickname was creating panic in the city. In the twenty-three days since the first abduction, four young women had been raped and murdered. Unlike most serial killers who start off slowly with wide intervals between crimes, Buono and Bianchi started at high speed. Now they would accelerate even more. By the morning of 13 November 1977, four more young women, going about the business of their lives, were already doomed.

That day, Angelo and Ken followed two young girls as they left the Eagle Rock Plaza Shopping Center to catch the bus home. The men were intrigued by the possibility of a double play orgy with young girls, followed by twin murders. The girls, Dolores Cepeda, age twelve, and Sonja Johnson, age fourteen, got off the bus. The two men immediately pounced. They flashed their badges at the girls and said a burglar was loose in the neighborhood. The girls were told they should accept a ride home from them as they were police officers. Dolores and Sonja, who had just stolen around a hundred dollars' worth of costume jewelry from shops at the plaza, were quite willing to cooperate so their crime would not be discovered.

Both girls had histories of being somewhat on the wild side, but they had never previously been in any real trouble. Like many young people from California, they were in a hurry to grow up and often dressed to look older than they were. Dolores, also known as Dollie, weighed ninety-six pounds, and Sonja, at four feet eleven inches tall, was thin at eighty pounds.

Arriving at the "satellite police station," Angelo's house, both girls were raped, sodomized, and killed. The stolen jewelry joined their belongings in the garbage bag. Their property went into the dumpster, and their bodies went into a ditch.

As time passed and they sought another victim, Buono and Bianchi noticed the heavily increased police coverage in the Hollywood area. Then Ken remembered the young woman named Kristina Weckler, who had spurned his advances when they were neighbors in an apartment house. Bianchi made an obscene phone call to her and then hung up.

A few days later, on 19 November, Bianchi went to Weckler's door and flashed his badge. He told her that he was a member of the police reserves and someone had crashed into her car in the parking lot. Would she come out to the lot and help him write up the report? When she reached the parking lot with Bianchi, she found Angelo Buono waiting for her. She was placed in Bianchi's car and taken away.

At Angelo's house, any restraints remaining on their behavior were released. They performed every sexual act on her body that they could think up. They also decided to try a different method of committing the murder. They filled a hypodermic syringe, which Angelo had stolen from the hospital during his visits to his dying mother, with Windex™. The Windex™ was then injected into her arms and her neck. Weckler went into convulsions but did not die.

Next, they dragged her into the kitchen. Because Angelo always ate out, he had no stove. However, a gas outlet for a stove was installed. She was forced to the floor and the gas pipe slammed against her neck. A plastic garbage bag was placed over her head. The bag and gas pipe were sealed against her neck with a cord. As Buono turned the gas on and off, Bianchi pulled the cord to strangle her. They managed to kill the young woman using two methods at once.

The following day, 20 November 1977, Kristina's nude body was found at Ramona Way and Nawona Avenue in the Glendale and Eagle Rock area. The corpse was on its side beneath a small tree. Investigators found ligature marks on her ankles, wrists, and neck, as in each previous case. She had bled from being sodomized. Puncture marks on both inner arms indicated she had probably been drugged and tortured. Around her breasts were numerous small bruises. Obviously, the killer knew the neighborhood and was able to place her corpse there undetected. The coroner's tests revealed no drugs in her body. However, it is unlikely they tested for Windex™.

At four p.m. on 20 November, the bodies of the two young girls were found. They were fifty feet down a hill off little-traveled, obscure Landa Street. They had been dead for a week. Rigor mortis had set in, and the faces had rotted. The five-point ligature marks were again detected. The bodies had been tossed over the edge and had rolled down onto a trash heap.

Police investigators found a boy who had seen the girls get off the bus near their homes. He had been on the bus and recalled seeing the girls talk to someone in a large sedan. The girls' parents and the priest of St. Ignatius School had set up search parties when they were first reported to be missing. One of the girls was known to be very frightened of strangers but very trusting and admiring of policemen. For the first time, the possibility arose that the killer or killers were posing as police officers.

The body of twenty-year-old Kristina Weckler was quickly identified. She had been an honors student at the Pasadena Art Center of Design. Friends remembered her as a quiet studious girl who often stayed home at night. She was known to be a very organized, tidy person.

On Tuesday, 22 November, the body of Jane King was found at the Los Feliz exit. She had been dead nearly two weeks.

As the result of the flurry of bodies, the Los Angeles Police Department announced they were forming a Hillside Strangler Task Force. Headed by Lieutenant Edward Henderson of the Los Angeles Police Department, it included officers from the Sheriff's Office and the Glendale Police Department. The task force quickly expanded to include thirty police officers and would eventually involve over one hundred. Investigators would collect over 12,000 "clue packages," each containing information on a given lead. The telephones of the task force quickly flooded with calls and tips, most of which were worthless, however well-meaning. A PATRIC (Pattern Recognition and Information Correlation) computer was purchased to aid the task force.

On Thanksgiving Day, 24 November 1978, the *Los Angeles Times* reported the murder of Jane King was probably linked to as many as ten other killings. That evening Ken and Kelli got into another fight. Ken lost his temper and hit her. Although he immediately went into his contrite act attempting to gain her forgiveness, she left the house.

The next day, the *Los Angeles Times* reported the strongest links in the Hillside case were between Yolanda Washington, Judy Miller, Lissa Kastin, and Kristina Weckler. The story pointed out their ages, body locations, the conditions of the nude bodies, and the sexual molestations they had suffered before death were quite similar. Each day for several weeks, the media would add and subtract possible victims from the Hillside Strangler list. The activity reflected the confused state of the investigation and the publicity surrounding it.

Buono and Bianchi took a few days off from their murder hobby over the Thanksgiving holiday. They also decided to switch areas from Hollywood to the San Fernando Valley to confuse the police. On 25 November, they resumed prowling. They spotted a young woman and followed her home. The woman, Lauren Wagner, lived with her parents, two sisters, and a brother. She was a very dependable girl and a business student at a local college. Always very prompt, Lauren usually arrived home by nine p.m. Her family described her as a loving and giving girl.

The two cousins exited their car and approached Lauren. It seemed she, unlike the previous victims, was alert enough to figure out that those men were the Hillside Stranglers, and she attempted to cooperate. However, once they arrived at Angelo's house, the usual rapes and assaults took place.

Using a new murder method, they stripped the wires from an electrical cord, taped them to her hands, and connected them to the power outlet. She was shocked several times but failed to die from electrocution. Finally, in frustration, they took her life as they had the previous victims using strangulation.

On Tuesday, 29 November, Lauren's body was found on a hill in the Glendale area. The corpse was found lying on her back, the upper part of her body in some brush but her legs sticking out onto the pavement of the street. Once again, the investigators found the five-point ligature marks. Her hands were still covered with the adhesive from the tape that had bound her. Several unusual, inch-and-a-half-long, double lesions appeared on the palms of her hands. Investigators speculated they were the result of some form of torture. They would not discover until much later that the marks were the result of an attempted electrocution.

The autopsy revealed Lauren Wagner had been sodomized before her death. Tests on the semen found in her body revealed only the blood type of the victim, which indicated the killer was a nonsecretor.

Investigators realized the two killers were becoming bored with simple rape and strangulation. Each crime was worse. The killers had become more and more obsessed with torturing, mutilating, and humiliating their victims, both before and after death.

Later in the day, Lauren Wagner was identified. That morning, her parents had found her car across the street from her home with the driver's door ajar and the dome light still on. A neighbor, Beulah Stofer, had seen Lauren park her car around nine p.m. and another car driven by two men pull up closely behind her's. The two men got out and apparently had an argument with her. Beulah heard Lauren cry out, "You won't get away with this!" Then she was placed in the car and driven away.

That same day, Mrs. Stofer received a threatening telephone call from a man with a New York accent. She said the man warned her to keep quiet about what she had seen. Beulah described the car as being big and dark in color, with a white top. One of the men was Latin-looking with bushy hair. The other, taller and younger, had acne scars on his neck. Although she felt she could identify the men if seen again, she had not called police. When she was a child, she had been raped and the sight of Lauren in trouble brought back all her terrors. However, when interviewed later by a detective, Mrs. Stofer was cooperative.

Another neighbor had also witnessed Lauren's abduction. She described two large figures and one small figure driving away in a large car. The witness described the auto as being light on top and dark underneath.

Previously, the killers had confined their activities to the Hollywood and Glendale areas. Now they had expanded into the Valley, and the city's panic level reached crisis proportions. Amoral politicians used the fear felt by citizens for personal gain. Office holders wanted the case solved so they could take the credit. Political candidates said the situation never would have occurred if they had been in office. Yet none had valid suggestions for ending the reign of terror.

Police began defining a victim profile. They knew the killers preferred a certain age of victim. The two youngest, Cepeda and Johnson, had tried very hard to look older, and the oldest victim, Jane King, looked much younger than her twenty-eight years.

Almost all the victims had been found nude. The exceptions were the two women murdered on 10 and 17 November, who were grouped with the Hillside victims by the media. All the victims had been strangled, and all had been bound or handcuffed prior to death. The bodies were found on hillsides where they had been dumped.

Police investigators were convinced at least two people were involved in the crimes. They reached that conclusion because of the difficulty of placing the bodies where they were found. Also, in most cases, sexual intercourse had occurred prior to death and had involved two men, at least one of whom was a nonsecretor.

On 25 November, the *Los Angeles Herald Examiner*, a Hearst newspaper with an almost legendary reputation for yellow journalism, published a description of the man witnesses had seen in Lissa Kastin's car. He was described as Caucasian or Latin with an olive complexion and acne on his face. He was twenty-seven to twenty-eight years old, six feet two inches to six feet three inches tall, weighing approximately 150 to 160 pounds. He had a thick mustache and a small black mark high on the left cheek. Even with that rather specific description, the murderer was still not identified.

However, as a result, several dozen men who are commonly

referred to as police groupies were arrested. Those were mentally unstable individuals who believed they were policemen or who liked to pretend they were. Often those individuals had very real-looking uniforms and vehicles that looked like police cruisers.

By now, the Hillside Strangler Task Force had fifty-eight members. They were working around the clock in an effort to stop the series of brutal crimes. However, they did not have any solid leads.

On 30 November 1978, the Los Angeles area newspapers published the sites where victims had been found. A circle was drawn around the locations to isolate an area. Unknown to police, at the center of the circle was 703 East Colorado Street, the home of Angelo Buono.

Buono and Bianchi were delighted with the Thanksgiving coverage of their depredations. At work at the title company, the women often raised the subject of the Hillside killer. Ken Bianchi would wink and say, "You never know. He could be anyone. Why, I could be the Hillside Strangler." The comment was passed along to police but, as one of thousands of such tips, was ignored.

On Tuesday, 13 December, the cousins decided to try a new scam and gain another victim. They placed a call from a public library telephone booth contacting an outcall service to send a girl to 1950 Tamarind Avenue. That was the apartment building in which Ken Bianchi lived. A few days before, Ken had asked the manager to show him vacant apartment number 114 on the pretext of wanting to move into it. After viewing the apartment, he placed tape over the security lock as he left. It allowed him later to gain access to the apartment.

When "Donna" arrived from the outcall service around nine p.m., she was told she was under arrest. The woman's true name was Kimberly Diane Martin. She was seventeen years old and a tough, experienced hooker. Five feet eight inches tall and stockily built, she was usually more than capable of taking care of herself. As she was led out into the hallway, she wrenched free and yelled for help. The two men then shoved her back into the apartment, where she hit her head on the floor.

They finally got her into a late model Mustang automobile, which a woman had entrusted Ken Bianchi to sell for her. Unknown to Angelo, Ken kept Martin's gold ram's horn necklace to give to Kelli. After killing Martin, they dumped her body on a steeply inclined vacant lot.

When Kimberly was late reporting back to the outcall service, a call was made to Dr. Lois Lee. Dr. Lee was a sociologist and founder of CAT (California Association for Trollops), a legal services and counseling organization for prostitutes. Dr. Lee went to the Tamarind address and found Martin's car in the lot. She then placed a call to police who said she could not file a missing person's report so soon. The police officer taking the incoming call also commented she was just a prostitute anyway. The comment showed a clear lack of understanding of the potential victims in the Hillside case by some members of the police force. It also revealed the insensitivity common among police officers dealing with crimes against "street people."

Dr. Lee went directly to the Sheriff's Office herself and demanded action be taken to find Martin. It took over two hours for a task force investigator from the Hillside group to arrive. When the information on the delayed reaction time was revealed in the local media, public confidence in the police fell to a new low.

When her body was found, Kimberly Diane Martin had a fractured skull. The corpse revealed evidence of being bound, gagged, and strangled. She was spread eagled on her back within sight of the Los Angeles City Hall.

Police traced the outcall service and the 1950 Tamarind address of Donna's trick. They also obtained Ken Bianchi's fingerprints, among many others, from the library telephone booth. Everyone in the Tamarind building was questioned, including Ken Bianchi. Apparently, the police did not manage to put the two items together. Some residents of the building had heard screams but had ignored them as a man and woman joking around. The cousins realized they had been very lucky to escape apprehension for the Martin murder. Fearing their luck was running thin, they decided to take a break from murder.

A week later, just before Christmas, Ken Bianchi moved out of his apartment. He had been living there alone since Kelli left some weeks before. He recently had lost his job for missing work too often. His employer at the title company had finally checked out his spurious cancer story and found him a liar.

Ken moved in with friends. He continued his attempts to become a policeman and took another ride-along with the Los Angeles Police Department in December. He asked the officers with whom he rode to show him the Hillside Strangler body sites. The officers did not know the locations and thought the request was unusual, but probably wrote it off to a perverse fascination with violent crime.

More and more, Ken was irritating Angelo. Angelo felt Ken wasn't as smart as he acted and was a little bit crazy. Ken had gone back to running his movie talent scout scam. Angelo thought Ken was far too interested in the media coverage of the murders. Both cousins, on the other hand, got a kick out of the reward money being offered.

Shortly after the beginning of the new year, Angelo's mother finally died of vaginal cancer. Although he had referred to her in the most derogatory terms for years, Angelo sincerely mourned his mother's death.

Angelo had started a new project of building an Excalibur car from a kit. The cousins would use the car in a future crime.

Even for serial killers, the mundane requirements of daily life continue. After losing his job at the title company, Ken took a low-paying job at the Alma Lodge nursing home. Although Ken and Kelli were still living apart, Ken attended the natural childbirth classes with her, anticipating the mid-February delivery of their baby. At the same time, Ken also was having sex with high school girls, as he and Angelo had always done. Ken was regularly using marijuana and Rush, a butyl nitrate sexual stimulant. In early February, because of his financial difficulties, his Cadillac was repossessed.

On Thursday, 16 February 1978, the two cousins were again cruising the streets. They spotted a young blond girl standing at a bus stop in Burbank. When they tried to force her into their car, another woman appeared and rescued the girl by creating a noisy scene. The second woman was Jan Sims, a Glendale schoolteacher. After she calmed the girl down and put her on a bus, she went to the police and gave them detailed descriptions of the Excalibur car, Buono, and Bianchi. The officer in charge chose to ignore her story, and it was never followed up.

Later that same day, Cindy Hudspeth drove her new Datsun automobile into Angelo Buono's shop to have custom floor mats made. Since she was job hunting at the time, Angelo talked her into going next door to his house with the promise of showing her information on a job openings list. Once inside, she was attacked by the men, who tied her up, spread-eagled her on the bed, and then proceeded to rape and sodomize her for nearly two hours. Finally, Ken Bianchi strangled her to death.

Wearing surgical gloves to avoid leaving fingerprints, they placed her body in the trunk of the Datsun. Bianchi drove the car, and Buono followed him in the Mustang. They drove to Angeles Crest, where Ken had once gone on a double date. Then, they pushed the car over the side of the road.

Exactly one week later, Kelli gave birth to a son. The boy was named Sean Bianchi. Ken was a proud father, although disappointed he had not been able to witness the birth. Kelli had developed complications and, as a result, had to have a Caesarean section. The baby was born with jaundice and remained in the hospital for several weeks.

During the next week, Mrs. Sims saw the Excalibur car again on Colorado Street in Glendale. She called police, who again chose to ignore her. Mrs. Sims finally remembered she had met Ken Bianchi before when he approached her in the parking lot of his psychology office building. If the police had followed up on her story, they could have matched his fingerprints with those in the Martin case from the telephone booth and from apartment 114 on Tamarind Avenue.

The failure to follow up and other police errors occurred largely due to poor judgment on the part of low-level uniformed officers. The panicked public had produced thousands of false leads, and the size of the task force, now expanded to ninety-three officers, was still insufficient to follow up on all those leads. That many police officers could not communicate effectively with one another. Many lacked the extensive homicide experience necessary in a case of that type. The PATRIC computer had proven inadequate at cross referencing information.

The usual infighting among the various law enforcement agencies continued. Some senior police officers took matters into their own hands and met privately with each other to circumvent the traditional rivalry between the LAPD and the LA County Sheriff's Office. They met and shared information in an attempt to solve the terrible series of murders. Some private citizens and many police officials felt the extensive and sometimes ghoulish media coverage actually hindered solving the case. They believed the task force was largely a capitulation to media pressure, which resulted in public hysteria.

Cindy Hudspeth's new Datsun was found with her body inside the day after her disappearance. Once again, the five-point ligature marks on the corpse were considered to be similar to the other cases. The body had suffered some additional wounds during the slide down the hill, bouncing around in the trunk, and finally being hauled back up the slope.

Cindy's roommate had reported her missing on 17 February. Cindy was described as a sweet, hardworking girl who was somewhat naive. The twenty-year-old was cautious and conservative, but rather trusting. Between her apartment and the college, she had been abducted and was never seen alive again.

One witness in the Angeles Crest area remembered seeing a reddish-orange sedan going up the highway about nine p.m. The driver had a full beard. It was later learned Ken Bianchi had worn a false beard that night. The sedan was followed by a second car, which was later identified as the borrowed Mustang.

When Ken moved in February, it was his fifth move in twenty-five months in California. He and Kelli had constant arguments. She moved around often and frequently stayed with friends. Kelli brought the boy to visit Ken but refused to live with him again. She remembered vividly their last night together and the beating she had received.

He got a job cleaning, sterilizing, and delivering surgical instruments at the Verdugo Hills Hospital. While a step up from his job at the nursing home, it was still far below the standard to which he had become accustomed. Bianchi lied on his job application about his credentials, and he listed Angelo Buono as a job reference. He also bought a $400 car from a fellow employee.

In March 1978, Ken Bianchi was interviewed twice more by police officers. A Glendale officer asked if he owned a police badge, which Ken denied. The mother of one of Ken's girlfriends called the Los Angeles Police Department about Bianchi and the strange look in his eyes. She also said he talked about the Strangler all the time. Two LAPD officers interviewed him for ten minutes and decided not to follow up further. Ken was calm, mentioned his application with the LAPD Reserves, and seemed to be an all-around likable fellow. The officers never checked the application, which had Ken's fingerprints on it. If they had, the case might have been solved far more quickly.

Angelo Buono was increasingly upset about the fact the police had now talked to Bianchi three times. Angelo told Ken if he was not more careful, he would shoot him.

On 29 March, Angelo Buono married again. Tai-Fun Fanny Leung, age twenty-one, had been born in Taiwan. She married Angelo so she could stay in the United States legally. Angelo was forty-three years old.

In March 1978, Kelli moved back to Bellingham, Washington, with Sean, now three and a half weeks old. She said she wanted to be close to her parents. Ken felt he was once again being abandoned by those he loved. He had been rejected by his real mother, his adored adoptive father had rejected him by dying, and his first marriage had failed because he thought his wife was cheating on him. Now Kelli was the fourth major person to abandon him.

Angelo told Ken he should follow Kelli. The advice was not based on a desire to see the young lovers reunited. Rather, Angelo's increasing concern about Ken's instability, arrogance, and big mouth was placing Angelo in a position where soon he must decide how to silence his cousin once and for all. Bianchi at first resisted following Kelli. A month or so later, Angelo flatly told Ken to get out of Los Angeles or he would kill him.

Ken renewed his efforts to reunite with Kelli. He telephoned and wrote, begging her incessantly to return. She refused to come back to Los Angeles under any circumstances. Finally, Ken prevailed on her to let him move in with her in Bellingham. Ken Bianchi arrived on 21 May 1978, one day before his twenty-seventh birthday. It had been only eight months since the first Hillside murder.

Back in Los Angeles, the police arrived at a dead end. The clues leading to a solution in a murder case are usually found at the site of the murder itself. When a killer moves the body elsewhere after the crime, the chances of solving the crime using traditional law enforcement investigative techniques are dramatically minimized. In the Hillside case, they had ten body drop sites but no murder site. Virtually no hard clues were available and, despite the number of people who had confessed, no viable suspects. At that point in time, it was obvious that, if Bianchi had remained in Washington and Buono in California and neither had killed again, the Hillside case would still be unsolved.

Consider a few of the components the police were examining. From the semen tests and the body locations, police were convinced two people, probably two men, had committed the crimes. In spite of the newspaper coverage, the victims had virtually nothing in common beyond their gender. Contrary to general belief, they were not all prostitutes. In fact, only three—Yolanda Washington, Judy Miller, and Kimberly Martin—were members of the world's oldest profession. One victim was black, one Hispanic, and the rest Caucasians running the gamut from very fair skin to very dark skin. None of the victims seemed to have struggled when first picked up by the killers. Many people in Los Angeles feared the killers were police officers.

The body locations and the bodies themselves revealed little evidence. A fiber found on the eye of Judy Miller was polyester of uncertain origin. Fibers found adhering to the hands of Lauren Wagner were untraceable. Also found were some animal hairs, probably from a cat. Lauren Wagner's hands revealed electrical burns indicating torture. The puncture marks on Kristina Weckler gave the impression of drugging and torture.

The Los Angeles County Sheriff's Office had a homicide conviction rate of more than seventy percent. The Los Angeles Police Department rated nearly fifty percent. Those were two of the better success rates for major American police agencies. Still, there was no break in the case.

It must also be remembered that the metro Los Angeles area is one of the largest, both in geographical size and in population, in America. Each of the numerous adjacent municipalities has its own independent police force. Also, the circumstances of the crimes revealed the killers were using the extensive freeway systems to cover large distances in short periods of time.

A number of psychiatrists attempted analysis and identification of the Strangler. The factors they mentioned were that the killer was in his late twenties or early thirties, lived alone, possessed an average IQ, and was unemployed or existed on odd jobs. Probably, he had been in trouble with the law in the past. The killer was described as passive, cold, and manipulative. Probably the child of a broken home, his own childhood was tainted by cruelty and brutality most likely at the hands of women. He was felt to be a bedwetter with a history of cruelty to animals, arson, vandalism, and alienation from others. The sexual gratification of the crimes was seen as the strangling, rather than the rape. Speculation arose that the rapes were not committed until after the victims were already dead.

Dr. Louis J. West, chairman of the Psychiatric and Behavioral Department at UCLA and director of the Neuropsychiatric Institute, was one of those who examined the case. Dr. West felt the killer was an individual living on the fringes of society. He was a man no one would suspect. West raised an interesting question about the police suspicion of two killers. He pointed out homosexuals murder by teams, but the traditional serial murderer was almost always a solo operator. He indicated if the murders were indeed done by two people, then the relationship between those two people was extremely unusual.

Such a relationship is called a *folie a deux*. This is a rare psychiatric condition in which two persons, who are usually relatives, share common delusions and act out the same psychosis.

Looking back, this seems an accurate description of the Buono-Bianchi relationship. Each contributed a portion of themselves to the fused identity of the Hillside Strangler.

By now, the case had received worldwide attention. As always, various psychics offered their services, some for a fee and others for the publicity. The LAPD did not use paranormal techniques on the case. Also, a German private detective came to Los Angeles from Berlin at his own expense. He was convinced he could solve the case. He believed it was the work of two Italians, probably brothers, both aged around thirty-five. His information was politely accepted, then he was put on a plane back to Europe. His theories were discarded.

The summer and fall dragged on. No new names were added to the list of victims. Slowly, the tension began to ease, but Hillside Strangler stories continued to appear in the newspapers on a regular basis.

In Washington, Ken Bianchi found another job as a security guard in a variety and hardware store. It was his eleventh position in seven years. It allowed him to apprehend thieves while leaving an opportunity for Bianchi to steal whatever he pleased. He did not remain long at the job. His next position was as an operations supervisor for Coastal Security, a company specializing in electronic alarm systems. Part of his responsibilities was to make patrols of the homes and businesses of the company's subscribers.

Bianchi's application for membership in the county sheriff's reserves was accepted. At long last, he had the official acceptance he so desired. He seemed to be occupied with establishing himself as a respectable citizen in Bellingham. Unknown to his friends and employer, Bianchi was using his position to continue his tradition of petty theft. He regularly pilfered items from the customers of the security company. When Kelli queried as to their origins, he told her they were gifts.

Bianchi had lost all sexual interest in Kelli. His sexual activity seemed to be limited to frequent masturbation with a small, rabbit fur rug. Kelli found the rabbit fur and told Ken she felt it was time they had a frank discussion about their sexual and emotional problems. She also found a stack of porno movies that belonged to Ken. Now deeply regretting her decision to allow Ken to come to Bellingham, she asked him to leave.

Ken fantasized about the "fun" he and Angelo had shared. Ken believed he could prove himself to be a perfect partner for Angelo if he were to do something on his own. He began searching for an empty house in the area and contemplating further murders.

Twenty-two-year-old Karen Mandie typified the best of young Americans. She was deeply ingrained with the work ethic. Even though her family had offered to pay her way through college, she insisted on working and earning her own money. She worked as a clerk at Meyer's department store where Bianchi had been employed. A warm, friendly woman, Karen avoided a wild night life in favor of working in her vegetable garden and spending time with her boyfriend.

Mandie's roommate, Diane Wilder, was much like her but slightly older. At age twenty-seven, Wilder loved studying various cultures of the world. She was especially fascinated by the Middle East. A pragmatic young woman, Wilder had already prepared her will.

On 9 January 1979, Bianchi called Mandie, who was not home. Diane took a message, and Karen later returned his call. Ken offered her one hundred dollars to house sit a local home. The burglar alarm for the house was under repair and would not be functional between seven and nine p.m. on Thursday, 11 January. He suggested she bring Diane along and warned her not to discuss the job with anyone to lessen the risk of burglary.

On 10 November, Bianchi called the sheriff's reserve headquarters and said he could not attend the law enforcement training class on Thursday night. In the meantime, he had made several trips to the Catlow house in the wealthy section of Edgemoor to prepare.

Thursday evening, Ken met the girls promptly at seven and suggested Karen accompany him inside to check out the house. When she started down to the basement, he strangled her with quick, deadly force. Next, he pulled the same trick with Diane Wilder and immediately strangled her. He then masturbated and ejaculated over the clothed bodies of his dead victims.

Bianchi dragged the bodies back upstairs and out to Karen's Mercury Bobcat, a small hatchback. Driving to a nearby cul-de-sac, he left the bodies heaped together inside the car. He walked back to the house and drove the security company pickup home.

By eleven p.m., the Meyer's manager was worried when Karen had not returned to work at nine p.m. as scheduled. He called her close friend, Bill Bryant, a university police officer. Bill knew about the housesitting job with Coastal Security for Ken Bianchi. At midnight, Bryant drove past the Catlow's Bayside address and past Karen's apartment. He could not see any sign of the girls or Karen's car at either place. He then called the Bellingham Police Department.

Police feared foul play. They called the owner of Coastal Security, who knew nothing about the Catlow housesitting job and suggested they contact Ken Bianchi, his trusted employee. By two-thirty a.m. on Friday, police questioned Bianchi, who said he had skipped the reserves meeting and simply driven around for a couple of hours.

Bellingham is a close-knit community where people know each other's habits. Friday morning at the girls' apartment, police found the note that Ken Bianchi had telephoned and a note with the Bayside address of the Catlow house. At Coastal Security, the key for the Bayside address was missing. Bianchi was responsible for all the keys and the information cards kept on each home. Ken had checked out a Coastal Security truck for the previous night, which he had failed to mention to police. By nine-thirty a.m., Police Chief Terry Mangan felt two murders had occurred.

Bill Bryant remembered he had once given Karen Mandie's

phone number to Ken Bianchi at Ken's request. About eleven on Friday, some sixteen hours after the women were murdered, Bryant called Bianchi, who vehemently denied ever having contacted him or asking for Mandie's number.

Meanwhile, Chief Mangan called a locksmith and entered the Catlow house about one p.m. Friday. Two detectives carefully combed the house. Bellingham might be a small town, but its police officers were well trained and conducted a thorough crime scene investigation. They found a still-wet footprint in the kitchen, which was photographed, studied, and preserved. Two pubic hairs found on the basement staircase were saved. Police learned Bianchi had called the neighbor who was watching the house and had told her not to go there Thursday night because armed guards would be on duty while the faulty alarm system was being repaired.

Just before noon Friday, police had the news media give descriptions of the Bobcat car and the two missing women. Around four-thirty p.m., a woman called and said she had seen the Mercury Bobcat in a dead end on her way to work that morning. It was still parked when she checked after work.

When police arrived at the cul-de-sac, they found what they had feared—the bodies of Diane Wilder and Karen Mandie. Footprints in the muddy area around the car were cast as evidence. A loose pubic hair found on Diane was carefully preserved and would prove a key link to the murderer. Each body was wrapped in a clean sheet. An initial examination found each had been bound, strangled, and subjected to other violence. The angle of strangulation appeared to be from behind and slightly above, as if the killings had occurred while the women were walking down stairs.

Police thoroughly cleaned the car. After testing, the carpet fibers on the girls' shoes were found to match carpet fibers in the Catlow home. A detailed examination of the car found a dent in the gas tank. Careful testing proved the dent had come from a rock in the driveway of the Catlow house. It was shown the car had to have carried three people in order to lower the shocks enough to hit that particular rock.

One witness had been driving on Thursday and had been cut off the road by a Coastal Security truck. Two Coastal Security trucks on duty that night had been accounted for; the third was

Bianchi's.

The police decided to arrest Ken Bianchi on suspicion of murder. They cornered him at a Coastal Security guard shack near the Bellingham dock area. Kenneth Bianchi offered no resistance. He acted as if he were innocent, the matter was a misunderstanding, and everything would soon be cleared up. Police impounded his Coastal Security truck. Inside, they found the information card for the Catlow house, the house key, and a woman's scarf. Diane Wilder had been fond of wearing neck scarves and had owned many.

When informed of the situation, Kelli Boyd could not believe the charges. How could Ken, the gentle lover and adoring father, also be a brutal murderer? She said he had never shown any signs of violence. Apparently, her memory failed her about some of the instances in Los Angeles. At the police station shortly after Ken's arrest, she answered questions as truthfully as possible. She felt it was the best way to get the real guilty party and to secure Ken's release.

Kelli hired Dean Brett as Ken Bianchi's attorney. Brett did not really want the case and agreed only to take it for a few days. As an attorney in private practice, he knew full well the case would be costly since it would take a long time to try. Also, he would not be paid by the city, county, or state until after the matter had been fully addressed and resolved. Kelli had to go to a private attorney because, at that time, Bellingham had no public defender system.

Naive, loving Kelli Boyd was about to get her first taste of the true nature of Kenneth Bianchi. Worried about Kenneth's cancer and his missing his treatments, she contacted the police to ask them to check on his physical condition. Doctors examined him but found no trace of cancer. In the Los Angeles hospital where he was allegedly receiving treatments, Bianchi had wandered through the halls or sat in a waiting room reading. He had apparently managed to validate the cancer story to others by stealing legitimate hospital forms and filling them in himself.

With Ken and Kelli's permission, police searched their home. They found many stolen items and, as a result, added a charge of grand theft to the impending murder charges against Bianchi. The latter charges were in limbo awaiting lab reports on the evidence found at the murder site and at the body location. Police also found Ken's California address on his driver's license and did a background check. They found a turquoise ring, which was later determined to match Yolanda Washington's. Also found was a gold ram's horn necklace belonging to Kimberly Martin. Police were disgusted to find a briefcase containing two hard-core sex books, several heavily stained pairs of men's undershorts, and a large towel. Those items indicated Bianchi had been masturbating frequently.

Kelli willingly gave police the clothes that Ken had worn on Thursday night. Semen stains had been found on the victims' clothes and on Bianchi's underwear. Menstrual blood was found on the inside of Bianchi's underwear.

Diane Wilder was having her period when she was murdered. Ken Bianchi's business card had been found in Karen Mandie's apartment. Karen's telephone number was found at Bianchi's house. At the dock area where Ken was arrested, police discovered a concealed coat belonging to Diane Wilder. The noose around Kenneth Bianchi was tightening rapidly.

Ken, meanwhile, denied everything and said he felt everyone was dumping on him. He claimed he was an innocent man. People who knew Ken Bianchi could not believe him capable of such violence.

By an odd quirk of fate, Bellingham Police Chief Terry Mangan was a close friend of the principal of St. Ignatius School in Los Angeles. The man who maintained the books for the diocese was the father of Sonja Johnson, a Hillside victim. The principal had contacted Mangan for information and advice when the girls had disappeared months before. Thus, Chief Mangan had become involved initially in the Hillside Strangler case.

By two-thirty p.m. on Saturday, 13 January, Chief Mangan was wondering if, perhaps, Ken Bianchi might be connected to the Hillside Strangler case. Bianchi, after all, had arrived in Bellingham after the last Los Angeles murder occurred. By eight the next morning, Mangan telephoned the following agencies requesting information on Kenneth Bianchi: Rochester, New York, Police Department; Los Angeles Police Department; Glendale Police Department; and the Los Angeles County Sheriff's Office. A Los Angeles task force officer made the connection between Bianchi's addresses and the Hillside murders. The hunt was intensifying.

When the task force realized a connection between Ken Bianchi and the Hillside Strangler might exist, they immediately sent several investigators to interrogate Kelli Boyd. On Sunday, 14 January, Kelli was officially questioned by the LAPD and the Bellingham police. Kelli was incredulous at the thought of Ken being the Hillside Strangler. She recalled all the fearful conversations about the crimes. She identified a photograph of Ken's repossessed Cadillac and the Los Angeles County seal on it. She said he had a badge that looked a lot like a police badge. She also informed them Ken's only friend in Los Angeles was his cousin, Angelo Buono. She made it clear she did not like Angelo Buono one bit.

Los Angeles police immediately put a tail on Buono. They interviewed Sabra Hannan, Becky Spears, and Jan Sims. On Tuesday, 16 January, police talked with Angelo in his home. The session was simply a preliminary feel-out-Angelo visit to determine what sort of a suspect they had and how hard he might be to crack. Twelve days later, on 28 January, they interviewed him again, but they still did not realize his house was the site of the Hillside murders. It wasn't long before Angelo figured out he was being followed and went to the police to complain.

Back in Washington, Ken Bianchi was suddenly claiming a faulty memory. He faced the death penalty in Washington. Police decided to play one cousin against the other.

On Tuesday, 6 February, at about five p.m., Angelo Buono was again questioned. He was interviewed about the restaurants where he talked to and picked up waitresses, Sabra Hannan and Becky Spears, the Foxy Ladies outcall service, and his cousin Ken Bianchi's activities. Police pressed Buono and accused him of being the second Hillside Strangler. They let him know witnesses were available and they had complete information on how the victims were killed. Angelo continued to deny he was a killer or that he had been associated with Bianchi's crimes. At a little after six p.m., Los Angeles investigators began a taped interview with Angelo Buono. They talked primarily about Bianchi, his movements, and habits. When shown photographs of the victims, he said he had seen them before but only on television. He was questioned extensively for over two and a half hours. He contradicted himself repeatedly and made a determined attempt to portray his cousin as irrational and dangerous.

Others were also interviewed. Candy Buono, Angelo's ex-wife, was more than happy to provide details about how Angelo had mistreated her and the children. She told them about Buono being very familiar with Landa Street. That, the most obscure body site, had been mystifying to investigators because it was such an out-of-the-way place. Angelo's son, Peter, said he was afraid his father would kill him if he said anything. Candy said she was convinced Angelo would kill anyone who crossed him.

The case was becoming more complicated on both ends. Back in Washington, Attorney Brett decided to stay on as Bianchi's lawyer. Even the busiest lawyer is usually reluctant to pass by a case carrying national publicity.

Bianchi now claimed amnesia for the night of 11 January. Distressed to think he might be a double murderer, Ken told Brett he was thinking of suicide from remorse. In early February, Brett called in a psychiatric social worker, John Johnson, to counsel Bianchi through his depression. Johnson listened to Ken's stated disbelief at the charges, about Ken's love for his parents, his love for women, and so on. To Johnson, Ken Bianchi appeared mild, intelligent, and sensitive. Johnson, who was not a physician or a psychiatrist, concluded he was dealing with multiple personality disorder. He shared his impression with Brett and then mentioned it to Bianchi. Ken, no fool, pounced on the idea.

Bianchi had done extensive reading on psychology. Like his cousin, he was a fanatic TV watcher. Previously he had seen the film *Three Faces of Eve,* a study of a woman with a multiple personality disorder. It was widely felt the comments of John Johnson, plus the reading Ken had done, plus films he had seen about the subject, paved the way for Bianchi to attempt an insanity plea based on a contention of a multiple personality disorder. However, some authorities believed Bianchi, indeed, suffered from the ailment.

Dean Brett, preparing for his case, accepted an offer by Dr. Donald T. Lunde, a forensic psychiatrist, professor at Stanford University, and author of *Murder and Madness,* to examine Ken Bianchi. Lunde's opinions were especially valued because of his bestselling books on murder, insanity, and the insanity defense. Lunde's initial examination of Ken was off the record and probably done as much to satisfy the doctor's curiosity as anything. He would be called in officially at a later date.

On 9 March, Bianchi, relaxing in his jail cell, watched the

movie *Sybil* on television. He carefully examined the psychiatric aspects of the film about an individual with a multiple personality disorder. When Lunde arrived on 11 March to examine Ken, he offered him two choices: the first was sodium amytal, a tranquilizer often used to reduce anxiety, or voluntary hypnosis. The hypnosis was supposedly to allow an exploration of Ken's faulty memory. Kenneth Bianchi might be a murderer, but he wasn't a fool; he knew he could fake his answers under hypnosis because he could fake being hypnotized. On the other hand, once the chemicals were in his bloodstream, he had no way to adequately control his responses. Ken chose hypnosis.

At that point in the Hillside case, like most serial murder cases, the psychiatric issues began surfacing. A decision was made to bring in six psychiatric experts. Of the six, two were retained by the defense, two by the prosecution, and two functioned as amicus curiae—friends of the court.

Dean Brett retained Dr. John Watkins, a psychiatrist with over thirty years' experience and a professor of psychiatry at the University of Montana. Watkins interviewed Bianchi in the presence of John Johnson, Dean Brett, and two Los Angeles detectives in mid-March. Video- and audiotapes were made of all sessions with Bianchi. Under hypnosis, "Steve," Bianchi's alleged alter-ego, spoke out. Steve hated Ken and Ken's mother. He related how Ken had walked in on Angelo killing a girl. He, Steve, made Ken kill several women because he thought they were his mother. It was apparent that at some point in time Ken Bianchi had studied Sigmund Freud. Bianchi made errors when Steve said Ken hated women, when earlier he had said Ken didn't hate anyone and was a nice guy. The Los Angeles detectives, observing intently, noticed the slip-ups and were convinced they were watching an elaborate charade.

A week later, Dr. Ron Markman, a Los Angeles psychiatrist who was also an attorney, examined Bianchi. No hypnosis was used. Bianchi spoke at length of his early life and of his time and memory lapses.

It should be noted here that one of the few psychiatric overview studies of mass murderers found certain common behaviors in their childhoods. As a group, they were bedwetters, fire starters, and animal torturers. Those traits can be extrapolated to serial killers, also.

Bianchi admitted being a bedwetter and killing a cat, but only one. He adamantly denied starting fires. He admitted to being a chronic liar but asserted he had it under control now.

Earlier in March, Kenneth Bianchi had entered a plea of not guilty by reason of insanity to the Bellingham double homicide. Markman suggested that possibly Bianchi was suffering from a temporal lobe seizure disorder. This is an organically based multiple personality disorder. Markman's conclusions were listed in an affidavit filed with the court. Later, an electroencephalogram, a series of skull x-rays, an echogram, and a spinal fluid tap all failed to reveal any basis for Markman's conclusion.

In the interviews, Bianchi continued to present the personality of the vulgar, foul-mouthed, abusive Steve. Investigators noted how Steve's personality strongly resembled that of Angelo Buono. He described the murders and gleefully told in great detail how he and Buono had alternated killing the victims. Initially, it had been Ken's plan to hold his silence and, with Buono's help, work up alibis for the Los Angeles killings. But now Bianchi had implicated his cousin once and for all. Buono somehow managed to make a phone call to Ken Bianchi and let him know that, if he testified, Kelli Boyd and Sean would be killed. Despite his denials, law enforcement officials knew Buono had been in touch with Ken subsequent to his moving to Bellingham.

Ken Bianchi was beginning to realize the only way to avoid the Washington death penalty was the insanity plea and implicating his cousin. About now, Angelo Buono must have begun bitterly regretting the fact he did not carry out his threat to kill Ken the previous year.

Meanwhile, Bianchi began attempts to get his mother and a girlfriend in Bellingham, Angie Kinneberg, to provide him with a backup alibi in case the multiple personality ploy failed. He kept a diary in which he wrote down various feelings, thoughts, and dreams. He knew full well the diary would be periodically examined by the psychiatrists.

The next psychiatrist to appear on the scene was Dr. Ralph Allison. The Santa Cruz-based doctor was considered an expert in the field of multiple personalities. He saw Ken beginning in mid-April 1979. Allison's techniques included age regression and hypnosis. In an early session, Ken, allegedly under hypnosis, told Allison he had just met Steve, who didn't like Mother Bianchi.

Steve was a smart aleck and a jokester. He spoke of Ken's parents always fighting and his mother hitting him. By the time Ken's father died, Steve had turned sour. He liked to abuse girls and had even knocked one down. After Ken's father died, Steve recalled his mother hitting him and ordering him around. At one point in the session, Steve became violent but was calmed by Dr. Allison.

Steve told Allison that he had killed the Bellingham girls in order to show Ken what it was all about. Steve liked Angelo very much. He said Angelo had killed five girls in Los Angeles. Steve admitted killing four others. Steve did the first killing, then they alternated. During the interview, Steve smoked incessantly but tore the filters off the cigarettes and smoked them unfiltered. When the session ended, Ken seemed surprised to find the torn cigarettes and informed the psychiatrist that he only smoked filtered ones.

By the end of the next day, Bianchi had told Dr. Allison that Steve's last name was Walker. Allison left convinced Bianchi had a multiple personality disorder.

The Los Angeles detectives sitting in on the interviews thought Walker might, in fact, be a real name. Checking Bianchi's background, they found a Steve Walker had applied in Bianchi's office during the time he was running his therapist's scam. Police also learned Bianchi had studied textbooks dealing with multiple personalities. However, the psychiatrists believed the use of a real person's name (Steve Walker) was not unusual.

Dr. Allison, trying to help Bianchi, taught him how to talk with Steve. However, it was later found his methodology had provided Bianchi with information on the subject, had altered his mental state, and interfered with future diagnoses. The police officers involved with the case were outraged. They felt Allison had given Bianchi a quick, comprehensive course in how to fake a multiple personality.

On 20 April, Dr. Watkins administered the Rorschach ink blot dissociative test to Ken Bianchi. Both Steve and Ken were tested under hypnosis, and each reacted in a different manner. Ken knew the test quite well from his previous studies, but he pretended he was unfamiliar with it. Steve saw gross, crude images in the ink blots. Ken saw pleasant, natural scenes. To Watkins, it seemed as if his diagnosis of multiple personalities was being substantiated. Those test results were later confirmed by an independent professor of psychology at the University of Chicago, who did not know whose tests they were.

In early May, Dr. Watkins gave an interview to *Time* magazine in which he referred to Ken Bianchi as a "very pure psychopath." Certainly, some aspects of a psychopathic personality were present: Bianchi's apparent inability to feel guilt and his inability to relate to human beings as anything other than objects for his gratification.

Bianchi seemed very pleased with the way things were going in his drawn-out legal situation. However, he continued to write in his diary about the dreams and realizations he was allegedly having. He also proposed marriage and a book deal to Kelli Boyd and marriage to Angie Kinneberg, his Bellingham friend.

At that point, the next move was with the prosecution. They brought in Dr. Martin T. Orne, head of the Unit for Experimental Psychiatry at the University of Pennsylvania Hospitals in Philadelphia. Orne was also a professor at the University of Pennsylvania. He was then considered the world authority on hypnosis. He testified on matters involving hypnosis at the trial of Patty Hearst, the erstwhile rich-girl terrorist of the mid-1970s.

Dr. Orne had four procedures he felt could help determine if a person was actually being hypnotized. Without informing Bianchi, Orne applied those procedures to him. Bianchi's responses to three of the four tests indicated he was faking. The fourth was inconclusive.

Orne set Ken up. He told Ken that he was puzzled by the fact Ken only had two personalities when multiple personality people usually have several. The next time Ken was hypnotized, he produced "Billy" in two forms as a thirteen-year-old boy and a frightened nine-year-old boy. During the session, Steve said he had killed one cat, one dog, and a lot of rats. The details were markedly different from what Steve had told Dr. Markman previously. Dr. Orne did not believe Bianchi suffered from a multiple personality disorder, nor did he believe Bianchi had, in fact, been under the influence of hypnosis.

The new character, Billy, had two origins. The first was at the age of thirteen when he took Ken's place at his father's funeral. Ken couldn't handle the idea of his father's death. The other origin was around age nine when Billy appeared as a liar since Ken was far too sweet to lie. Billy knew of Steve but considered him a bad egg and didn't want anything to do with him. According to Billy, Steve had sexual problems and could only become aroused with a woman when he knew he was going to kill her, when he killed her first, or in situations when he was able to tie her down before having intercourse with her. Billy was quite willing to discuss Steve's killing and mistreatment of women. Billy didn't bother with girls; he was not interested. Billy's basic idea of life was to be left alone and to have fun. He did, however, like to steal.

Ken sensed Dr. Orne was less gullible than his predecessors and was not buying the multiple personality story. Bianchi responded by trying to set up his diary to make it look like Dr. Watkins and Dr. Allison were to blame for the multiple personality scam. From childhood, Ken had always tried to blame someone else for what he had done.

The next new member of the squadron of psychiatrists was Dr. Charles Moffett. He was specifically hired to advise the judge in the case. Moffett had his first interview with Bianchi in late April. His report to the judge emphasized Ken's history as an abused child and the circumstances of the Bellingham murders. Ken continued to deny any knowledge of the Bellingham crimes. He maintained he was aroused only by mutually agreeable and amorous sex.

Steve now related another version of the Bellingham murders. Steve took the girls inside the Catlow home and showed them around. Downstairs, he suddenly pulled a gun on them, made them lie on the floor, and tied them up. He took Karen into the bedroom on the bed, searched her, and took a can of Mace from her pocket. He left Diane lying in the bathroom on the floor. Both girls were then untied one at a time and told to remove their clothing. When they were naked, he re-tied them. Next, both young women were raped. He said he used condoms. Both girls were untied and told to redress themselves. Steve then tied them up a third time and strangled them, first Diane and then Karen. Steve carried each body upstairs and put the corpse in the trunk of the car.

Steve then drove the security company truck to a nearby school and walked back to the Catlow house. He drove the Bobcat to the cul-de-sac, where it was eventually found. Walking back to the truck, the personality of Steve receded and Ken Bianchi's personality returned. Ken said he could not figure out why he was even in that area. It should be noted the account of the murders differed significantly on many points from the earlier account.

Dr. Moffett began seriously questioning the theory of multiple personality disorder, in part because Steve and Ken seemed such superficial characters of good and evil rather than real people. Most of the developed personalities in a multiple personality case are, in fact, as ambivalent about various moral values as if they were, indeed, separate and distinct individuals.

However, Dr. Moffett began to believe Ken might be a delusional psychotic, possibly schizophrenic, of an undifferentiated variety. Moffett felt Bianchi should be considered insane under the law. He indicated that, although Bianchi intellectually knew the difference between right and wrong, the combination of his grandiose ego, dissociation, and lack of awareness of the violent aspects of his own being would not permit him to effectively control and govern his own actions. In that way, the man could be considered a killer and insane.

Back in Los Angeles, the investigation of the case continued. Markust Camden, the witness in the Judith Miller disappearance, identified a picture of Angelo Buono and said he would testify in court that Buono was involved in the abduction. However, Camden had been voluntarily admitted to the Richmond State Hospital in Richmond, Indiana. This is a mental health facility and, therefore, Camden's reliability and impeachability on the witness stand were now open questions.

Beulah Stofer, the next-door neighbor and witness in Lauren's abduction, had finally agreed to cooperate with the police. She immediately picked out photographs of Angelo Buono and Kenneth Bianchi from a pile of mug shots.

Meanwhile, law enforcement officials began to scrutinize Angelo Buono. They found teenage girls were often at his home. Also, he enjoyed the more exotic denizens of the Hollywood street scene. However, police still had no concrete evidence to link him to the Hillside murders.

On 21 April 1979, police investigators obtained a search warrant and thoroughly searched the house at 703 East Colorado. They did not find any fingerprints, not even those of Angelo Buono.

They decided they simply did not have enough evidence to

arrest Buono at that time. However, they felt he might be a cyclic killer and they had a strong obligation to the public to warn them about Angelo Buono. Knowing it was distasteful and running the risk of a lawsuit from Buono, authorities leaked his name to the local media as a major suspect in the Hillside Strangler murders. They felt it would be worthwhile if even one life was saved.

As a result of the untoward publicity, Buono's life began to crumble. His new wife, Tai-Fun, left him and moved in with her parents after his allegedly murderous activities became public information. He also began to receive anonymous threatening letters in the mail. Buono, not to be outdone, turned those letters over to police and demanded protection.

In Bellingham, Dr. Saul Faerstein of Beverly Hills was appointed as an advisor to the judge on 1 June. Faerstein did not believe in multiple personalities and was convinced Ken Bianchi was competent to stand trial. He explored Ken's childhood and adolescence thoroughly and delved into the Bellingham crimes. Bianchi said he had lost his virginity when he was sixteen years old to a high school tramp in Rochester. He remembered her as a skinny girl with large breasts who was known to be very promiscuous. He recalled it as a pleasurable experience and even remembered he had used a condom. He related to Faerstein that most of his sex education came from the street, and he considered himself rather conservative. Bianchi also admitted he frequently looked at girly magazines and pornographic material, becoming aroused as a result.

Bianchi further related how his alter ego, Steve, had used a white cord, which was used in hospital traction cases, to carry out the Bellingham murders. He said he had taken Ace bandages, rope, and condoms with him in his truck to the scene of the crime. After the two women had been raped, the condoms were dropped in the toilet and flushed away. Both girls were face down when he strangled them.

Ken recalled Steve gathered all their books, the murder materials, and other items and placed them in a trash bag. He also recalled he straightened up the bed and the house and searched thoroughly for any evidence at the scene. Diane's scarf and coat were placed behind the truck seat. On Friday after the murders, he hid the coat and scarf behind the guard shack at the terminal, where they were later found and where he was arrested.

Faerstein's comments are quite interesting.

[Bianchi] manifests symptoms and behavior consistent with several categories of mental disorders. Ken Bianchi is diagnosed as having a Personality Disorder with features of sociopathy, explosiveness, and narcissism. He also can be characterized as having a Sexual Deviation Disorder with features of sexual sadism and violence.

Faerstein's inquiries again revealed Bianchi's fascination with police and law enforcement. As a boy, Ken had often drawn pictures of police officers during his psychological tests. His dream was to be a policeman. He had applied for law enforcement positions in New York, California, and Washington, but was always rejected. Dr. Faerstein wrote:

All these rejections by law enforcement agencies made him bitter. In the long string of murders he committed, he demonstrated he had mastered the science of law enforcement, and that he was a better policeman than any policeman on the force. He left no clues. He went undetected for over a year. So in the process of achieving his victory over the female authority figure [his mother] by killing her surrogates, he also vanquished the male authority figure by eluding the police, sheriffs and detectives.

By late June, Ken Bianchi had been talking to psychiatrists and psychologists for three and a half months. Dr. Allison continued interviews with him to learn about Billy and also would uncover a fifth personality called "Friend."

In July, Dr. Donald Lunde was concentrating on the California murders. It was planned that Bianchi would be extradited to that state after his trial in the Bellingham cases.

To Ken Bianchi, the fact he had a normal subjective memory about every part of his life and an objective memory only about the murders made him feel as if he were in some way less responsible. He certainly did not feel emotionally involved. Some psychiatric theory indicated that perhaps his troubled mind could only handle the difference between his moral code and his actions by such an internal trick.

Dr. Lunde had Ken describe the layout of Angelo's house to check for credibility. He felt that Ken

is suffering from a Dissociative Reaction, extremely severe, bordering on psychosis... Whether or not Bianchi represents a true case of multiple personality is debatable, in my opinion, but certainly the psychological dynamics of his very disturbed personality structure are similar to those which have been described with respect to multiple personality, which is simply a sub-type of Dissociative Reaction.

After the doctors had finished their interviews with him, Ken Bianchi suddenly stopped writing in his diary. After all, now only he was interested in reading it.

The summer drew to a close, and the Northwestern autumn closed in. On 19 October, a sanity hearing was held in the Bianchi case at the Whatcom County Courthouse in Bellingham. Both audio- and videotape recordings were made, although direct broadcasting of the hearing was not permitted. Ken Bianchi appeared in court well dressed, but underneath his three-piece suit was a bulletproof vest. The prevalent feeling was that the citizens of the community might, indeed, take matters into their own hands in dealing with the murderer.

Bianchi's attorney entered a plea of not guilty by reason of insanity on his behalf. Drs. Watkins and Allison indicated at the hearing that Bianchi had multiple personalities and, in their professional opinions, was not competent to stand trial. The other physicians, however, felt he was nothing more than a psychopathic killer who could take life without remorse. The split in the ranks of the psychiatric resource raised other issues. The most important of which was the question of exactly what role psychiatric testimony would play during the trial. As in several other cases that we have discussed, the act of murder when repeated over and over becomes more of a psychiatric issue than a justice issue.

Drs. Faerstein and Orne indicated Bianchi, in their opinions, should stand trial and was competent. Dr. Orne's systematic dissection of Bianchi's hypnosis act proved to be decisive. The judge declared Kenneth Bianchi competent to stand trial. One of the facts that helped to guide the judge's decision was the finding by the detectives that Steve Walker, Ken's alleged alternate personality, was, in fact, a real person.

Attorney Brett had analyzed the evidence and felt no question of Ken Bianchi's guilt remained. The pubic hairs, the carpet fibers, and numerous other physical evidence constituted overwhelming proof against him. Ken Bianchi had difficulty accepting his guilt and his lawyer's opinion. He wept frequently during the hearing.

Meanwhile, the Los Angeles County district attorney's office was offering Ken a deal, which had been arranged by Dean Brett. If Ken were to plead guilty to the Washington murders and to some of the Hillside killings, he would get life with the possibility of parole and could serve his time in California. The California prisons were allegedly more humane than those in Washington State. He would spend up to thirty-five years incarcerated in California, then be transferred to Washington State to serve the life terms there.

In return for the deal, Ken Bianchi was to agree to testify truthfully and completely against his cousin, Angelo Buono. He would openly name Angelo as his accomplice, at which time a warrant could finally be issued for the arrest of Angelo Buono. The Los Angeles police were ready to move in on Angelo the moment they received word of Ken's decision and his naming of his cousin in open court.

Dropping his multiple personality attempt, Kenneth Bianchi accepted the arrangement. He named Angelo Buono as his accomplice in open court. In return, he was sentenced to two consecutive life sentences for the Bellingham murders. In California, he would have to plead guilty to five murders: the first, fourth, seventh, ninth, and tenth of the Hillside killings. At long last, the murders of Yolanda Washington, Jane King, Kristina Weckler, Kimberly Martin, and Cindy Hudspeth would be solved and the cases closed.

Buono's arrest came literally within minutes of his being implicated by Ken Bianchi. He was forty-five years old. Buono, of course, claimed he was innocent, but when the police went to arrest him, they took along the media.

Among the evidence collected at the time of arrest was Angelo Buono's wallet. Contained in the wallet were numerous photographs of young women. Impressed in the leather was the perfect outline of a badge. The impression was a serious clue about the police ruse, and the officers were somewhat surprised the usually careful Buono left it.

A psychologist friend of one of the arresting detectives predicted Bianchi would probably tell the truth at that point but would not do it again. In the weeks to come, it was predicted, he would start lying again and would probably contradict his original statement several times.

All the principal investigators on the case gathered in the courthouse in Bellingham, Washington, to interview Ken Bianchi and to test his usefulness as a cooperative witness. Under California law, the accused in a criminal case cannot be convicted solely on the basis of an accomplice's testimony.

This is a part of what is commonly known as the "admissions contrary to interest" rule of criminal procedure. However, if the accomplice's testimony is corroborated by any other evidence—be that evidence direct, physical, or circumstantial—then the accomplice's statement can be used to convict his partner or partners.

Ken Bianchi began his narration of death. He first spoke of the Yolanda Washington case, the first of the duo's crimes. He told the investigators Yolanda's body had been covered by a big log. However, no log was found on or near her corpse. Ken denied the turquoise ring, which had been found in his Bellingham home and confiscated as evidence, was the property of Yolanda Washington.

He went on to tell the truth about Judy Miller's murder. He recalled the foam over her eyes came from Buono's car seat business. That was an important clue and began the process of linking Buono to her death. When speaking of the death details themselves, he showed no sign of emotion and spoke with great calm. He said the body dump site was selected because Angelo knew the area from having a girlfriend nearby.

Bianchi spoke briefly of the incident involving Peter Lorre's daughter. He said the young woman had been allowed to live only because of the notoriety of her father. The police were surprised she had almost become a victim and certainly intended to verify the story.

Ken then began lying. He spoke of luring Kristina Weckler out of her apartment with the offer of going to a party. Once she was in the car, each man grabbed an arm. He also said Kristina wasn't handcuffed until they got to Buono's house. He did, however, tell the truth about using a needle filled with Windex™ and then killing her with gas.

The gruesome details began to accumulate. Police officers, as is often the case in such crimes, were forced to listen to an almost endless litany of death and violence. Bianchi then recounted Lauren Wagner's abduction and death.

By now, it was becoming obvious a modus operandi was emerging. The Miller and Washington abductions were the only two where Bianchi was not in the car at the time of the pickup. The several variations of the police ruse became obvious. It was also clear Buono and Bianchi took turns pretending to be the police officer. All of the victims seemed to have taken it for granted that the other man in the car must also be a police officer because the women were convinced the one who accosted them was. The times of death were invariably between eleven p.m. and two a.m.

The victims had all been on foot and usually alone when approached by the killers. All of them, except Lauren Wagner, willingly got into the car. Many victims were told they were being arrested for something that made the handcuffs an acceptable accessory. Washington, Miller, and Martin were being arrested for prostitution. Kastin was being taken in for questioning in a burglary, and Johnson and Cepeda for being out late. The other cases were all similar. King was offered a ride home by a reserve policeman, and Weckler was told by a reserve officer that her car had been hit. Cindy Hudspeth had been lured into the house by a job offer.

Once the victims were in Buono's house, the killings took place in the spare bedroom on the floor. Kenneth Bianchi had three main reasons for committing the murders: to obtain sexual arousal, to be aroused by knowing the end product of intercourse would be death, and to eliminate witnesses to his deviance. He was uncertain in his mind whether the sex or the killing itself was the primary motivator, or a variation of both. If he is consistent with most rapists/murderers, the violence is the primary motivator and the sex merely the vehicle.

The police officers believed that, prior to Kenneth Bianchi's coming to California, Angelo Buono had never committed murder. It was not hard to believe Angelo was the one who organized and planned the crimes and Ken was the follower and errand boy. Ken insisted Angelo was the one who had figured out how to pick up the girls, how and where to kill them, and how to dispose of the corpses. Ken appeared in his recitation to be a nowhere man, a sort of human chameleon, who could, on command, become whatever someone else wanted him to be. Ken did admit, however, that he chose the dump site for the body of Cindy Hudspeth.

The investigators believed, on the whole, Ken told the truth in the session. It was almost as if he had to purge himself one time before lapsing back into his basic personality. Police were describing Ken Bianchi at that point as "a superb con man" and a manipulator.

Twenty-four hours later, Ken Bianchi was back in Los Angeles. The LA County Sheriff's Office chartered a Lear jet for the trip from Washington. The Los Angeles County Attorney had compiled a twenty-five-count indictment against Buono and Bianchi. On Monday, 22 October 1979, Ken Bianchi was officially sentenced for the California murders. He received a total of six life sentences, five of those for killings and the sixth for conspiracy to commit murder. An additional five years was added for having sodomized a victim. Under California law, even with the accumulation of six life sentences and five years, parole was theoretically possible. California has the most liberal parole statutes in the United States.

Angelo Buono, meanwhile, was housed in the special security section of the Los Angeles county jail. Ironically, his son, Peter, was in the cell next to his awaiting trial for grand theft. When Kenneth Bianchi arrived, however, they placed him in an entirely separate part of the jail, and the two men had no contact. Angelo was contemptuous of Ken and described him as a "lazy bullshitter."

Another prisoner asked Angelo why he had killed all those young women, and he allegedly replied, "They were no good. They deserved to die. It had to be done. But I only killed a couple of them. I ain't worried. My cousin's gonna go into his little nut bag." The inmate hoping to gain an advantage for himself, reported the comment to the jail authorities at the first opportunity.

The Washington state law enforcement authorities had treated Bianchi with a soft approach because of their suspicion he was

mentally ill. The officials in Los Angeles took an entirely different tack with Ken. Questioning and requestioning, endless rec-
itations of the crimes, and an unremitting search for details were
the rules of the day.

Finally, Bianchi began to fold in upon himself as it became
obvious he could not face the reality that he might, indeed, be a
multiple murderer. On 11 December, Kenneth Bianchi developed
a second man theory in the Bellingham murders. In a letter, he
wrote about walking in while another man was hanging the girls,
but the autopsy and other evidence proved the idea false.

Ken was in frequent contact with his mother. She and her
husband moved to California from Rochester to be closer to him.
Mrs. Bianchi did, indeed, love Ken. However, she was horrified
by the crimes with which he had been involved and perpetrated. She finally began to accept the very real possibility that Ken
was guilty. She was most hurt by accusations of her being a child
abuser. To be fair to her, the De Paul reports could have misunderstood her point of view. Was she irrational in her desires, or
merely conducting herself in a manner that women in her cultural and ethnic group would traditionally seek for church, children,
and a home in a better neighborhood?

If Kenneth Bianchi was emotionally damaged by the age of
three months when he was adopted, then any normal punishment would have appeared to him as rejection. He could, indeed,
have been frightened almost into irrationality by the terror of
normal childhood discipline. He could have perceived those incidents as child abuse.

Kelli Boyd had become fearful of making commitments to
other men. How could she be sure of her judgment when she
was so totally fooled by the vicious, murderous Kenneth Bianchi? How could she ever teach Sean about the human side of Ken
without telling him about the dark side and without Sean hat-
ing his father? Kelli came to hate Ken for what he did to her, for
his crimes, and for his refusal either to admit his guilt or to seek
psychiatric care while he was in prison. She decided she would
never allow Ken Bianchi to see Sean again.

Ken undoubtedly saw that as simply one more in his lifelong
chain of rejections. Also, he denied the murders because he felt
Sean would grow up to loathe him as a killer. Ken appeared to
love Sean deeply. Kelli Boyd had begun dating again, and the fact

she was seeing other men hurt Ken even more.

Bianchi continued his claims of innocence and refuted his previous confessions. Five of the Los Angeles murder charges against him had now been dismissed. He no longer had to fear the death penalty, since he had already been sentenced to the other five Los Angeles crimes.

Ken must have felt terribly guilty for testifying against his sometime father-figure, Angelo Buono. Ken was concerned he would be known as a "K-9," or snitch, in prison. That can sometimes be a death sentence. He hoped by making inconsistent statements, feigning loss of memory, and generally acting bizarre, he might be declared insane, placed under psychiatric care, and eventually be released. It would relieve the pressure on him in the Buono case if his testimony were seen as tainted.

Meanwhile, the lawyers in the Buono matter continued to jockey for position. Pretrial hearings, trial delays, and several firings of his lawyers took place. Because of Ken's conflicting accounts, no one could be certain what Bianchi, who was the main case against Buono, would finally say when he arrived on the witness stand.

An erstwhile playwright, Veronica Lynn Compton, contacted Ken in early June 1980. She wanted his help with characterizations for her fictional play about a female mass murderer. The twenty-three-year-old woman was a dark, Latin siren with emotional problems. After several letters of entreaty, she gained his consent.

They carried on long, erotic conversations during Ken's unmonitored telephone calls and extended visiting hours. Discovering they both loved necrophilia and real-life murders, Ken played her along with amorous poetry. However, Ken had other plans for her. With Compton in the picture, Ken no longer needed Kelli Boyd, and he ceased contacting her.

Ken told Veronica how proud he was of killing those women. He described it as being "like a kid going down the street, and you see all these candy stores, and you can pick any candy that you want, and you don't have to pay for it, and you just take it. You just do what you want. It's the greatest."

Soon, Veronica began to fantasize about living with Ken and murdering people by the dozen. That had been the purpose of Ken's long, involved seduction of her. He suggested she use the theme she had developed in her play as a way to save him. She should go to Bellingham and murder a third girl. If she did so using the same modus operandi, including leaving semen on the body, it would show the Washington authorities had the wrong man. Veronica, believing herself in love with Ken, agreed immediately. Ken managed to provide a sample of his semen by masturbating into the tip of a rubber glove and smuggling it out to her.

Going to Bellingham, Veronica had trouble finding a suitable victim. She checked into a hotel and bolstered her courage with liberal doses of wine and cocaine. She came up with a disguise, including a pillow to make her look pregnant and a blond wig. Scouting for victims in a local bar, Veronica managed to lure a woman back to her hotel room. She went into the bathroom, returned with a length of cord, and looped the cord around the woman's neck. Fighting for her life, the woman flipped Veronica off and fled. Veronica panicked, called a taxi, went to the airport, and flew back to Los Angeles.

Several days later, the woman, recovering from the attack, finally went to the police with her story. Veronica was arrested in Los Angeles a few days later. Bianchi lost interest in Veronica immediately after her arrest. Veronica later fell in love with another killer with whom she also corresponded.

A few months afterward in Bellingham, Veronica Compton was tried, convicted, and received a life sentence for attempted murder. The press referred to her as the "Copycat Strangler." Her incarceration brought to an end one of the strangest sidelights to one of the strangest murder cases in the annals of crime.

Back in Los Angeles, Ken Bianchi continued to protest his innocence. He ignored the detailed and accurate confessions given by him that included facts only the killers would have known.

On the legal front, preliminary hearings alone lasted nearly a year. A main focus was the fact the only hard evidence against Angelo Buono were the fibers taken from the eyes of Judy Miller. Expert chemists found no significant difference between the Miller fibers and fibers taken from Angelo's shop.

Buono was bound over for trial on ten counts of first-degree murder. Bail was denied. In an attempt to affect the jury, Buono had requested a female counsel and received Katherine Mader as one of his two attorneys. A bright, respected graduate of the

University of California at Davis, Mader was known as a tireless researcher and investigator.

Another interesting trial aspect was the judge allowing photographs inside the courtroom. For some years, California had permitted both film and still photographic coverage of criminal trials. Although that practice has now become common, it was then a rarity in American jurisprudence.

In June 1981, two legal moves occurred that would have a major impact on the trial. First, the nonmurder charges were separated from the ten murder counts. Although they could have been tried together, it was felt trying nonmurder offenses at the same time as capital crimes might prejudice the jury. The nonmurder counts included charges of pimping, pandering, sodomy, conspiracy to commit extortion, oral copulation, rape, and false imprisonment.

The second issue addressed was the question of hypnotically induced or enhanced testimony. As hypnosis left the arena of sideshows and entertainment and become an aspect of the psychiatric profession, it found its way more frequently into American criminal courts. The controversy, briefly stated, is this: How does the defense know whether testimony given under hypnosis is testimony enhanced or invented? Hypnotically implanted testimony might very well pass a polygraph exam because witnesses truly believe that is what they saw.

In a convoluted but fair-minded decision, Superior Court Judge Ronald M. George denied the prosecution request that several witnesses who had been hypnotized be allowed to testify. However, he also concluded, after exhaustive reviews and pretrial testimony with the six psychiatrists, that Ken Bianchi could be compelled to testify because he had faked being hypnotized.

One of the amusing aspects of the psychiatric testimony was made by Dr. Allison, who now had modified his opinion of Ken Bianchi. Allison had gone to work as a prison psychiatrist and, because of that experience, had concluded that criminals often do lie. Given that amazing revelation, one only wonders in what nirvana Dr. Allison had previously lived.

Angelo Buono's defense team was very pleased that Ken Bianchi would be compelled to testify. They felt it would be easy to impeach him as a witness because of his repeated lies. Ironically, the prosecution was also pleased; they needed Ken's testimony to convict Angelo.

On 6 July 1981 in open court, Kenneth Bianchi continued to recant his previous statements and denied having killed anyone in Los Angeles. He said he probably faked the multiple personalities, he was not sure he committed the murders with Angelo, and he probably lied when he confessed. His earlier statement that he had his lying under control seems to have been a lie. Back on the stand in the afternoon, however, he boasted of the killings, described them in gory detail, and thoroughly implicated Angelo.

The ruling on hypnotized witnesses sharply limited the prosecution's resources. Many of the potential witnesses, including Catherine Lorre and Markust Camden, were seen as questionable. The search for physical evidence continued.

Another bizarre chapter in their case was about to begin. On 13 July 1981, in a move that would stun the nation, Los Angeles County Assistant District Attorney Roger Kelly asked for all charges against Angelo Buono to be dismissed. His rationale for the surprising move was based on the overriding question of the credibility of Ken Bianchi. His boss, District Attorney John Van de Kamp, agreed. It is usually the practice, when the prosecuting authority requests a dismissal, the trial judge will grant the request in the interest of justice.

On 21 July, eight days later, Judge George handed down his decision. In a thirty-six-page ruling, he exhaustively discussed the legal precedents for dismissing a case of that type and the law concerning homicide in California. He indicated, even with Bianchi's many contradictions, Angelo Buono was always named as being involved with those crimes. He noted the district attorney's office knew of Bianchi's shakiness when charges were filed against Buono. The judge enumerated the many circumstances pointing to Buono, including the witnesses, the physical evidence such as the badge imprint in Buono's wallet, and so on, that would corroborate an accomplice's testimony. Judge George hinted the motivation for the move to dismiss might have been less of an interest in justice than Van de Kamp's and Kelly's concerns for their legal reputations and their political futures. Van de Kamp was running for the office of California's Attorney General.

Saying he felt a dismissal would not be "in furtherance of justice," the motion to dismiss all charges was denied. Judge George compelled the prosecution of Angelo Buono and warned the district attorney's office that he expected a thorough and complete prosecution. The media and the public supported the judge's decision. When criticized by some lawyers, Judge George pointed to the ample precedent for the action.

The district attorney's office formally withdrew from the Buono case. Prosecution was handed to a team from the office of the California Attorney General. Lawyers Roger Boren and Michael Nash, and Investigator Paul Tulleness, examined the evidence and concluded the case could be successfully prosecuted. It was their opinion the key to the case was the fiber evidence on the brutalized body of Lauren Wagner. Fibers found on her hands and wrists were identified as coming from the carpet in Buono's spare bedroom. Other fiber evidence was also identified as having come from Buono's house. Despite the fact the case was largely circumstantial, they felt it would be enough. The new team was so disgusted with the attitude of Roger Kelly that he was never again consulted.

In the fall of 1981, Angelo, still in jail, signed over his house deed to a neighbor. The new owner bulldozed the house and cleared the lot a few weeks later. Now the prosecution could not show the actual murder site to a future jury.

As the date for Buono's trial neared, another serial murder case was in progress in the same courthouse. William Bonin, sometimes called the "Freeway Killer," was charged with the sodomy murders of twelve young men. Their naked and mutilated bodies had been found alongside local freeways during a five-year period ending in 1980.

In mid-November a few feet down the hall, the trial of Angelo Buono began. Over 350 people were examined before twelve jurors and eight alternates were seated. The jury was composed of seven men and five women, of whom six were black, two were white, and four Hispanic. The voire dire took three and a half months. The jurors were largely middle-class working people, and their employers had agreed to pay their full wages for as long as the trial lasted.

The remaining pretrial issues were cleared up. Bianchi's statements to police in Bellingham were ruled inadmissible because he was not under oath. Yet the defense reserved their right for purposes of impeachment to examine him on those statements. As a result, his confession was not allowed to come in the front door but was readily admitted through the side. The defense's main hope was to prove Ken Bianchi a massive and consistent liar who had made false statements and accusations about their client. Their approach, however, allowed the prosecution to defend Bianchi's truthfulness by showing that much, if not all, of what he had said was true. The jury was allowed to hear the tapes of his confessions.

The defense, attempting to prove Angelo Buono a gentle and considerate lover, brought in a woman who testified Angelo had once attempted anal sex with her but stopped when she complained. That opened the door for the testimony of Becky Spear, Sabra Hannan, and Toni Lombardo, a teenage girlfriend, to demonstrate Angelo's sadism and vicious cruelty.

Angelo Buono, now forty-eight years old, granted an interview to a local television station. He protested his innocence, portraying himself as a good citizen being railroaded by the authorities. Investigator Paul Tulleness had uncovered Angelo's criminal record, which portrayed him as a bully and a thief since childhood. Tulleness had also interviewed Candy Buono and others and learned the lurid details of Angelo's rape, incest, and sexual brutality.

The physical evidence continued to mount. The Mustang automobile used in the abduction of two victims, Cindy Hudspeth and Kimberly Martin, was located. Another layer of support was added to the testimony of Ken Bianchi.

In June 1982, the moment for which everyone had been waiting arrived. Kenneth Bianchi took the stand. He was the 200th witness in the case against his cousin. On his first day on the stand, Ken developed selective amnesia and denied knowing anything about the murders. At night in his cell, he seems to have reflected on the fact that by doing so he was violating his plea bargain agreement and was now facing incarceration in Washington, a prospect he did not relish.

The next day, he began to talk but could not resist the temptation to add the occasional lie. During his entire testimony, he never once looked at Angelo Buono. Bianchi was on the witness stand for five months, including forty-five days of intense cross examination.

The Hillside trial reached its first anniversary on 16 November 1982. The jurors had been working together so long they were now bringing each other birthday cakes.

In December, the jury was taken to 703 East Colorado, where Angelo's house had once stood. They also visited the apartments, the abduction and body sites, and other relevant locations. The guided tour of death was conducted at night so the jury could have an authentic feel about the locations at the time of the murders. Angelo as the defendant had the right to go along. However, security considerations required he be handcuffed and shackled if he exercised that right. He declined, allegedly to avoid prejudicing the jury. By April 1983, over 1,000 exhibits and 250 witnesses had been presented. After seventeen months, the prosecution rested.

In another ironic twist, John Van de Kamp, the former Los Angeles County district attorney, had been elected the California attorney general and was, once again, in charge of prosecuting the case he had attempted to dismiss two years before. Roger Kelly, the assistant district attorney who had started the fuss, had been transferred to Compton, California, the equivalent of a lawyer's Siberia.

Behind the scenes, Angelo Buono was feuding with his lawyers. Angelo did not want any defense made at all. He felt the longer the trial lasted, the more damaging the evidence against him would become. He wanted to gamble the jury would feel the prosecution had failed to put forward an adequate case. His lawyers prevailed, and a defense was made.

The defense theory was Bianchi had committed the murders alone or with a different accomplice. They proceeded to verbally attack the witnesses as they were presented. Markust Camden was attacked because of his history of mental health problems, but Camden did an excellent job on the stand.

Much of the physical evidence was extremely gruesome. Color photographs of the living and dead victims covered a huge piece of plasterboard, and a scale model of Angelo's house was made. Those exhibits were brought out only when needed.

The defense called Veronica Compton. She related the details of an alleged conspiracy between Ken and herself to frame cousin Angelo. However, the prosecution demonstrated that her manic states, emotional displays, and powerful anger at Ken impeached her testimony completely.

Finally, on 2 August 1983, the defense rested. The last of the trial motions were cleared up. Court adjourned for two weeks to allow the attorneys to prepare for final arguments. The trial proper had lasted twenty-two months.

On 5 October 1983, Angelo Buono celebrated his forty-ninth birthday, and final arguments began. The defense attacked Kenneth Bianchi, accusing him of doing the crimes alone. In a move that may not have been wise, they went on to describe sodomy, oral sex, sex with young girls, and bondage as normal in modern California.

The prosecution presented twelve damning points against Angelo Buono. Those involved the circumstances of the murders, Buono's use of incriminating evidence, various eyewitness situations, fiber evidence, and the Buono/Bianchi relationship. The prosecution told the jury that more than enough evidence to convict Angelo had been presented even if they did not believe Ken Bianchi.

The longest criminal trial in American history to that date was coming to a close. After two years and $2 million, the jury began its deliberations. No friends or relatives of Angelo Buono were ever in court except to testify.

Judge George sequestered the jury until a final verdict was reached. Also, he allowed the jury to return a verdict on each count as it was decided. Although the action was unusual, the judge felt, if an alternate juror had to step in for any reason, the process would avoid having to start deliberations all over again.

On Friday, 21 October 1983, jury deliberations began. Ten days later, a verdict of guilty in the first degree was reached in Lauren Wagner's murder. On Thursday, 3 November, the jury said Buono was not guilty of Yolanda Washington's death.

Two days later, the jury found Buono guilty of murdering Judy Miller. "Special circumstances" that linked the Wagner and Miller killings were cited. A recent California law had been passed in response to the public furor over killers such as Charles Manson and Sirhan Sirhan being eligible for parole. It mandated that one murder conviction meant a sentence of twenty-five years to life in prison. If special circumstances were found to link a second murder to the first, then conviction carried a sentence of death in the gas chamber or life without parole. Buono now had two connected murders against him.

On Monday, 7 November, the jury found special circumstances in the verdict of guilty in the Dolores Cepeda and Sonja

Johnson deaths. In the afternoon, Buono announced he was firing his two attorneys. Later that day, he was found responsible for Kimberly Martin's death.

Guilty verdicts came in two days later on Kristina Weckler, Lissa Kastin, and Jane King.

On 11 November, the jury was deadlocked on deciding Cindy Hudspeth's case. The judge ordered the jurors to resume deliberations. On the way to the hotel, one woman juror had chest pains and was taken to the hospital. She recovered and the case resumed three days later. On 14 November, the jury reached a guilty verdict on Hudspeth.

In all, the jurors cited seventy-two instances of special circumstances linking the nine murder convictions. Judge George refused to grant Buono's request to defend himself during the penalty phase of the trial. Angelo Buono took the stand for the first and only time on Tuesday, 16 November 1983. He said his "morals and constitutional rights has been broken." Only two character witnesses could be found to testify on Buono's behalf. One was his sister. The other was a long-term acquaintance who had once asked Buono to burn down a man's house, but Buono had refused.

Determining Buono's guilt had dragged on for nineteen days. Only one hour was needed to spare his life by setting punishment at life without the possibility of parole. The jurors, who had been sequestered twenty-eight days in all, avoided a long death sentence argument when those in favor of it relented their opposition.

Friends, family, and others wrote to Judge George, begging him to impose the death penalty on Buono. However, the judge's powers did not include upgrading a sentence.

On 9 January 1984, over twenty-five months since the trial began, Judge George pronounced formal sentence on Angelo Anthony Buono II. Judge George told Buono he regretted not being able to sentence him to death. Noting that both cousins were incapable of feeling any remorse, he stated, "and ironically, although these two defendants utilized almost every form of legalized execution against their victims, the defendants have escaped any form of capital punishment."

That same day, Judge George confronted Kenneth Bianchi in court. By his deliberate efforts to sabotage the case against Buono,

Ken had violated his plea bargain agreement. The judge ordered Bianchi back to Washington to serve his life sentences there.

In late 1984, the California Supreme Court excluded hypnotically induced testimony and applied that ruling retroactively. The wisdom and foresight of Judge George in excluding such testimony was vindicated. If he had allowed the testimony, the Buono convictions would have been reversed and a retrial would have been necessary.

Angelo Buono, serving his first year in Folsom Prison, sought protective custody status. Fearing death at the hands of other convicts, he refused to leave his cell even for exercise. Buono died of a heart attack on 22 September 2002 while alone in his cell. His body was cremated.

Several hundred miles to the north, Kenneth Bianchi served his time in Walla Walla Prison. He stayed away from other prisoners. Bianchi married a Louisiana pen pal in September 1989. His latest parole attempt on 18 August 2010 was denied. Ken will not be eligible for parole application again until 2025.

Bianchi changed his name twice to avoid being recognized in prison. Yet, in the end, like his cousin, he will always be known as the Hillside Strangler.

WAYNE WILLIAMS: THE ATLANTA "CHILD" KILLER?

> For you, or for me…the missing child distorts totally, the universe, but, for Authority, it is a statistic and, for bureaucracy, a detail. Only when these details and statistics begin to multiply is a public danger perceived.
>
> James Baldwin
> *The Evidence of Things Not Seen*

Like a phoenix rising from the ashes of the Civil War, modern Atlanta is the heart of the New South. From the mid-twentieth century, it had been the site of one of the greatest economic and cultural resurgences in the history of the United States. Yet underlying the rebirth were many of the problems that plagued southern America. The home of enormous wealth, it was also the home of crushing poverty. The most enlightened city in the region in terms of race relations, it also held firmly to the old stereotypes and bigotry of southern America.

Those dichotomies produced a surface stability that laid uneasily over the specter of racial strife. The elections of black mayors and governmental officials helped to ease that somewhat. However, it took only the slightest spark to detonate an explosion of anger, bigotry, and hatred.

Wayne Bertram Williams, only convicted of the murders of two young black adults, has been called "the Atlanta Child Killer." Williams was accused of being one of the most heinous murderers America had ever seen. From 1979 through 1981, he allegedly took the lives of twenty-nine black individuals in the metropolitan Atlanta area.

As events unfolded over the next two years, millions of words were written concerning every aspect of the crimes. Throughout the ordeal, misinformation, misidentification, and misunderstanding constantly plagued attempts to investigate and to solve the case.

One item that needs to be clarified immediately in order to make the case understandable is the misnomer of calling it the "Atlanta child killings." Both the local and national media went to great lengths to portray the victims of those crimes as innocent preteens. Nothing could be further from the truth. Although some victims fit the definition, the majority were streetwise, sophisticated, ghetto youths. That does not in any way diminish the horror of the crimes, but from the outset created a misunderstanding about the crimes and the environment in which they occurred.

Many victims came from an environment totally alien to the average white American. The poverty-ridden subculture of inner-city blacks often bears only a passing resemblance to mainstream life in America. Things normally looked upon almost with horror are taken for granted. It is rare for a male to reach adulthood without being charged or convicted on a criminal matter. Drug and alcohol abuse are facts of daily life. Sexual deviance is tolerated, if not accepted. Despite the labors of churches, civic groups, and the community, honesty and truthfulness are not held in significant esteem. Despair is normal.

Violence is an accepted fact of life. At every level, the child in this setting is exposed to violence. Problems are solved, disputes are settled, and agreements reached using one's hands and weapons. Violence is the greatest cause of death of urban blacks between the ages of fifteen and twenty-five.

On 28 July 1979, the bodies of two young blacks were found in the Niskey Lake area of suburban Atlanta. They were subsequently identified as fourteen-year-old Edward Smith who had been shot to death and thirteen-year-old Alfred Evans whose apparent cause of death was strangulation.

The police reports on Evans, however, listed the cause of death as "unknown," which was later changed to "probable asphyxia." Probable asphyxia means either that a person has stopped breathing as the result of death or has died as a result of not breathing. It does not in and of itself indicate foul play. Yet, time after time, the authorities investigating the "Atlanta crimes" would list probable asphyxia as the cause of death and imply murder.

The two young men were both dressed, according to authorities, in black ninja-type outfits. A story made the rounds that the two had been at a marijuana party. At the party, Evans in a fit of rage shot Smith to death, and one of Smith's friends, outraged by the killing, strangled Evans. That does not account for the disparity in the dates of their alleged disappearances. Smith supposedly disappeared on 20 July and Evans on the twenty-fifth. If the marijuana party story was true, where was Smith between the twentieth and the twenty-fifth?

The Smith/Evans case, although now considered the first of the Atlanta killings, did not draw significant attention from either the media or the public.

On 5 November, the decomposed body of Milton Harvey was found in a local dump. He had been missing since early September. He was young, male, and black.

On 21 October, nine-year-old Yusuf Bell, a bright child who read the encyclopedia for fun, left home to run an errand for a neighbor. His body would be discovered a few weeks later.

The following spring, the body of twelve-year-old Angel Lanier was located tied to a tree across the street from her home. Lanier, also young and black, was originally from Chicago. She had left the Illinois city largely due to problems with the police involving narcotics. Her body was found with a pair of adult women's panties, not her own, stuffed down her throat. She had been strangled with an electrical cord.

The following day, 11 March 1980, Jeffrey Mathis disappeared while running an errand for his mother. Witnesses later came forward and alleged they saw the ten-year-old getting into a blue car. Another witness later reported he had seen Jeffrey alive on 24 March. The witness claimed when he went to the police, he had to insist they take his statement. The indifferent attitude of the police in the early cases is understandable but not acceptable. One of the many tragedies in the lifestyle of the ghetto is the police become jaded and uninterested after seeing acts of senseless violence over and over. After a time, their attitude becomes as accepting as that of those they are charged with protecting.

A few weeks later on 18 May, Eric Middlebrooks, who had been a witness in a recent robbery case, disappeared and was found dead almost immediately. He had been beaten to death. A series of peculiar V-shaped wounds appeared on his upper torso. A family member later said his death was probably related to his impending testimony in the robbery case.

On 9 June 1980, Christopher Richardson left home to go swimming. He disappeared as if swallowed by the earth. His bones were found the following January.

Thirteen days later, seven-year-old LaTonya Wilson was abducted from her bed in the middle of the night. Her body was discovered by a party of volunteers searching the area in October.

After the 22 June abduction of the Wilson girl, the FBI entered the case. Their legal rationale was a suspicion she had been transported across a state line. That would qualify as a federal crime and allow the Bureau a point of entry.

The next day, Aaron Wyche also disappeared. His body was found on 24 June underneath a nearby railroad overpass. Police concluded he had fallen from the bridge. That seemed extremely unlikely considering the fact the bridge had a sidewalk with a waist-high safety barricade. Wyche was also known to suffer from a powerful fear of heights, making it very unlikely he would have climbed on the barrier. Acrophobic children do not normally choose high bridges as playgrounds.

The eleventh victim in the series was nine-year-old Anthony Carter. He was still playing in the street at one-thirty in the morning on 6 July. He was found stabbed to death the following evening.

The local law enforcement agencies were still not terribly concerned about those "crimes." Unless a body was actually found, the children were considered to be runaways. The approach created a lag in investigation quite similar to the one seen in the Gacy crimes in Chicago. However, unlike the Gacy case, public reaction was much more immediate.

One of the things police officers attempting to solve a crime dread the most is the intrusion of politics into an investigation. The Committee to Stop the Children's Murders was formed in May 1980 with the best of intentions by sincere parents of the murdered and missing children. The group was highly critical of the quality of the police investigation. However, it very quickly became a vehicle for individuals to gain media attention by taking cheap shots at the police. There is no question that the investigation was often poorly handled. Yet, one wonders whether any police agency, large or small, could have done it any differently or any better. It is easy to criticize the efforts made in a situation like this. It is not so easy to provide legitimately better ideas.

The Atlanta Police Department had been destabilized for several years. Metropolitan police agencies are always at risk when it comes to politics. Political power struggles between police commissioners and police chiefs for ten years had resulted in divided loyalties and poor morale among the street officers. The result was a police force plagued by inefficiency, confusion, and poor communication. The added pressure of the changing demographic and social structures of the new Atlanta left local law enforcement in shambles.

Lee Brown, the first black Public Safety Commissioner of Atlanta, felt the pressure from the media and the Committee to Stop the Children's Murders. He felt that for two reasons: first, he was in charge of the police department, and second, he was black and the victims were black. He responded by forming a five-member police Task Force to investigate the crimes. The Task Force would later grow to thirty-five, plus nearly forty FBI agents. The FBI worked independently and did not always share the results of their investigations with the Atlanta Police Department.

An arbitrary date of 25 July 1979 was chosen as the starting date for the "child murders." The eleven deaths between the formation of the committee and the arbitrary date, which coincidently happened to be exactly one year before the formation of the Task Force, became the basis of what would be perceived as the Atlanta death list.

The list was another of the many distractions strewn throughout the history of the case. The list gave the impression those were all the murders of young people or blacks in metropolitan Atlanta during the period. Nothing could be further from the truth. Scores of other murders, some of which fit the criteria for inclusion on the list, were never added.

Only two young, black females were included on the list: Angel Lanier and LaTonya Wilson. They seem to have been added not so much because of similarities to the other killings, for they had virtually none, but rather because their mothers belonged to the committee.

At that point, the criteria were that the victims were young, black, and poor. The criteria did not appear to have ever been formulated in writing. They changed in response to official whim and political pressure. Later, the informal definition would confuse many of the issues in the case. An old Southern saying goes, "Be careful not to muddy the water around you, for someday you may have to drink it."

On 30 July, Earl Terrell set out to go swimming. Like Christopher Richardson the month before, he was not seen alive again. Later, a strange story surfaced about a telephone call from a man who, by the sound of his voice, was white saying he had Terrell and would return him for $200. The man never called again.

On 20 August, Clifford Jones, a visitor from Cleveland, left the house where he was staying and went looking for aluminum cans. Later in the day, he was seen entering a local laundromat widely known to be a gathering place for homosexuals. Before dawn the next morning, his plastic-wrapped body was discovered lying next to a trash dumpster near the laundromat.

Five alleged witnesses said they had seen Jones strangled in the laundromat or saw his body placed by the dumpster. The killing followed a sexual molestation. The suspect in the case, a nineteen-year-old black man, was never arrested.

After the Jones killing, public outcry was joined by governmental indignation. The fact that Jones and his family were visitors to Atlanta was often mentioned. The tourism and convention business, which was vital to Atlanta's economy, was threatened. Now it was more than a case of black youths being killed. It was a dagger pointed at the heart of the city's economy.

Ten-year-old Darron Glass disappeared on 14 September 1979. As of 2021, he has not been seen again, and none of the bodies found has been identified as his.

Charles Stevens was a twelve-year-old drug dealer. He disappeared on 9 October and was found the next day in an Atlanta suburb. He had been suffocated.

The police as yet had no significant leads and were apparently making no progress at all. Community outcry became increasingly hostile toward the authorities. Citizens' groups were formed to search for the bodies of those children still missing. The first such group located the body of LaTonya Wilson. Still the murders continued.

One well-intentioned but futile response became the imposition of a ninety-day, eleven p.m. to six a.m. curfew for those under the age of sixteen. Questions of constitutionality notwithstanding, the curfew was worse than useless. It invited violation, especially by children of single-parent families, and ignored the fact that most of the victims disappeared during the day. Additionally, fifteen murders occurred after it began.

Not surprisingly, given the traditional minority attitudes about law enforcement in general and the specific circumstances of the Atlanta case, public attitude toward the Task Force was generally rather negative. That attitude was exacerbated by the lack of responsiveness by investigators to citizen input.

The late summer and early fall of 1980 was as racially tense a period as any since the 1960s. All around the country, attacks on blacks were increasing. Street murders in Buffalo, New York City, and Salt Lake City; the shooting of Vernon Jackson in Fort Wayne; and other equally senseless crimes fostered an attitude of suspicion and mistrust throughout America. The Atlanta situation was the focal point.

Many Atlanteans attributed the change in attitude to the conservative approach of the new administration in Washington, DC; economic conservatism was leading to repression. When a day-care center boiler exploded in Atlanta in late summer, conspiracy theories were rampant. A later finding that the explosion was an accident was generally disbelieved.

Nine-year-old Aaron Jackson had been a friend of Aaron Wyche. On 1 November, the corpse of Aaron Jackson was also found under a bridge. The cause of death was "probable asphyxia."

On 10 November, Patrick (Pat Man) Rogers disappeared. He was listed as a runaway until his body was located floating in the Chattahoochee River.

An interesting aspect to Rogers' death was the fact that several months later, two Atlanta police officers came to his mother's house to serve an arrest warrant on him for burglary. Apparently, death was no bar to prosecution in Atlanta.

The tide of death continued into 1981. On 3 January, fourteen-year-old Lubie Geter disappeared. Geter had been in trouble with the authorities for truancy and drug use. His body was discovered on 5 January in a wooded area. He had been stripped to his underwear, and sexual assault was assumed.

On 22 January 1981, Terry Pue, described as being an exceptionally tough kid, disappeared. He was found the next day strangled and dumped in a remote rural area.

Eleven-year-old Patrick Baltazar set out for downtown Atlanta on 6 February. His parents never bothered to file a missing person's report, because they considered him unpredictable and assumed he was all right. The next time they saw him was a week later on 13 February. His partially frozen corpse had been dumped behind an office building. Missing for a week, he had been dead around seventy-two hours and had been strangled. Again, the question comes up: Where was the victim between the time he "disappeared" and the time of death?

As mentioned above, one of the persistent problems with the so-called Atlanta child murders is a disparity in dates. In several instances, a three-date sequence—the first date being the date of the disappearance, the second when the body was found, and the third the official time of death—raises unanswered questions. The time of death was sometimes several days after the disappearance. One more time, the period between the abduction and the death appears inconsistent.

Thirteen-year-old Curtis Walker vanished on 19 February. His decomposed body was located on a bank of the South River on 6 March.

On the evening of 2 March, Joseph "Jo-Jo" Bell left a local community center with two black males. His body was also discovered on a bank of the South River on Easter Sunday, 19 April.

On 13 March, Timmy Hill disappeared. Hill, age thirteen, had a history of drug abuse, running away, and homosexuality. His body would be found on 30 March in the Chattahoochee River. Hill was acquainted with Jo-Jo Bell, the previous victim.

The next day, 31 March, another body was pulled from the Chattahoochee. Eddie Duncan, a twenty-one-year-old black male, was considered to be mentally challenged. Like Hill, his body was discovered wearing only underwear. He had disappeared on 20 March. It was notable that Duncan was an adult. Another discordant note had been added to Atlanta's symphony of death.

Five days after the disappearance of Duncan, Michael (Mickey) McIntosh, a twenty-three-year-old ex-con with a fondness for the company of homosexuals, disappeared. Mickey was acquainted with Jo-Jo Bell, another victim. Mickey's body was found on 20 April.

On 30 March, following another five-day lapse, Larry Rogers disappeared. Larry's body was located in an abandoned apartment house on 9 April. Fully clothed, with no signs of sexual molestation, Larry's cause of death was ruled by the medical examiner as "probable asphyxia."

On 12 April, twenty-eight-year-old John Porter was found stabbed to death on an Atlanta sidewalk. An adult, mentally ill ex-convict, Porter was later added to the list of victims.

By the spring of 1981, one of the most tragic side effects of the Atlanta case could no longer be ignored. Childhood development experts, educators, and parents noticed an increasing level of fear among children, both black and white. At a time in their lives when they should be experimenting and exploring their world, children were becoming fearful, introverted, passive, and overwhelmed by the fear of death.

The media hype became a deluge of terror. The portrayal of the victims as being literally jerked from the street into waiting cars and driven away to a horrible death was having its impact on Atlanta's youth. Because of that mindset, the children were given the traditional message about not getting into cars with strangers. The evidence, however, suggested many of those murders were not "stranger" crimes. As a result, the children should have been taught to be wary around people they knew. That was not done. Whether the technique would have saved lives will never be known.

In March, the *Atlanta Constitution* published what was allegedly an FBI psychological profile of the "Atlanta killer." The Bureau later denied releasing the document. It ran as follows:

Wanted: a man or woman about 40 years old, single or childless, with at least a high school education. A reliable employee who has frequent contact with children, perhaps even on the job, and lives in a lower middle-class racially mixed neighborhood. A loner, with few close friends and virtually no sense of humor. Extremely neat. Brought up in a broken home by an abusive mother. May believe it is an act of mercy to kill poor black children and thus remove them from a bad environment. May have expressed condolences to some of the victims' families; may even have attended a funeral or two.

The national media focused more attention on Atlanta than

any time since Sherman burned the city in 1864. Concerned citizens nationwide held vigils and prayer meetings and sent donations to help the people of Atlanta. No other serial murder case had been attended by the vast influx of money that came into the Atlanta community. The Atlanta mothers' committee solicited funds allegedly for extra police and investigative resources and to aid the families of the victims on the official list. Considerable controversy arose over the distribution of those funds. Auditing procedures were apparently nonexistent.

It seems great tragedies bring out the best and the worst in people. Like scum rising to the top of a pond, the con men and freaks came to Atlanta. Illegal fundraising, publicity seeking, and political power grabbing became a part of life for a city in pain.

Finally, in 1981, the Georgia Governor's Office of Consumer Affairs warned the mothers' committee to stop soliciting funds. The committee retaliated with criticism of the city government of Atlanta, the Georgia Governor's Office, and the Reagan administration in Washington. The bucks kept rolling in.

Twenty-one-year-old Jimmy Ray Payne disappeared on 22 April 1981. Payne, a convicted felon, was acquainted with at least two of the previous victims. He was found five days later floating in the Chattahoochee River.

On 11 May, William (Billy Starr) Barrett, on parole for burglary, vanished. His body was located on 12 May. The cause of death was listed as strangulation, although he had been stabbed several times after death.

Twenty-seven-year-old Nathaniel Cater, another convicted criminal, disappeared sometime around 22 May. His body was found on the twenty-fourth.

Several months earlier in March 1981, the FBI indicated they were proceeding from the assumption that more than one killer was prowling the streets of Atlanta. Their stance was that eleven of the twenty killings were the work of one person, three others a copycat, and the remainder were individual unrelated crimes. Those numbers would indicate eight different murderers.

Speculation was rife. Patterns of various types were sought, sometimes found, and then discarded. The only real pattern was the victims were black and poor. Investigators looked at questions of sexual molestation, size, hair style, personal habits, and whether the body of the victim had been cleaned after death and before being dumped. Tiny, tantalizing threads ran through a few deaths here and there. Yet no thread led back to the murderer.

When faced with the tangled problem, the law enforcement agencies involved in the search went back to basic techniques. One of those was the time-honored stakeout.

By eight p.m. on the evening of 21 May 1981, three Atlanta Police officers and an FBI agent were staked out at the James Jackson Parkway bridge. Several bodies had turned up in the Chattahoochee River near the area, and it was thought another might appear.

A rookie police officer named Campbell parked under the north end of the bridge on the Cobb County side. FBI agent Gilliland waited in a chase car four-tenths of a mile north on the west side of the road. To the south on the Fulton County side, another police recruit named Jacobs stood beside the bridge. The fourth officer, Holden, sat in a second chase car behind a liquor store at the south end of the bridge. There was a slight rise nine-tenths of a mile north of the bridge. Then the road leveled off and headed downhill toward the bridge. At the north end of the bridge was an expansion joint that made loud clanks as any vehicle crossed it. Also at the north end was a side road that headed east along the river.

Around three a.m., Officer Campbell supposedly heard a splash in the river. The Atlanta child murders were on their way to being solved, at least in law enforcement minds.

What happened after the splash was heard was not clear. The officers' reports proved inconsistent, and Wayne Williams' account varied widely from theirs.

In his version, Jacobs said Officer Campbell radioed him about the splash. Jacobs looked up at the bridge and saw a car approaching slowly from the north end with its lights on. It was a 1970 Chevy Chevelle station wagon. From his position, Jacobs said he did not see any car lights illuminate the trees around him as they should have if the car came over the rise from the north.

The car crossed the bridge and drove into the liquor store lot on the west side of the road. Holden and Jacobs said the car then turned around and recrossed the bridge heading back north. However, Jacobs admitted he ducked under the bridge to avoid being seen. Holden pulled out and followed the car north.

The second version had Campbell hearing the splash, looking down, and shining his flashlight on the water. He saw the point of entry and the concentric circles spreading out from it. Campbell said he then radioed Gilliland, who had not seen a car pass his position nor had he heard the splash. Campbell saw car lights come on at about the point where he thought the splash originated. He did not hear the expansion joints make any noise as they should have for the car to cross onto the bridge.

Gilliland said he first saw the car when it was coming back north, followed by Holden. Gilliland maneuvered his car between the wagon and Holden. One and a half miles north of the bridge on the entrance to Interstate 285, Gilliland turned on his siren and lights to stop the car. Wayne Bertram Williams was driving the car.

For nearly two hours, Williams was questioned about what he was doing on the bridge that night. Williams claims at no time did the officers read him his Miranda rights. That has never been disputed. Williams said he was looking for the address of a woman named Cheryl Johnson. He had a business appointment with her scheduled for later that morning, but he was looking for her address now. No one has ever been able to locate the woman, and the telephone number Williams had with him for her was incorrect.

Williams said he did cross the bridge but earlier before the time the officers heard the splash. He said he did not turn around in the liquor store lot. He continued six-tenths of a mile south toward a Starvin' Marvin gas-convenience store. There, he used a pay phone and picked up some cardboard boxes for his mother. Then he crossed the bridge going north and was finally stopped by the police.

Two hypotheses have been suggested to resolve the conflict among all the reported events of the early morning. First, Williams, at some point in time, drove north with the victim, Nathaniel Cater, either alive or dead. He crossed the bridge from the south and turned immediately right onto the side road. Down the road was a guard shack at the entrance to a power plant area. Nearby was a boat ramp to the river. Williams drove down the boat ramp to the water's edge. He either killed Cater or rolled his already dead body into the river.

Williams then returned to Jackson Parkway. After stopping at the stop sign, he headed south moving slowly from a dead stop. At that moment, a beaver splashed the water. Beavers often disturb residents in the area with their loud splashes, as Park Service officers could attest from the many complaints they received. Williams' tires hit the expansion joint one at a time, making a noise to which the police were not accustomed. Any other noises went unheard because Campbell was preoccupied with the splash. Thus, as Williams' lights "come on" as Campbell claimed, the headlights did not illuminate the trees at Jacobs' position, and no car passed Gilliland.

The second scenario had Williams driving south across the bridge following two more vehicles. Williams went to Starvin' Marvin's, used the phone, picked up the boxes, and headed back north. Meanwhile, another vehicle left the power plant, stopped at the intersection, and pulled slowly onto Jackson Parkway going south. The beaver splashed the water, and the car lights were seen as in the first example. The expansion joint made the different sound. The driver crossed the bridge and started to pull into the liquor store lot but changed his mind. That car then proceeded south.

At that moment, Williams passed the entrance to the liquor store lot headed north. Holden, who had momentarily lost sight of the vehicle that had just entered the lot and then continued south, emerged from behind the store and followed Williams. He assumed Williams' was the car he saw seconds earlier.

The medical examiner's initial workup indicated Cater's body could have been in the water prior to 22 May. The conclusion using that date was influenced by his being told in advance the splash was heard on the morning of 22 May, thereby bringing the date of Cater's death into question.

After the questioning, the decision was made to release Williams. His vehicle had been searched with his permission. He was cooperative with the officers on the scene.

Wayne Williams was born on 27 May 1958. The only child of middle-aged parents, he lived a life of parental indulgence and was thought by many to be a spoiled kid. His parents referred to him as "the miracle child" and indulged his every whim. He had been an honors student, a Cub Scout, and active in church. His greatest fascination was with various aspects of the media. A somewhat talented photographer, he had also started his own low-power radio station by the time he was twelve.

Like several other convicted serial killers, Williams had a fascination with police work. He purchased a car resembling an unmarked police cruiser, added police lights and a scanner, and raced to the scene of every accident or crime he heard about. On the scene, he would take photographs and attempt to sell them to local news operations. In 1976, he was arrested but not convicted for the crime of impersonating a police officer. That same year, his parents, because of underwriting Wayne's expensive hobbies, were forced to file for bankruptcy. Doting parenthood can be an expensive proposition.

Wayne had no close friends and no girlfriend, and he does not appear to have dated steadily. He seems to have spent most of his time racing up and down the streets of Atlanta to the scene of the latest disaster.

Physically, Williams, a light-skinned Black American, stood about five feet seven inches and weighed 160 pounds. He had never shown the slightest inclination to athletic endeavor. Later, some of the things he would be accused of doing seemed unlikely for an individual of his physique and prowess.

Williams had attended Georgia State University for one year before dropping out. An enterprising young man, he was featured in *Jet* magazine when only nineteen. He started many elaborate projects but failed to finish any of them. One of those was a talent agency that brought him into contact with hundreds of young people.

Next to electronics, Williams' greatest interest was music. A self-styled promoter, he attempted to start a singing group called Gemini. The group was intended to be young blacks in the style of the Jackson Five. Recruiting flyers for males between eleven and twenty-one years old were distributed in Atlanta area shopping malls by kids hired by Williams. The marketing would bear negative fruit later when it was pointed out that connections existed between some victims and shopping malls.

Wayne Williams is remembered for a tendency to play fast and loose with the truth. He was constantly exaggerating his own importance and embellishing stories about his life. His ability to look and act sincere stood him in good stead. He seemed to have an uncanny ability to make himself popular with children.

After the incident on Jackson Parkway, Williams was under constant surveillance. He was aware almost immediately of that fact. The following day, 23 May, neighbors say Wayne Williams and his father, Homer, burning large quantities of photographs and negatives in a backyard barbecue grill. Law enforcement authorities had no right to stop their actions. However, it is interesting to speculate what those photographs portrayed. Like Ted Bundy before him, Williams seems to have developed a sudden interest in domestic cleanliness after being placed under surveillance for a crime.

A few days later, Wayne celebrated his twenty-third birthday.

On the morning of 3 June, Williams was picked up at home by FBI agents and voluntarily went to their headquarters for further questioning. Although not placed under arrest, he did receive a Miranda warning and signed the waiver. The FBI failed to inform the Atlanta Police Department that they had Williams in their custody. After twelve hours of questioning and two polygraph examinations, Williams was again released.

By that time, the local media had become aware Williams had been questioned. They joined the police in staking out the Williams family home. By evening, Wayne, taking a leaf from John Gacy's book, led them all on a merry chase through the streets of downtown Atlanta and up to the front door of Police Commissioner Lee Brown's home. Locking himself in the car, Wayne proceeded to honk his horn and shout obscenities at the house.

The following morning, Williams held what must be considered the most unusual press conference since the decline and fall of Richard Nixon. Inviting reporters to his home, he proceeded to tell them the police who had stopped him at the Jackson Parkway bridge on the night of 22 May accused him of killing Nathaniel Cater. The problem with the statement was Cater's body was not discovered until 24 May. At the time Williams was stopped, no one knew Cater was dead, except the murderer.

Wayne then distributed and read out loud a five-page resume supposedly detailing his varied accomplishments in the community. The document was later discovered to be largely false.

He also committed an incredible faux pas, which was to haunt him later. He told reporters he had submitted to three polygraph exams and the FBI had informed him his answers on the exams were false. By discussing the polygraph tests publicly, he made it possible for them to be introduced in evidence when he went to trial. He concluded with a lengthy protestation of his innocence and accusations of harassment by police authorities and the media. Later in the day, he hired a local attorney named Mary Welcome.

On Wednesday, 5 June, FBI agents and members of the police Task Force armed with search warrants, conducted an exhaustive search of the Williams home. A number of items were confiscated, including a yellow blanket, a purple robe, fibers from a carpet and a bedspread, and hair from the Williams' dog. At three-thirty a.m. on the morning of 6 June, Police Commissioner Brown conceded they did not have enough evidence to make an arrest.

For the next two weeks, the street in front of the Williams home became a media circus. Williams, like John Gacy, was acquainted with many public officials, politicians, and media staffers. He made the best of those connections by constantly keeping his name in front of the public and waging a war of accusations on the various law enforcement personnel involved in the investigation. He was quoted in Time magazine for 15 June 1981 as saying, "If all this boils out to be nothing, I have been slandered by the police and the news media." Was this a Freudian slip when he said "if" instead of "when," or was he aware that his life was, indeed, at risk?

In the days to come, Williams sought the spotlight, then filed lawsuits against it. He created conflict even inside the media on the issue of whether he should be publicly named as a suspect. Some media representatives felt that, because he had not been arrested or charged, he should not be named. Others felt his press conference made him a public figure.

At the same time, his actions created an atmosphere of political turmoil. The chief prosecutor, Lewis Slaton, declined to authorize an arrest warrant, because he felt the case was not solid enough. He made statements to that effect several times in the days preceding Williams' arrest. Slaton's hesitance led to a meeting at the Georgia governor's mansion, which nearly resulted in his removal and the appointment of a special prosecutor. Meanwhile, the FBI, which had said in April that four of the murders had already been solved, continued to press for an immediate arrest.

Finally, on Sunday evening, 21 June, Wayne Bertram Williams was picked up at his home, placed under arrest, and charged with the first-degree murder of Nathaniel Cater. He was held without bond in the Fulton County Jail.

The people of Atlanta breathed a collective sigh of relief. The feeling was widespread that the Atlanta child killer had been apprehended. The question now became whether enough proof existed to justify the feeling.

On 23 June, a grand jury convened in the matter of Wayne Williams. At the hearing, some of the evidence against Williams was revealed. First, Williams had allegedly stopped on the Jackson Parkway bridge; and second, dog hair and bed and carpet fibers found on the naked corpse of Nathaniel Cater were consistent with hair and fibers taken from the Williams home. The case against Wayne Williams was based entirely on circumstantial evidence.

After the hearing, Williams was returned to jail where he continued to be held without bond. On 17 July 1981, the grand jury handed down an indictment formally accusing Wayne Williams of the willful murders of Nathaniel Cater and Jimmy Ray Payne. One irony of the indictment was, at the time, Payne, who like Cater was an adult, had not been listed by the medical examiner as a murder victim. Rather, his death was considered to be the result of "probable asphyxia."

After Williams' arrest, the Task Force and the FBI operation were quickly downscaled. A major media campaign, apparently designed to reassure the citizens of Atlanta, harped constantly on the idea that since the arrest, no more "child killings" had occurred. Subsequent evidence proved the assertion to be untrue.

The FBI had said in April that several people were involved in the long series of murders and claimed to have solved four of the crimes. Now the Bureau seemed to be convinced of Williams' guilt on all of them.

Six months lapsed between the indictment and the time Williams went to trial in December 1981. The time was filled with the usual infighting as a result of the magnitude of the case and the presence of several lawyers at the defense table. The typical salvo of suppression and discovery motions was exchanged. Mary Welcome, who had been hired by Williams on 4 June, had never tried a murder case of any kind, let alone a major serial murder case. She initially sought and received the services of Tom Axam, another black Atlanta attorney, as co-counsel. After Welcome and Axam discovered they had irreconcilable difficulties in working together, Axam was fired. A Mississippi criminal lawyer named

Al Binder was brought in to fill the void. Binder, a seasoned criminal lawyer who had tried several homicide cases, did most of the actual trial work.

During his long months in jail, Williams tried to keep his business enterprises running by mail. He failed. He also said repeatedly the whole thing was "a terrible mistake." On the other hand, he did not offer a viable alibi.

Despite the publicity, many people continued to have doubts about Wayne Williams' role in the crimes. Camille Bell, the mother of Yusuf Bell, an early victim, volunteered to work on the Williams defense team. She was quite convinced that the killer of her son was not Wayne Williams.

On 28 December 1981, the trial began. The jury selection process lasted five days and, on 5 January of the new year, a jury of eight blacks and four whites was seated. The jury was carefully sequestered during the entire trial process.

Opening arguments began immediately. Famous black American writer James Baldwin described the spectacle of a major murder trial as a "visceral Roman circus." He said people could not be impartial or suspend judgment and to ask people then to dismiss their perceptions during a trial denies people those faculties at a time when they needed them the most. All too often it seemed a person was found guilty at the moment of arrest rather than at trial.

An issue quickly raised was the manner of death of Jimmy Ray Payne. The original death certificate issued the previous summer had listed the manner of death as unknown. After the indictment and before the trial, the manner of death was changed to read "homicide."

An unusual aspect of the Williams trial was the absence of psychiatric testimony. That was compounded by the prosecution's failure to present a believable motive.

The actual trial evidence was largely built around the so-called fiber evidence. Fiber evidence is circumstantial at best. In the Williams case, a considerable number of questions arose as to whether the state of "best" was achieved. Thousands of pieces of fiber evidence were excluded, while several hundred were presented. The evidence was largely based on carpet fibers. An attempt to convince the jury that those fibers came from the Williams' home and their vehicles was fraught with problems. The analyst who examined the fibers in the Williams case had also handled the fiber evidence aspect of the Ted Bundy case, an interesting irony.

The prosecution's major contention was the trilobal fiber found in the Williams' carpet and on Cater's body was rare. Actually, the fiber was one of several that made up the blend in the Williams' carpet. The fiber itself was common and was used in home and apartment carpets, in commercial stores, and in automobile floor mats.

The state's fiber case had other problems. Some of the victims on which fibers were found were pulled from rivers. Rivers carry millions of fibers from many sources in their waters. Also, the entire fiber case was built on finding fibers supposedly from Williams' environment on the victims. However, only one fiber similar to those in Payne's red undershorts was found in Williams' car.

It should be remembered that professional law enforcement agencies themselves repeatedly caution about the dangers of using only fiber evidence in a situation of this type. The FBI's own manuals state clearly that evidence of this type should be backed up with noncircumstantial proof in order to obtain a conviction.

In the fourth week of the trial, prosecutor Lewis Slaton petitioned the court to allow the admission of "prior acts cases." A list of ten of the "child killer" victims was presented to convince the judge that the evidence in those cases, although not sufficient to convict Williams on them directly, should be admitted into evidence on the Cater/Payne cases. That would allow the prosecution to establish a pattern in the homicides leading to the conclusion Wayne Williams had done them in addition to the two with which he had been actually charged. After considerable deliberation, the judge, who was sitting on his first murder trial, decided to allow the "pattern evidence" to be presented.

In the ten cases on the pattern list, the prosecution tried to show fiber links and commonalities among the victims. The victims were black males, most came from broken homes, and they had been murdered.

On the other hand, the victims on the pattern list were significantly younger. The actual causes of death varied from stabbing and bludgeoning to the now legendary "probable asphyxia." Cater and Payne had been found in the river, and nine of the ten on the list on dry land. Only two of the ten had had any of the trilobal fibers found on their bodies.

Strong reason was apparent to believe the real purpose for the introduction of the pattern list was not to establish a true criminal pattern. Rather, it allowed the introduction of otherwise inadmissible evidence and shored up the significant weaknesses in the Cater/Payne evidence.

The prosecution contended all the murders occurred in the Williams family house. The idea borders on the unimaginable. First, it would mandate Homer and Faye Williams, both retired, were not only aware of the crimes but almost certainly participants. Second, it would defy the evidence presented in several of the cases as to locations, times, and places of victim abductions and deaths. That was particularly true in the case of Clifford Jones, the young man who an eyewitness saw murdered in a local laundromat. It also called into question the Jackson Parkway incident. If Williams had murdered Cater in his home and was dumping the body, why was he headed toward his home at the time he allegedly threw Cater's corpse from the bridge?

At the trial, no witnesses would testify they saw Wayne Williams stop on the bridge or saw him throw anything into the water. It was all inferred. The prosecution said Williams sneaked onto the bridge with his lights off. He traveled so slowly that Campbell did not hear the clank-clank of the expansion joint. Then, Williams removed Cater's body, which was two and a half inches taller than he, through the tailgate of the station wagon. He lifted it over the four-foot-high and one-foot-wide bridge railing without leaving a mark on the nude body or on the bridge. His eleven-year-old car ran so smoothly that Campbell, who was positioned under the bridge, did not hear it. Williams returned to the car, turned his lights on, and drove over the bridge. He turned around in the liquor store lot and drove at a normal speed back across the bridge.

Defense attorneys tested the expansion joint. They drove a car back and forth across the bridge at various speeds. The expansion joint always made a loud clank audible to a man beneath the bridge. The man testing it could hear the noise even over the daytime surrounding sounds.

Witnesses were produced who stated they had seen Wayne Williams with various victims over time. Most of the testimony involved sightings at Cap'n Peg's, a local seafood drive-in restaurant. Williams denied ever having been in Cap'n Peg's. That denial was extremely questionable considering the fact the proprietor identified him as a regular customer and Williams on one occasion had used the restaurant address as the headquarters for his Gemini musical group.

Blood stains found in the Williams station wagon were identified as belonging to the blood groups of two of the victims. The finding does not mean the stains were their blood, only that the blood came from the same types.

The defense produced a former Atlanta policeman who testified the two officers on duty at the Jackson Parkway bridge the night of 22 May had been drinking and were known to have been sleeping.

A series of witnesses were then produced giving various perspectives on Williams' personality. One male witness testified Williams had once offered him twenty dollars for sex. He also placed Williams in a game room at the same time as Timmy Hill, one of the victims. Another witness testified a business associate of Wayne's was effeminate. He also said he had never known Williams to date girls or to even think about them.

Wayne Williams always denied being a homosexual. A young woman interviewed before the trial stated she had dated Wayne, but they had never been lovers. On the stand, she said they, indeed, had been sexually active with each other.

Wayne's father, Homer, painted a different picture of his son during his testimony. He denied the allegations of hostility and tension between himself and his son. He also raised questions about the availability to Wayne of various cars possessed by the family. If Wayne did not have a car, it is impossible to see how he could have committed the murders. However, Homer also stated the two Williams family cars had shown an average of 4,000 miles a month on the odometers. He had no valid explanation for the excessive mileage.

Further, when questioned about the burning of the photographs in the barbecue grill, Homer said it was a common practice and occurred sometimes two or three times a week.

In a departure from most serial murder trials, Wayne Williams was allowed to testify in his own defense. The prosecution pulled out all the stops in dealing with Wayne. Slaton spent hours discrediting various aspects of Wayne's story. He showed the inconsistencies in Wayne's statements about the night of 22 May. He also discredited Wayne's statements about his relationship with his father. Slaton introduced a magazine article containing an interview wherein Wayne had been critical of his relationship with Homer.

After three days on the stand, serious cracks developed in the defendant's composure. He responded to questions by calling the district attorney derogatory names and referred to two FBI agents as "goons." Slaton used the outburst to demonstrate what he called Williams' split personality.

Throughout the trial, no testimony was ever introduced to prove where or when any of the victims were killed. No eyewitnesses came forward to connect Williams to any abductions or murders. Persons who had told police other versions of the crimes were not asked to testify.

Faye Williams, Wayne's mother, testified the relationship between her husband and son was not as portrayed by the prosecution. She said they never argued in public.

On 26 February, the closing arguments began. The prosecution portrayed Williams as a pathological liar who killed "over and over without any apparent motive." The jury was reminded of Williams' outburst on the stand and told it showed "a raging explosion inside him." The prosecution conceded their case was circumstantial but called it "an overabundance of circumstance pointing to Wayne Williams."

Defense attorney Al Binder rose to respond. He pointed out the many inconsistencies in the state's case. First, he emphasized the fact the entire case was circumstantial. Then he attacked the so-called pattern cases. Third, he reminded the jury the defense was not compelled to prove innocence, but the prosecution was compelled to prove guilt. He aggressively attacked the flaws in the fiber evidence and pointed out to the jury no motive had ever been established. Last, he stated there had never been a black mass murderer.

The state in rebuttal once again raised the point that the killings had supposedly stopped with the arrest of Wayne Williams. In an attempt to respond to the motive issue, the jury was reminded of the testimony of an acquaintance of Williams' named Roland Lee Toland. Toland had testified earlier in the trial that

Williams had told him that doing away with one black male child would significantly affect the population of blacks in Atlanta.

Finally, on the evening of 26 February, after nine weeks of testimony, the case went to the jury. The feeling in the courtroom was the prosecution had compensated for the lack of quality evidence by introducing a vast amount of weak evidence.

The jury deliberated for two days and, finally, on 28 February 1982, brought in a verdict of guilty on two counts of first-degree murder.

Georgia, once the most criticized state in the South for its use of the death penalty, did not have a death penalty law at the time. Wayne was, therefore, sentenced to two consecutive life sentences for the deaths of Nathaniel Cater and Jimmy Ray Payne.

The end of the trial did not end the controversy. Homer and Faye Williams continued to criticize the investigation, the lack of evidence, and the conduct of the trial.

The appeal process began immediately. However, by the end of 1982, Williams had severed his relationship with both Al Binder and Mary Welcome, his two defense lawyers.

The Atlanta newspapers continued to say the killings stopped with the arrest of Wayne Williams. They did not seem to notice that at least seven killings consistent with the police parameters for the "child killings" occurred in the first six months after Williams' arrest.

Williams, still in the Fulton County Jail, requested he be sent to the Georgia State Penitentiary at Reidsville. Reidsville is considered by many to be the harshest and most dangerous prison in the South. Williams felt the inmate population at Reidsville would present less of a threat to his safety. He feared younger inmates in a facility like Alto Reformatory would be more likely to attempt to gain a reputation by killing someone with as much notoriety as he now had.

The FBI had withdrawn, and, on 1 March 1982 the Task Force was shut down. The cases of twenty-four murder victims, including John Porter who had never been listed previously, were closed with the notation "cleared by arrest." Two days later, under enormous public pressure, Public Safety Commissioner Lee Brown reactivated the Task Force to address the many unanswered questions. He protected his credibility by combining the Task Force with a specialized homicide unit.

By late 1982, many of the unresolved issues were surfacing again. The mothers of several victims requested repeatedly that Williams be brought to trial for the deaths of their children. The prosecutor refused to do so, calling it a waste of time and money. The mothers filed a federal suit in December 1982 requesting the federal court to mandate prosecution on the untried cases. They were unsuccessful.

The case of Patrick "Pat Man" Rogers was administratively closed with a notation that fiber evidence linked his murder to Wayne Williams. His death was the twenty-fifth homicide directly attributed to Wayne Williams.

A request for a new trial was denied. An appeal to the Georgia Supreme Court resulted in the upholding of Williams' conviction in December 1983.

Because of its emotional content, the Williams case continued to be one of the most controversial murder trials of the twentieth century. Media attention focused on the acts of various police authorities during the conduct of the case. Many issues were never resolved. Many alternate suspects were never questioned, and no hard evidence had ever surfaced. It is impossible for anyone other than Wayne Williams himself to say whether he is guilty and of what. What is known is that the two-year nightmare in Atlanta appeared to come to an end in June 1981. Many do not believe that it came to an end in the way it should have.

The publication in 1983 of *The List* by former Atlanta policeman Chet Dettlinger did nothing to ease the controversy. The book was meticulously plotted and researched. Later nominated for a Pulitzer Prize, it raised many questions about the fairness, honesty, and completeness of the investigation leading to Williams' conviction. Dettlinger pointed out patterns among the victims that had never been revealed to the jury, including connections with homosexuality, child pornography, drugs, and street crime. Those activities focused attention on an entirely new group of suspects, some of whom were in prison, some of whom were dead, but many of whom were still living in the metro-Atlanta area.

In the spring of 1985, a CBS television docudrama aired. It attempted to make the case Wayne Williams was nothing more than an innocent man who had had the misfortune to be in the wrong place at the wrong time.

By the fall of 1986, it became clear that, more than any other serial murder case, ongoing attention might very well lead to the exoneration of Wayne Williams. The prestigious ABC television program, *Nightline,* carried an entire program dedicated to raising issues about the Atlanta case. It pointed out the alternate suspects who had not been questioned, the trial witnesses who were known to have perjured themselves, and the deceptive techniques used by the prosecution to gain conviction. During the program, the foreman of the jury was interviewed and said that if the fiber evidence had been presented in a proper fashion, it might very well have led to a hung jury or acquittal.

The Williams controversy will undoubtedly continue until all the concerns raised by law enforcement professionals and the bereaved families have been aired and resolved in a public forum. In the meantime, Wayne Williams remains in prison.

By law, Williams is eligible for parole after serving seven years on each sentence. His last parole request was denied on 20 November 2019. He can request again in November 2027.

The question haunting the case remains. Has Georgia locked up a monster, or has it incarcerated an innocent man and allowed the monster(s) to walk free?

PORTRAIT OF A SERIAL MURDERER

What changes a human being into a serial murderer? What makes him tick? Who's to blame for his development? These are questions with no simple answers. Yet some possible explanations have been analyzed, and clues to future solutions await research. A major conclusion is obvious: Three main factors are involved in the development of a human being.

One is the effect of the family situation on the child. Researchers stress the importance of early bonding and the formation of healthy relationships within the family. They see in the home life the origins of the pattern an individual uses to deal with personal interactions throughout life. Thus, family life, or lack thereof, is vitally important. Many such influences were examined in reviewing the lives of six serial murderers. This chapter will detail how family influences can lead to a potential serial murderer.

The second set of factors is the least understood: genetics and biochemistry. Still in its infancy, research into these subjects is rapidly increasing. They will have a major impact on how crime and criminals are perceived in the future. The next chapter will explore their connections to criminology.

The third area is the society in which the child is raised. Some standard reactions in discussing crime are that poverty leads to crime, or television causes violence, or some other equally simplistic solution. The chapter entitled "The Whole Bloody Mess" will examine societal factors.

Common Threads

We can now see a series of common threads running through the lives and careers of the serial murderers examined here. Those detailed are not significantly different from the scores of other serial killers known to law enforcement agencies and the public. The serial murderers in this book were chosen because they were the most completely researched. Many serial murder cases exist, but few seem to capture the public imagination the way these individuals have. Like Jack the Ripper himself, these criminals cause a strange fascination.

The greatest difficulty in doing an overview study of serial killers is the lack of adequate information, background, and research on this burgeoning problem. Law enforcement agencies conduct investigations for the purposes of apprehension and prosecution. Correctional authorities investigate and research to determine the nature, circumstances, and length of incarceration. Nonfiction writers occasionally do additional background inquiry to more fully understand their subjects. Academics have researched various types of criminal behavior. No one, however, seems to have looked at the overall picture or attempted to define the serial killer in the context of society. This has been the nature of our attempt.

One of the problems with comparison studies is one virtually never finds points of universal applicability. The conclusions drawn here apply to most of the killers analyzed in this book. We have researched many other serial murderers who are not included, but whose attributes fit the general pattern. It is also important to remember the sample group from which these conclusions are drawn is very limited. The comparisons are submitted here to encourage further and more extensive research by various professionals concerned with criminal justice.

The common characteristics we have found in serial killers will also be present in criminals as a group and in a large segment of the noncriminal population. The reason for an attempt at definition is to narrow the possibilities, to enhance the probability of detection, and to know the warning signs before tragedy occurs. In this chapter, we will discuss behavioral patterns. Later, other biological issues will also be examined.

Although only time will tell, it is highly probable many of the common attributes identified will reoccur in future cases. The characteristics enumerated here, in addition to the law enforcement profiles, provide a clearer definition of these criminals as a personality type. In this chapter, we will weave all the threads together to provide a portrait of a serial killer.

Family Dynamics

To begin understanding the nature of serial murderers, it is obvious we must look first to their family backgrounds. Parental influence has been written about for centuries. Unlike Athena in Greek mythology, human beings do not spring full-grown from the brow of their parent. We are the product of our heredity and the environment in which we live. Serial killers have parents who have commonalities.

Some things are obvious as common denominators among the parents of these individuals. The parents tended to be second- or third-generation descendants of European immigrants. They possessed a strong work ethic and a conservative value system. Each generation of parents attempted to better themselves and the lives of their children. The parents were willing to work long hours pursuing their goals.

Like many people of their generation and ethnic backgrounds, the parents of the serial killers seemed to have been politically conservative and personally private. That may be attributed to the fact they often worked long, hard hours and did not have much time or energy for outside social activities at the end of the day. They also tended to be financially frugal, saving their money or investing it in homes and property. Those were not the families of impoverished ne'er-do-wells. They were lower middle-class people struggling to climb the social ladder.

It was not unusual to find both parents working outside the home. However, that was not the norm in the 1950s to 1960s. Women had flooded the workplace during World War II, but most of the mothers returned home at the end of the war. The couples studied here needed both people working to get ahead.

In most of the families, one partner in the marriage was dominant. The struggle for dominance is a traditional factor in Western marriages. Rightly or wrongly, the male is usually the primary decision maker. However, with few exceptions, such as the Gacy family, the dominant partner in the marriages of the serial murderers' parents was the female.

Each of the families in question was under some sort of stress. Sometimes the stress was financial, as in the case of the Bianchis, but more often it was emotional or health related. Among the mothers, the stressors included divorce, unwed motherhood, inability to have children, or becoming pregnant late in the childbearing years. The fathers experienced divorce, becoming a widower, becoming a father late in life, and alcoholism. Those misfortunes would affect the attitude of the dominant parent toward the child, with that parent being overprotective.

Most of the parents who were divorced or widowed remarried. These days, remarried parents attempt to create a new family unit from the two broken families. Discipline is a shared responsibility. However, in the era when our subjects grew up, the birth parent retained the responsibility for discipline. That tradition created an even greater confusion about parental roles. The disciplining of the children was a major issue in every case.

The predominant religion in each family was Catholicism. Often the child attended Catholic schools or had Catholic teachers at public school. While millions of children of Catholic families have no problems with the church's teachings, a youngster who has negative personality issues can be affected. The faith's strong emphasis on individual responsibility for one's actions often left a heavy burden of confusion on the growing child. The church expectations were far higher than this child could achieve, leading to poor self-esteem. The use of confession, especially on the young, and the emphasis on guilt on the psyche of an angry youth could lead to acting out aggressively. That religious confusion would give rise to feelings of inadequacy, which would interact with his personal identity problems later in life.

Unhealthy Bonding

Research in psychology and medicine indicates the bonding between an infant and its parents in the first few months of life is extremely critical. Those contacts and relationships will largely determine what the child's personality will be like as an adult.

For the serial murderers, an imbalance existed between the roles of the two parents, with the mother usually being dominant and overprotective. The almost smothering attention usually focused on the health of the infant. Normal childhood ailments took on cataclysmic importance. As a result, additional tension was created between the parents, which the child inevitably sensed.

Frequent trips to the doctor and great amounts of medical attention resulted from the health obsession. Additional financial stress occurred. Eventually, one parent developed considerable cynicism and sometimes a negative attitude toward the child.

Another byproduct of the inordinate attention to health issues was a child who, early in life, developed an excessive concern with bodily functions and self-image. The intense focus created a significant type of manipulative behavior. The child discovered his parents could be influenced by the raising of health issues. One parent was played against the other to gain attention and to avoid discipline. The dominant parent usually prevailed, thereby creating a reservoir of distaste by the subordinate parent for the child and contempt by the child for that parent, as in the case of Ted Bundy. The key personality trait of manipulation continued throughout life, producing trauma and inevitable pain for all involved.

A negative relationship was also created between the dominant parent and a series of physicians. To prevail, the manipulative child periodically had to prove the doctor wrong when the physician said no ailment was apparent. Over time, the primary parent became cynical about medical care and convinced only she knew what was best for her child. Feigned ailments are common among serial killers, both as children and adults.

Another aspect of the complex intrafamilial structure was a relentless search for parental approval. That approval proved forever out of reach. The problem centered on the parent being overinvolved in the child's life and, therefore, having expectations outside the bounds of reality. As a result, the child, who was expected to be perfect, was not capable of performing up to the level of his parents' demands.

Over time, the dominant parent became an object of dislike, contempt, and finally hatred. An increasing need to assert independence was usually met with a tightening of the apron strings. The growing child inevitably came to feel like a kitten in a cardboard box. Enormous energy was expended attempting to escape, only to be placed back in the box time after time.

Social Services

In a few cases, early contact with some social services agency caused problems. The interaction was usually initiated by neighbors concerned about child abuse or neglect, or by attending physicians frustrated by unsuccessful experiences with the family unit. None of those children was ever removed from the home or placed in an institution. Physical child abuse was not usually an issue, but unwanted intrusion was. The resultant hostility toward "outsiders" became a fact of life early on. It is impossible to discount this as a contributing factor to a generally antiauthoritarian attitude.

The social services agency invariably recommended the entire family unit seek mental health counseling. That was always rejected. The attitude was partially influenced by the traditional belief in taking care of one's own family and solving one's own problems. The other side of the situation was the prevailing social attitude in the 1950s and 1960s concerning the use of psychiatrists. A person did not go to a psychiatrist unless the conclusion had already been reached that he or she was crazy.

Solitary Childhood

Even before kindergarten, the child became aware he and his family were "different." That led to the early formation of a loner attitude and a poor self-image. Other problems inevitably resulted, such as solitary or aggressive play habits and an inappropriate fixation on adult companions. The future serial murderer did not seem to have been the type of child who had a best friend or even close friends. It is probable he filled his life with fantasy companions. Fantasy would also be an important component in his future crimes.

Although it does not seem siblings were a matter of major concern in the criminal lives of serial killers, at the same time we are reluctant to simply dismiss them out of hand. This is an area where biographical research is woefully inadequate. However, as with any small child, the arrival of younger brothers and sisters creates resentment and competition for parental time and attention. His role as the center of attention is usurped, and he is on his own. His questions have not been answered, and he feels unprepared to deal with the world. Again, he feels alone.

Late in the preteen and early teen years, attempts were made to encourage the child into more sociable activities. Ironically, those attempts were usually made by the submissive parent. Several serial killers were Boy Scouts, had newspaper routes, or did odd jobs around the neighborhood. Yet even here, no significant friendships with other boys developed. Underneath the trappings of those activities, the child remained lonely, unhappy, manipulative, and frightened. The pattern of outward sociability balanced by internal insecurity followed the individual throughout his life.

Early Problems

Serial killers exhibit early problems, providing warning signs for predicting future criminal behavior. Because of the lack of analyses about serial killers, we have used comparison studies involving similar criminal groups. Studies of mass murderers, which we consider applicable to serial killers, indicate an early pattern of animal torturing and killing. Neighborhood or family pets were tortured, mutilated, and killed. The lack of positive nurturing in infancy is manifested in the child's inability to nurture or, indeed, to tolerate the needs of other living beings. Cruelty toward defenseless creatures is very possibly the earliest warning sign in the development of violent aggression.

Some other aspects of the mass murderer studies also may be relevant to serial killers. Bedwetting and arson are common characteristics. Some serial murderers have admitted to childhood incidents of bedwetting. No biographical research exists to address the question of whether they were arsonists. We can only hope future research in this area will be comprehensive and exhaustive. The key to solving any problem is to have as much information available as possible. Even those things that appear on first examination to be irrelevant may, in fact, hold the answer.

Parents know virtually all children experiment with petty theft. Most children are caught, punished, and never steal again. Sometime between the ages of five and fifteen, all the serial killers we have studied became petty thieves. They did not stop even if caught. Those thefts were rarely significant in monetary value but were important in understanding the overall pattern of behavior. We have avoided using labeling terms such as psychopath in our analyses. However, one of the things these individuals seem to have in common with the classic definition of a psychopath is they do not learn from punishment.

Various kinds of theft become an integral aspect of their behavior throughout their lives. Even while committing brutal and heinous murders, these offenders are also petty thieves. While that may seem inconsequential, moral philosophers have often described murder as the ultimate theft.

The dominant aspect of any American childhood is school. As students, these individuals tend to be indifferent and inattentive. That is not to say they are not bright. Often IQ tests indicate they are quite intelligent. The lack of an adequate attention span, an almost instinctive rebellion against authority, lack of fear of discipline, and the stresses of an unstable home life lessened their chances of being good students. We will be discussing some biochemical causes for these behaviors in the next chapter.

Awareness of Sexuality

Years before puberty, these individuals have a much greater awareness of human sexuality and their personal sexuality than normal children. That awareness may come in part because of the early, almost morbid, interest by the parents in health and bodily functions.

The children's awareness of sex did not indicate sexual sophistication. Quite the contrary, their ignorance concerning the basic truths about sex often left them confused and unhappy. Sexual knowledge and information came from the street. Often, their parents were no more knowledgeable than the children themselves. Because the children had no close friends, they had no one with whom to talk about the matter. Since most of those individuals were the oldest child or only children, they did not have older siblings to advise them, either.

No pattern of overt sexual activity as preteens existed, however. On the other hand, certain isolated incidents were worthy of note. As a child, John Gacy was caught "playing doctor," was sexually molested by a friend of his father's, and was masturbated by an older, mentally challenged girl who lived in his neighborhood. Ted Bundy deeply resented his stepfather, because he perceived his mother's repeated pregnancies as painful. He did not understand where babies came from but sensed it was Johnny Bundy's fault.

It is interesting to note the early connection between sex and pain. Many people have a similar unconscious connection. Fortunately, few go the next step and establish a correlation between pain and sexual gratification.

Medical and social researchers have long been aware the teen years for a human male are extraordinarily difficult. The biological changes are far more rapid than the emotional growth leading to maturity. One powerful indicator of that difficulty is the extremely high rate of suicide among adolescent males. The biological disruption of puberty added another burden to those already troubled youths. Those lonely, confused, hostile, young men now lost their last sole anchor—being mamma's little boy.

The transition from boy to man in our society is not celebrated with the rites of passage our "less civilized" forebearers used to denote manhood. One major criticism by anthropologists about Western civilization is the confusion over when a boy becomes a man. One moment, as if he were a child, he is being told to clean up his room, and the next he is an adult who is given the car for a weekend date. That ambiguity, when coupled with the twisted self-image of the individuals discussed here, inevitably led to greater problems.

The identity problem was not eased as they grew older. A lack of healthy male bonding, too much time spent alone, and the general sense of inferiority from which the individuals suffered continued to separate them from healthy relationships. They were never outstanding athletes or scholars. Most of their relationships continued to be with older people, even though the role of the dominant parent had now begun to recede.

In most of the cases we have studied, the moderating influence of the male parent was gone by the middle teen years. The male parent may have died, gotten divorced, simply left, or given up. In any case, the family arena now had two combatants—mother and son.

One final note about sexuality. There are numerous cases of homosexual serial killers: John Gacy, Henley and Corll in Texas, and others. It appears they also have the powerful attraction to the female parent. That attraction is complicated even further by a rage toward the male parent and a sexual attraction toward other males.

Few documented cases of any magnitude involve female serial killers in the United States. Thus, it is impossible to calculate the influence of female sexuality on homicidal behavior.

Mother and Son Relationship

The change in that relationship, in our opinion, is critical to an understanding of these individuals, their lives, and their crimes. The pivotal point comes in the middle teen years and revolves around the changes in their relationship with their mothers. The mothers had been the dominant presence in the children's lives, whether the women themselves were dominant or submissive. Their impact was most keenly felt in the family structure. The fathers were more remote, and their primary role was outside the home. The fathers were seldom the family disciplinarians.

The mother of a serial killer is perceived by her murderous son as a "whore/goddess." Mother as a goddess is the first source of love, food, and nurturing that the infant encounters. She is the giver of all things, the ultimate expert on what is best for the child, and the person whose approval is most sought in the early years. In these families, this role is even more pronounced. When the mother is the dominant parent, her word is final in all decisions, whether involving health, peer relationships, school attendance, or self-image for the child. When she is submissive, as in Gacy's case, she is still the ultimate protector from the abusive father, the soother of tears and fears.

As the child enters the teen years, he begins to see the family situation in a different light. The overattentive motherly love begins to stifle his growing sense of independence. However, attempts to separate from her influence are met with resistance and, probably, the implied threat of loss of love and approval. Since the child has an unstable self-image, this desire to develop himself becomes confused with self-doubt about his abilities to function on his own.

By this time in his life, our future serial killer is thoroughly enmeshed in the following syndrome. He, the young adult, wants to assert his freedom and independence. Because of the pattern established from early childhood, however, he also has a poor self-image and desperately needs the reinforcement coming from his mother. She, on the other hand, is now in the position of saying the price of love is the loss of freedom. This inevitably leads to a situation where he cannot escape, finally resents, eventually hates, and never resolves his feelings for his mother.

The whore aspect develops when the child realizes his mother is human. To him, the goddess is perfect and, since she has wanted him to be perfect, he has tried so very hard to please her. To discover the goddess has flaws shakes the basis of his universe. If she is imperfect, then he, who has never been able to meet her standards, must be very imperfect indeed. To his unsophisticated sexuality, if she is not a goddess, then she must be a whore who has deceived him for years. Once that transformation from goddess to whore begins, it moves inexorably and includes all women.

It is no coincidence this change in attitude toward his mother occurs simultaneously with an increasing interest in pornography. For our purposes, we are not talking about Playboy, Penthouse, and the so-called "men's magazines." Rather, the concern here is hard-core pornography: bondage, sadomasochism, and the darkest aspects of human sexuality.

That interest in pornography is lifelong. It apparently fills the need for sexual stimulation and information. Although the murderers are obviously reluctant to speak about it, we conjecture these individuals are also frequent masturbators. In several cases, an interest in women's lingerie is also seen. When found out and punished by the dominant parent for this behavior, they do not stop.

Relationships with Women

The whore/goddess syndrome carries over into the man's attempts at dating. Since he had lost his original goddess, his mother, he sought a new one. Often it was a virginal female who was his ideal of what an innocent woman should be. Continual disappointment resulted when the man discovered that his ideal woman had flaws because she, too, was human. At the same time, he was not averse to having sex with the "whores" in high school, but he would never marry one of them.

When he married, he carried that attitude with him. The man's self-image told him he was unlovable. But the man sought a virginal woman to love and marry. When he found such a woman and married, or at least had sex while dating, the woman no longer was a goddess. A goddess would not have loved him, because he was so flawed and imperfect. Therefore, the woman was a whore. If she was a whore, she could not be trusted and eventually must be rejected. Also, the more he thought of the woman as a whore, the less sexually attractive she was. Sexual interest waned, and he moved on to others. Thus, the man was never monogamous in a relationship but demanded absolute fidelity in his partners.

His habits continued to be secretive and irregular. Inevitably, his actions would further strain the marriage or relationships. The serial murderer lied, manipulated constantly, threatened, intimidated, coerced, and abused. Everything in the relationship had to go his way and, to guarantee that, he made and enforced the rules. Failure to comply would bring a swift response.

Feminists may say this is the traditional male behavior pattern in Western civilization. That may be true to an extent. The serial murderers' need to control their environment, however, goes far beyond that of even the most aggressive of traditional chauvinists. This is not attitude or philosophy of life; this is pathology. Part of this mode of behavior is obviously predicated on the fact these individuals by their very nature are unable to trust or love anyone.

Personal Characteristics

Another facet entered during the teenage years: ambition and big dreams. That ambition manifested itself in three forms: political, financial, and/or social. It was also related to the desire for power over others. Yet those youthful dreams never materialized. The killers' chronic inability to follow through on even the simplest of plans always brought the men down. As adults, the men had one exception: the ability to plan and carry out murder. That they did very well.

One of the most striking aspects of their personal characteristics is their unusual sleep patterns. As a group, serial killers often have erratic and very limited sleep patterns. A few hours around dawn usually suffices. The hours when most people are sleeping are taken up by restless movement. Prowling the streets, driving for hours, they move through the night like nocturnal hunters.

These individuals appear to possess a higher degree of energy than the average person. That is also reflected in the fact that, when employed, it is quite common for them to have multiple jobs. Later in their lives as the criminal behavior emerges, the work aspect diminishes in importance. Their time and energy are taken up by the hunt for victims.

Despite all this movement and the inevitable contact with others, they continue to be solitary, almost reclusive, individuals by nature. They exhibit an apparent lack of new emotional relationships once they become adults.

They may enter new relationships, but these are more likely to be part of their overall masquerade of normalcy than sincere commitments to other people. We agree with some recent research that indicates people of this type do, indeed, have the ability to form emotional relationships. However, we see this ability as limited in extent and as occurring and ending in early life.

Significant relationships with these individuals are difficult to the point of impossibility because of their totally rigid way of dealing with life. Nothing is ever their fault. They portray themselves as eternal victims, striving nobly against overwhelming odds. They see conspiracies against their success everywhere they turn. They fail through no fault of their own, but rather because of being abused by a malevolent universe.

This is another of the grandiose ideas that are a hallmark of these serial killers. It takes as much ego to think that you have been singled out by the universe as it does to think that you rule the universe.

The inability to carry out long-term planning is also shown in their attempts at higher education. They will usually succeed in gaining admission to some institution of higher learning, sometimes even to the level of law school, as with Ted Bundy. A favorite subject is psychology. This discipline fascinates them as it allows them to spend endless hours studying their favorite subject, themselves. It also seems to provide them with an opportunity to intellectually excuse their behavior. It provides supporting evidence for their belief in a person being controlled by fate and not by his own actions. On the other hand, like a big game hunter reading up on lions, psychology gives them an opportunity to study their quarry.

They never seem, however, to succeed in completing academic programs. After at most two years of school, they drop out. They do not lack intelligence or ability but are incapable of disciplining themselves and following through to completion.

Self-discipline is an interesting issue in analyzing serial murderers. On the face of it, they appear to be very disciplined individuals. Yet their impulse control is minimal to the point of nonexistent in many settings. All are capable of towering rages at the slightest provocations. Their daily activities may conceal this rage, but the brutality of their crimes is ample evidence of its existence.

Hunger for Power

In virtually all serial murder cases, the killers have a strong interest in police, law enforcement, and authority figures. Police and soldiers, because they carry the power of life and death with them, are subconsciously seen by most of the murderers as the ultimate power figures.

Much has been made of the fact that mass murderers like Charles Whitman and infamous assassins like Lee Harvey Oswald learned their skills in the military. Yet none of these serial murderers has a history of military service and, indeed, they lack the rudiments of patriotism. Even John Gacy with his Fourth of July parties seemed to be carrying out a part of his personal charade rather than demonstrating a sincere love of country. There is no evidence that these individuals even apply for military service. Despite their fascination with law enforcement, they seem to be reluctant to face the discipline, structure, and control that military service requires.

Their fascination with law enforcement is detectable in another area of their lives. As a group, serial murderers tend to be avid television watchers, and their preference goes to police stories, such as *Baretta, Serpico,* and *Starsky and Hutch.* They are fascinated by portrayals of the rogue cop out on the street, making and enforcing his own laws. This image has many aspects they find attractive. These television police officers are individuals who prowl the night, searching for "Evil," who fight alone, rely on no one, and make up the rules as they go along. Avid thrill seekers that they are, serial killers are gratified by the high drama portrayed on television. Car chases, shootouts, and such fare fend off the boredom and monotony of their everyday lives.

While rejecting authority for themselves, the killers are determined to impose it on others. In most cases, they pretend either to be police officers or to project a law enforcement image in order to lure their victims to their deaths. Bundy, Gacy, and Buono/Bianchi each had a badge and other police paraphernalia and routinely impersonated police officers. This is a facet of the same hunger for power over others that is at the bottom of most of their behavior. They are obsessed with control. That obsession is nothing more than a mirror image of their feeling they are powerless and their lives are out of control.

The knowledge gained from their interest in law enforcement has a significant byproduct. These criminals are difficult to catch. With the knowledge of police techniques they obtain, these killers can anticipate law enforcement agencies and stay ahead of them. The most interesting case of this is Ted Bundy, who worked for the Seattle/King County Crime Commission studying rapists and murderers. What he learned no doubt allowed him to elude authorities while committing the thirty-some murders for which he is thought responsible.

Demand for Stimulation

One of the universal items we have discovered about the serial killers is the incessant demand for stimulation. Rich, complicated fantasy lives require constant input. The short attention span and lack of self-discipline we have discussed above, combined with a hunger for ever greater stimulus, are some of the center posts of the serial killers' nature.

One response to boredom is the use of drugs and alcohol. At some point, usually in their early twenties, most serial killers we have examined begin to use either alcohol or drugs in some form. Their abuse tends to accelerate, but given the secretive nature of these individuals, it is usually not detected. We are not implying these individuals become addicted to hard narcotics. That is not the case. What we have seen, however, is a repeated pattern of low-grade chemical dependency, usually in the form of barbiturates, marijuana, and alcohol.

Like most young adults, the individuals we studied have a pattern of increasing separation and distancing from their parents. This is nothing unusual or extraordinary on its face. Yet we also note these are individuals who, as a group, had a dependency on or hostility toward their parents far more extreme than the norm. When they arrive at a point where they can distance themselves, the actual pattern of crime begins shortly thereafter.

First Kills and Invisibility

The killers at the time of their first crimes have usually come into what passes for maturity for these individuals. Most of the time, the men will be stabilized in a job and not transients as such. Much has been made over the years about transient killers, and certainly, most serial killers are highly mobile within their community. Yet they are not transients.

One of the ways serial killers may cover their trails is to become what some have called "invisible men." Using their manipulative skills, they will create dramatically different impressions, even among a closely knit group of coworkers. They will also have multiple jobs, change jobs often, or be self-employed. This is consistent with the solitary pattern in that individuals in our society have more contact with others through work and the workplace than any other aspect of life. Serial killers do not stay long in jobs, therefore they make no close friends and reveal their true selves to no one.

This is the major reason why these murderers are so difficult to apprehend. They look and act on the surface like ordinary human beings. They hold jobs, live in nice surroundings, and look neatly groomed. They often join some publicly recognized group, such as a political party or civic organization. Also, serial killers tend to be highly articulate and extremely manipulative. They are the neighbor next door. They can leave a trail of false and mistaken impressions about themselves with almost everyone they meet.

Their habits do not usually change significantly after they begin killing. Virtually nothing in their outward behavior would indicate to the friends and family of such individuals that they are committing repeated murders. Part of this is attributable to the fact they have solitary habits and no close friends, and they make a practice of being dishonest and secretive in all their relationships.

Their night habits continue to be extremely unsettled. Night roving, prowling, and sometimes window peeking are seen repeatedly. They are often cruising the streets until the wee hours of the morning. Personal vehicles loaded down with police apparatus and radios and a thorough knowledge of law enforcement procedures allow them to stay one step ahead of the authorities. It is interesting to note the group that most avidly reads new information, theories, and textbooks on law enforcement is not law enforcement personnel but criminals.

Sometime between the ages of twenty-five and thirtyfive, the pattern of homicides begins. They have usually passed through a series of increasingly violent steps toward the act of murder. They often stalked potential victims on the street and peeked in windows at random. That led to stalking plus an actual, but harmless, approach to a potential victim. Next might be following the person home on the sidewalk and then walking on by as the person entered his or her house. Later, a victim's dwelling is entered, and the victim raped in the faceless dark. Finally, a victim is killed. Those few who have spoken openly about their crimes usually say something to the effect that the first killing was an accident, a mistake, or self-defense.

However, this does not end the process, for once the killings start, they tend to increase in frequency and brutality. The sense of power obtained by playing god with the life and death of the victim becomes boring. A new thrill must be added. The violence used in killing the victims becomes ever greater and more bizarre. Here enters the never-ending variety of ways to take the life of another human being.

The previous chapters detailed the specific techniques each developed. What we have done in this chapter is to portray the general background of serial killers to put them into context with the rest of society. Each step of their lives brings them closer to the point of murder. Yet they do not exist in a vacuum. They act on the lives of others and vice versa. As we said in the first chapter, serial killers may not consider themselves members *of* society, but, absolutely, they are *in* society.

Predicting Violence

We have attempted to identify things that can allow society to predict, with some reasonable degree of accuracy, the potential for this type of violence. The similarities we have uncovered taken individually are neither unusual nor extraordinary. However, when all the factors come into play and the individuals at the center of this storm are finally triggered, a bloodbath ensues.

It should be remembered that portions of the descriptions we have just given about serial murderers will also fit thousands of honest and law-abiding, if somewhat eccentric and unhappy, citizens. Many people have in their backgrounds being unloved or overprotected children, shattered homes, physical brutality, alcoholic parents, manipulative parents, and an introduction to violence at an early age. Many people are addicted to drugs and pornography. Many people have unusual sleep, movement, and employment histories. They are not serial killers.

Our descriptions of family and personal characteristics, however, are part of the makeup of serial murderers. We must determine what are the added ingredients that produce a killer.

Tempting though it is to follow the traditional moral attitudes toward crime and criminals, we are left with an incomplete picture in these cases. In singular murders, something happens to take a human being across the line once to kill another person. Something else causes him to stay across the line and repeat his crime without guilt or remorse. Yet these are not madmen no matter how much defense attorneys would like to portray them as such. The factors that can predict homicide and serial homicide are beginning to be understood.

The greatest of unanswered questions remains: What happens in the minds and spirits of these individuals to make them breach that invisible line into the realm of multiple murder? In the next chapter, we will offer some theories about that leap.

Born to Kill?

Mass murderer Richard Speck had a tattoo on his arm that said, "Born to raise hell." Perhaps, more appropriately, it should have said, "Born to kill."

The question of how the mind and body are interrelated has been around for years. As a corollary, mankind has searched for answers as to what makes a person a criminal. Ironically, early ideas of people being "born" to be criminals because of "bad blood" may not have been too far afield.

Connections between Body and Emotions

The search for the areas of the brain controlling bodily functions and emotions has long intrigued humans. The ancient Greeks believed the heart was the center of the intellect and the liver the center of emotions. In the late fifteenth century, Leonardo da Vinci speculated about functions of the various parts of the brain. Over 100 years later, Rene Descartes claimed the mind was bound to the body through a specialized brain structure that was truly the seat of passions, not the heart.

Phrenology, first proposed by Franz Joseph Gall and expanded by Johan Kasper Spurzheim in 1800, concluded that the lumps on the skull corresponded to the brain shape, which likewise was molded by moral and intellectual faculties in the different brain areas. The size and shape of a certain lump indicated the strength or weakness of a given moral value.

The idea that the brain contained electrical impulses first appeared in 1780. Expanded in the 1800s, the concept led to relating behavioral responses with changes in the neurochemical activity at certain sites in the brain. If one could alter the brain neurochemical changes, through drugs or physical means, one could modify behavior.

When Darwin published his theory of evolution in 1859, his ideas were extended into the social sciences almost immediately. The bestial behavior of some criminals was said to be remnants of primitive man still reproducing in a modern age. Cesare Lombroso, an Italian physician, spent the last quarter of the nineteenth century studying convicts and asylum inmates, looking for a "criminal" body physique. He believed certain people were born morally and physically primitive. His followers tried to differentiate people into criminal or noncriminal type by their appearance. Lombroso felt such "criminaloids" varied in their tendency to commit crime from nonexistent to irresistible urges.

Lombroso's work was the basis for the "reformatory movement" in penology. He felt crime often was caused by bad biology or society, not just from malicious intent. His idea challenged the classic doctrine of the free but "guilty mind." If crime was caused rather than freely committed, then punishment was not deserved. Rehabilitation was the group's goal. The concept led to the science of criminology, the search for the causes and effects of crime.

Other theories followed. In 1901, Charles Goring described the existence of criminal tendencies in everyone to some extent, more due to heredity than environment. Forty years later, E.A. Hooten found criminals and noncriminals differed physically, as did criminals convicted of different crimes. Hereditary inferiors naturally drifted to bad environments, and the weakest or worst of them surrendered to social stresses and committed crimes.

Hooten correctly predicted the biological explanation would not be popular for three reasons. First, Fascism was on the rise, with its lethal perversion of the study of human biology. Second, it was easier for people to accept sociological causes of crime because they felt those could be cured. Last, biological and psychological theories were new, making criminologists uneasy with them. Thus, sociology took over crime studies in the 1940s.

Also, in that decade, physiognomy, the study of facial features and expression as indicative of personal character, became popular. William Sheldon expanded the idea to include how physique correlated with behavioral traits, temperament, disease susceptibility, and life expectancy. His three "somatotypes" were standardized for men and rated on a seven-point scale. He felt physique did not cause crime but could be correlated with it.

One obvious difficulty in assessing heredity versus outside forces in developing criminals is the quality of measurements and study samples. Often, some of those early theorists were on the right path but lacked the technology to adequately measure or to assess their ideas.

Analyzing Heredity

The issue of how to utilize technology to study and support theories is still the case today, although genetic research is rapidly increasing. As has been stated, humans can create vast technologies but still do not understand the brain, the source of our existence and accomplishments.

Genetics is the branch of biology dealing with heredity. Of basic interest are chromosomes, rod-shaped bodies carrying genes. Genes contain the hereditary characters to determine such things as how a person will look and, as many believe, what basic personality he or she will have. Each human cell normally possesses forty-six chromosomes, both sex and non-sex chromosomes. Each person obtains some chromosomes from his mother and some from his father. In terms of sex chromosomes, males usually possess one X and one Y chromosome (XY) and females have two Xs (XX).

In the mid-1960s, research appeared concerning a possible linkage between abnormal sex chromosomes and criminal behavior. Polysomy Y (XYY) suddenly looked like the perfect answer to some causes of male crime. Early studies found the XYY syndrome was more common among individuals in prison for various crimes than in the general population. The condition was correlated with greater than average height, mental retardation, and occasional, unpredictable outbursts of extreme violence. Subsequently, it was found to occur at the rate of 1:700–1,000 live male births. However, its occurrence was more than fifteen times higher among prison inmates. Some researchers concluded the extra Y chromosome predisposed males toward aggression.

Later studies showed XYY males were not more likely to commit crimes of violence. Their crimes usually tended to be against property rather than against persons. The prevalent opinion now is that they are not as bright as some criminals and are more likely to be apprehended and incarcerated than normal XY male criminals. The brighter XYY criminals may not be detected as readily, so their numbers are unknown. Thus, the percentage of XYY males who are criminals versus those who are not criminals cannot be determined. The numbers present in institutions do not infer that XYY males truly commit more crimes than XY males.

Klinefelter's Syndrome (XXY) was also found to be more frequent in institutions than its 1:1,000 live male births would indicate. The XXY males have a somewhat higher crime rate than XY males, but less than XYYs. Also, with Klinefelter's Syndrome, the men tend to be taller, possess normal intelligence, but have some coordination impairment, delayed verbal skills, and short-term memory deficits.

It is important to remember that many individuals with sex chromosome abnormalities lead normal lives. Then there are the extreme exceptions. John Wayne Gacy Jr. has Klinefelter's Syndrome. He had an intelligence level in the very bright range, was a highly successful businessman, and was prominent in the community. However, Gacy was one of the leading serial murderers of his time in this country, creating one of the inconsistencies that upset attempts to predict human behavior from studies. The other serial murderers analyzed in this book do not appear to have been tested for chromosomal abnormalities. The results might have proved extremely interesting.

Genetics and Crime

Can a genetic predisposition to commit criminal acts be found? To try to determine the answer, many studies have been conducted on children adopted at a young age and, thus, raised away from the biologic parents. The goals were to see if crime or alcoholism was inherited. The results found a correlation between alcoholic biologic fathers passing down a tendency toward alcoholism to their sons. Less inheritance appeared in sons if only the biologic mothers were alcoholics. Little effect of either parent's alcoholism on the daughters was uncovered.

The studies found a smaller genetic correlation for criminality between parents and sons. If the biologic parents were both criminals and alcoholics, a significant number of sons had alcohol abuse only or criminality only, but no excess of both traits in the same individuals. A link between alcoholism and criminal acts appears due to the effects of alcohol on social behavior. For some studies, it was concluded a good home environment could reduce or eliminate any genetic inheritance for criminality.

To separate the impact of environment from heredity, adopted children are still being studied. Whether the children would show more traits of the adopted or biological parents became the focus. Several recent studies confirmed an adopted child whose biological parent was a criminal was more likely to commit property crimes. This was especially true for boys. Since other social and environmental factors varied in the research settings, the genetic link is possible, but other factors need to be better delimited before final conclusions are drawn.

Studies on twins have provided hints at a biological, as well a social, connection to criminology. For identical twins, if one twin engaged in criminal activity, the chance was fifty percent the second twin would also commit crimes. Also, identical twins had more delinquent peers than nonidentical twins. How much is social versus biological in cause has yet to be determined.

Other biochemistry topics possibly related to criminal propensity are under research. These include testosterone, Premenstrual Syndrome (PMS), the genetically linked and more severe Premenstrual Dysphoric Disorder (PMDD), postpartum depression, and neurotransmitters. Other study areas include diet, food allergies, sensitivities, vitamins, minerals, and environmental toxins. All have been associated to some extent with criminal activity.

So far, no specific gene has been identified as causing an individual personality trait. Yet personality traits seem to be inherited. Any mother can describe whether her baby is naturally a happy or a fussy baby. Perhaps the evidence will come as technology expands to unravel the mysteries contained in genetic coding. Researchers accept that the hereditary makeup a person possesses when he enters the world will be modified to some extent by the familial and societal setting in which the person is raised.

Brain Chemistry and Aggression

A closely related area has been the subject of intense scrutiny—the effects of brain chemistry on personality. While this is not a biochemistry textbook, it is necessary to say a few words about how the brain functions to understand the effects of body chemicals on aggression.

The brain operates by electrical and chemical processes. In response to some stimulus, electrical impulses are sent along the nerves. However, the brain is not one continuous nerve, but a series of nerves. When the electrical message reaches the end of one nerve, its message must be passed across a gap to the start of the next nerve. It is in this gap that neurotransmitters operate to convey information between cells. These transmitters are affected by drugs, alcohol, and some hereditary problems. In addition, neuromodulators in the gap area amplify or dampen the activity of neurotransmitters.

This complex process is one of the keys to understanding human behavior. What happens between these nerve endings has an enormous effect on nearly all bodily functions. However, the nerve endings and gaps are extremely small, and modern technology is in its infancy as far as being able to see what happens there. Much must be inferred from measuring the minute amounts of various chemicals present before and after various stimuli are applied and deducing the mechanics of how they appeared.

Three basic types of neurotransmitters exist: catecholamines (dopamine and norepinephrine), serotonin, and acetylcholine. Catecholamines have been implicated in aggression. Changes in the level or metabolism of serotonin also have been correlated to alterations in emotional behavior, especially aggression. Stimulation of certain brain structures with acetylcholine has produced aggressive or murderous behavior.

It is thought neurotransmitters share some functions. Thus, researchers cannot say one particular neurotransmitter causes aggression. Also, neurotransmitters are present throughout the body. Dopamine helps transmit impulses from the brain through the nervous system to the muscles. Serotonin is in the brain, the bloodstream, and elsewhere, such as in the retina of the eye. By measuring the amounts of certain chemicals in various parts of the body for many people, a normal level can be estimated. When more or less than normal is present, this can be studied to see if there is a correlation among differences in human behavior.

For example, serotonin is correlated with dominance relations in certain subhuman primates and in humans. The dominant primate males tend to have more present. In humans, serotonin levels found in whole blood tend to be elevated in power-oriented people. These are not just people who happen to be natural leaders, but persons who are very hard-driving, competitive, impatient, aggressive, distrustful, and confident. It would be interesting to have been able to measure Napoleon or Hitler for his serotonin levels. Also, people placed in a position of power in stressful conditions, such as military officers in combat, have a rise in serotonin during the stress period, then a falling back to near normal levels afterward.

These same brain chemicals and genetic problems are intertwined with other personality and body traits. Brain chemistry is involved with schizophrenia and manic depression, which may both be inherited. Foods affect neurotransmitter levels in the brain that regulate appetite. One cause of obesity and of bulimia, the eating disorder in which a person gorges on food and then vomits to empty the stomach, is low levels of serotonin. Anorexia nervosa, Cushing's disease, depression, and many of the mood changes associated with stress, the menstrual cycle, and pregnancy are related to the effects of steroids on nerve cells in the brain. Even too much of a sweet thing known as aspartame, commonly found in some artificial sweeteners, can raise certain brain chemicals involved in mood and behavior.

Brains and Behavior

The brain structure and function can impact human behavior. New studies comparing the brains of violent offenders with those of other people show differences in both structure and function. Small sample sizes, however, have limited how many generalized conclusions can be drawn. Early and chronic exposure to stress such as abuse, neglect, and violence may produce brain physiological alterations affecting how people respond to stress. If the exposures are prolonged, the person may be less sensitive to cortisol, the brain hormone created to respond to stress. Cortisol levels should lower after the stressor is gone, but continued high levels can produce aggression.

Within the body, these brain chemistry irregularities can come from two major sources: internal, inherited problems or externally induced through foods eaten, drugs ingested, or injuries to certain brain areas. The inherited genetic abnormalities are somewhat beyond our power to alter at the present time. It can be argued that the diet and health care received by a pregnant woman can enhance a baby's chance for a normally functioning body at birth. However, other factors affecting random genetic alterations are not fully understood.

External factors can be more readily controlled. Just by

changing the diet to include more nutrients at one large juvenile detention facility, violence was lessened by fifty percent in one study. As many as six million American children suffer from depression, which is often linked to aggression. Poor diet and various drugs from aspartame to cocaine can aggravate the condition. Although not totally preventable, accidents, especially head injuries, can alter an individual's personality and aggression levels.

Aggression

What is aggression? Aggression is forceful, attacking behavior. It can be either self-assertive and self-protective in defensive situations or destructively hostile to others or to oneself. Violence is intense, destructive force used to injure, damage, or destroy. All living creatures can show aggression under the right conditions. However, few besides humans show violence toward their own species.

Two main types of aggression are defined: affective and predatory. Affective, or emotional, aggression includes such displays as irritability, intermale aggression, territoriality, and maternal reactions. It activates the autonomic nervous system, which involves heart rate, pulse, breathing rate, and skin sweat, and has certain associated threatening and defensive postures. Used against one's own species, it is a response to external or internal threatening situations. Predatory aggression is usually against other species. The animal exhibits little autonomic arousal and often concentrates on the prey so intently that other sensory input goes unnoticed. Aggression can cover a wide range of acts. What one person would regard as aggressive behavior would not be so designated by another.

In discussing aggression and criminal behavior, it is important to remember the men discussed in this book are the worst of the worst modern murderers. They committed the most killings, got away with them the longest, and showed no remorse for their actions. These are the subjects in greatest need of research into their activities and into what makes them tick before preventive steps can be contemplated. To do so, emotional reactions to their crimes must be set aside and the men themselves be studied objectively.

Brain chemicals are involved in aggression, but their role is unclear. Decreased serotonin levels have been correlated with aggressive situations. Suicide victims and patients who made violent suicide attempts were found to have lower levels of serotonin in their brain stems. However, it is not clear whether the lower readings were the cause of the aggression or a resulting byproduct. High levels of enzymes that produce catecholamines are predictive of high levels of aggression. Certain externally administered drugs can increase aggressive behavior. Several neuroregulators are involved in the initiation and carrying out of aggressive behavior. No one regulator has been found to be the sole cause for any specific type of aggression. It is a shared duty to be sorted out through future research.

The reader may wonder why little has been said about female criminals. The reason is simple. They occur in such small statistical percentages when compared to the general female population that very few studies have been done about their criminal tendencies. Low serotonin levels, known to be involved in aggression, are strongly suspected of being the cause of Premenstrual Syndrome (PMS). Around forty-four percent of females incarcerated for crimes commit those crimes in the week before or the week of their menstrual cycle. This is the time when the PMS symptoms are at their peak. Further research is needed in this area.

It has been postulated that females have a higher "boiling point," a higher threshold level they must reach before they become aggressive. Some indications show, with the general change in sex roles and male-female stereotypes, women are becoming less inhibited about responding aggressively when provoked. This would be good in the sense of women protecting themselves when they are potential victims. In 2019, however, women committed about seventeen percent of all US serial murders. Their rise as perpetrators of crime would be a negative result of the "sexual revolution."

It should be noted that aggression and criminality are not the same thing. A person can be aggressive without being a criminal. On the other hand, most criminals are aggressive. Society is concerned with aggression because it can lead to criminal behavior.

Predicting Criminal Behavior

If criminality is at least partially genetically determined, what are the implications for predicting those "born to kill"? If a specific gene or set of genes were identified as leading to criminal behavior, how would society react? Currently, ten percent of the criminals commit at least fifty percent of the crimes. If those repeat offenders were biologically predisposed to a life of crime, then dealing with those few individuals would dramatically lessen the crime problem. The results could be manipulated by those in power for good or for evil.

In some ways, that situation is already happening. Individual genes for specific physical abnormalities, such as Down Syndrome, have been identified. If we assume gene mapping will ultimately identify a criminal gene or genes, the negative side is apparent. Pregnant women in families with one or two generations of criminals might be required to undergo abortions or be sterilized. Society then could eliminate the problem at the start. If a child were born to such a family, he would face stigmatization from neighbors, school personnel, and peers. That could lead to the quandary about whether the child would naturally become a criminal, or just fulfill the social prophecy and pressures due to categorizing him as born with "bad genes." The circle would be complete to earlier times when the good guys in the movies commented that Billy had to become an outlaw because there was bad blood in his family.

On the positive side, those few who might become criminals could be headed off at the pass. Gene altering in vitro is a distinct possibility. Already fetuses are being operated on for a variety of conditions, from hydrocephalus, or water on the brain, to correcting motherfetus Rh factor differences. It may be possible in the future to alter the genes for criminality in the womb to lessen or eliminate any predisposition toward criminality. Children born into "crime" families could be tested to see if the genes were present. If they were, the children and families could undergo counseling to build self-esteem and to head off aggressive behavior and other early signs of incorrect tendencies, such as compulsive lying and petty theft. The children could be taught methods for coping with anger and frustration to lessen the chances for violence later.

The field of genetics is here to stay and will obviously expand. It will be up to each society to decide how to regulate the potential results. Whose rules or conscience will be followed? The tremendous good or evil such studies can produce is at stake.

Society and Serial Murderers

How does society view these modern predators, the serial murderers? It has only been in the last few decades that the serial murder phenomenon has really caught the public's attention. While authorities vary on the number of serial killers operating in the United States each year, the number of victims continues to grow.

An enormous number of people are affected by the serial murderers, from victims to both the victims' and killers' families and friends. The United States leads the world in the number of serial killers, with California and Texas experiencing the highest number of victims. Yet, very little research beyond psychiatric reviews has been conducted on these men.

American society has always been the champion of the little man, struggling for upward mobility. It has been suggested multiple killers are "losers" who struggle to achieve social and economic goals. When they fail, they kill out of frustration. To compound this social struggle, the serial murderers come from a troubled background involving their illegitimacy, adoption, or institutionalization when young. Their murders help them achieve their ambition of a rapid rise in social recognition. These murderers are not insane; they are acting out a grudge.

That view is one opinion taken from one of the few books to even examine multiple murderers. A great deal more research is needed.

Addiction and Brain Chemistry

What causes a person to murder repeatedly? Can a person become addicted to crime, especially to murder? To explore this idea, we must look at the nature of addiction in a physiological aspect.

In a normally functioning brain, built-in systems maintain a balance between the punishment and the reward factors. Every reaction to stimuli involves both systems. For example, if we are startled, the punishment centers that act on dissatisfaction, frustration, and pain put us on alert. But the reward centers for satisfaction, gratification, and pleasure help us assess the level to which our systems should react. When the punishment sectors are irregular, we are not afraid enough. When the reward areas are not functioning properly, we overreact to a situation.

Complete override or destruction of either aspect leads to death. In experiments in which animals could press a lever to stimulate only the pleasure centers in their brain, they did so as much as 7,000 times per hour. The animals never felt satisfied, continuously stimulating themselves. Finally, they ignored food and water until they became exhausted and died.

Such is the basic effect of heavy doses of drugs, alcohol, and other addictive habits on the brain. They interfere with the biochemical processes to the detriment of the body. If we use cocaine as an example, we can see how it affects three major neurotransmitters: dopamine, serotonin, and norepinephrine. These three are also involved in depression. We must go back to the discussion of the brain's nerve endings for a moment.

When stimulated, one nerve ending releases one (or more) neurotransmitter, which fills the gap, stimulates the next nerve ending, and thus transmits the message down the line. When the stimulation ceases, the neurotransmitter is resorbed back into the first nerve ending where it is stored, ready for use the next time.

With cocaine and other drugs, the pleasure centers are overstimulated. The person feels euphoria, an overwhelming sense of well-being and physical comfort. However, over time as the body attempts to restore the brain chemical balance, the excess neurotransmitter is washed out of the body. The nerve endings are depleted of the substance, which leads to depression. Ultimately, the brain's normal survival drives of hunger, sleep, and sex urges are disrupted. Eventually, a variety of medical problems result.

Cocaine addicts are being treated with antidepressant medications. These block cocaine euphoria and reduce the craving for cocaine. As less cocaine is used, the brain begins to readjust to normal chemical levels.

This type of addiction involves the external ingestion of drugs and alcohol. Another type of addiction may be produced internally.

The brain naturally produces three categories of opioids: enkephalins, endorphins, and dynorphins. Enkephalins are the weakest of the three. Endorphins are naturally produced morphine. Dynorphins are among the most potent opioid peptides. The opioid peptides affect hormonal functions of the catecholamine neurotransmitters.

Since the first naturally produced opioids were isolated in 1975, studies have flourished on their analgesic, or painkilling, properties. It is known that the plasma concentrations of enkephalins and endorphins rise with exercise. While endorphins do not seem to have a major influence on the cardiovascular response to exercise, they do regulate breathing in high-intensity exercise. Also, all three affect pituitary hormone secretion at rest and during exercise.

Vigorous exercise produces a feeling of well-being. Chronic physical activity can reduce anxiety and depression and raise self-esteem. Some argue this is due to a "distraction" hypothesis, in which exercise diverts the person's attention from stressful stimuli. Another view is exercise raises the level of neurotransmitters in the brain, which makes a person feel good. The third theory is exercise releases endorphins that reduce the sensation of pain and produce euphoria.

Runner's high has been compared to the euphoria from drugs. Endorphins may be the cause of the altered states of consciousness some people experience during intense exercise, especially long-distance running. Both are functions of brain biochemistry, but the drug euphoria may be related to neurotransmitter levels, whereas the exercise high involves opioids. In either case, the person "feels good."

Obviously, people can become physically addicted to drugs and alcohol. It has been said people can become addicted to exercise. In either case, if the drug or exercise is not forthcoming after chronic availability, the person feels depressed. A physical dependence for exercise and its naturally released opiates has been demonstrated in mice, with addiction symptoms similar to morphine. Natural endorphins, like externally administered opiates, are highly addictive.

Proving the existence of runner's high in the laboratory has had mixed results. Anywhere from ten to seventy percent of long-distance runners say they have experienced the runner's euphoria. Psychosomatic techniques—giving people a placebo and telling them that they will feel good—will also increase endorphin levels. Like the runner's high, this placebo effect works on certain types of individuals.

Whatever the exact cause or the specific brain chemistry involved, the fact exists that certain people become addicted. A definition of addiction says if the stimulus is stopped, the individual will experience withdrawal symptoms. These include anxiety, restlessness, irritability, nervousness, guilt, muscle twitching, a bloated feeling, and sleep disturbance.

If people can become addicted to alcohol, drugs, or exercise, can they become addicted to other behaviors?

Addicted to Murder?

One reason people go to horror movies or ride frightening carnival rides is the "rush," the excitement they feel during and immediately afterward. This involves euphoria produced by brain biochemistry: the neurotransmitters and opiates. Whatever the technical biochemical process involved, the person himself feels great and that is the major concern.

Professional criminals describe the "rush" they feel when going through the procedures involved in their crimes. Thieves tell of the excitement when planning a burglary. Rapists and murderers feel an extreme stimulation in stalking their victims. To them, the chase and the look on the victims' faces are often more important for the euphoria they produce than the actual sexual encounter or murder of the victims.

If there is a genetic predisposition and/or a chemical imbalance which makes some people addictive personalities, then the possibility that people can become addicted to crime must not be overlooked.

It has already been shown alcoholism can be inherited. Extensive studies on children born to alcoholic parents from 1930 onward have been possible because alcoholism has been a societal problem for years. Therefore, the number of parents and children needed to form a statistically significant sample were available.

The same size group for two generations of drug abusers is only now appearing. The drug explosion of the 1960s provided the addicted parents who had children from the late 1970s and onward. Would it not be logical to assume there may be a predisposition toward various drug addictions besides alcohol? This theory could be tested using adoption studies similar to the ones for alcohol and criminality heritability.

As far as crime is concerned, once the initial thrill is felt with the individual's first crime, the feeling was found to be pleasurable. It was associated with the physical procedures involved in the crime—the planning, stalking, look on the victim's face, and so forth—and the new criminal would like to feel that good again.

Could not serial murder become addictive? Playing god with the life or death of a victim produces an incredible emotional surge. With any such intense emotions, the brain chemistry system becomes a factor. Murderers describe how they feel the urge to kill build up inside them when they are between victims. They tell of the incredible release and draining of emotions they experience after the act is completed. These are the same symptoms drug users or heavy exercisers express. Like the rogue tiger that first tastes human flesh, the serial murderer will not cease his killing until stopped by external factors, such as jail or death.

Murderers and Psychiatric Labels

Can anyone commit serial murder and be sane? This is the most frequently asked question about these killers. The answer for nearly all the cases is yes, they are sane. All the killers have what are commonly referred to as "personality disorders," but they do not meet the legal criteria for insanity. The insanity defense will be discussed shortly. As has been noted, these murderers do know the difference between right and wrong; they just don't give a damn.

This leads to our efforts in this book not to place a psychological label on these people: schizophrenic, psychotic, psychopathic, or so on. Even among those in the psychiatric profession, disagreement exists on how the terms should be defined, on what behaviors to include in a particular category, and how to diagnose people and place category labels on them. This is why psychiatric testimony in court cases seems so confusing; no one can agree on the name of the problem. Thus, we have tried to describe the serial murderers' behaviors and some of their thought processes without the biases created by psychiatric classifications.

It was also felt after beginning our research that these men were a rapidly expanding modern breed of killers who may not really fit the old definitions of psychiatric problems. They have aspects fitting parts of several disorders. Therefore, to avoid the confusions caused by bringing in several titles, we decided to explain these criminals to the reader by their actions alone.

For those who feel the need for a classification, such an attempt will be presented at this point. We again caution that titles can be misleading and often miss the nuances of individuals, their behaviors and thought processes.

The closest, single, psychiatric label that would define serial murderers is "psychopath." A psychopathic personality is a person whose behavior is often amoral and asocial. It is characterized by irresponsibility at home and work; a lack of remorse or shame for his actions; perverse, impulsive, often criminal behavior; and other serious personality defects. The psychopath is egocentric in the extreme; his wants and needs are of prime importance. He has a clear absence of emotion when he deals on an interpersonal level with other human beings. Yet he is often good at manipulating other people, at being charming when he chooses.

As early as 1835, a person displaying mania without mental defects was categorized as "morally insane." Lombroso described the condition as a variant of epilepsy. His daughter proposed that psychopaths "differed from ordinary people because they hated the very persons who to normal human beings are the nearest and dearest ... and because their inhuman deeds seemed to cause them no remorse." In this century, it has been called "psychic immaturity." A psychopath can be both charming and successful. He can be an impulsive, aggressive, emotionally isolated person with an extreme craving for excitement that is unrestrained by social norms or conscience.

This is a person capable of committing any crime he wants and not feeling a twinge of guilt—a totally emotionally cold person.

Physical Responses to Punishment

One interesting aspect of the psychopath is his slower-to-react autonomic nervous system. He does not exhibit fear in response to danger as a normal person would. His pulse rate, skin conductance, and so on is much lower. This is an important factor when lie detector tests, which depend on autonomic responses to distinguish truth from falsehood, are considered. A psychopath could easily pass a polygraph test.

This also explains why a psychopath does not learn from punishment. Punishment, whether verbal or physical, depends on the autonomic reaction to stress and pain to act on a person's conscience or fear systems to produce corrections in behavior.

If a person's reaction system is geared low, he does not fear the punishment and, thus, learns no lesson from it. If he does not fear punishment, then he feels no link between his actions and some reprisal in the future. The longer the time span between his actions and the societal recriminations, the harder it is for the psychopath to see any connection between them. He does not understand why he is being punished.

His low arousal system is the main factor in his attraction for emotionally stimulating situations. His cool nerves make him able to handle extremely intense emotions, especially anger, which another person could not tolerate. He loves adventure and thrills. The studies that have been conducted on psychopaths indicate this low arousal level is probably related to the levels of certain brain chemicals in their bodies.

Parental rejection and inconsistent punishment have been correlated with psychopathology. It is unclear whether a person predisposed to psychopathology is the cause of parental rejection or the psychopathology results from it. If a child's fear system is low, then the parents might try one type of punishment, get no results, then try a different type the next time. To the child, this would appear to be inconsistent discipline or rejection, when it could be just the parents trying to find some discipline system that works.

If such a child receives inconsistent punishment and rejection regularly, he becomes accustomed or desensitized to it. This could explain his lifelong tendency to commit acts that appear painful and ignore risks.

It has been found that persons diagnosed as psychopaths have other childhood similarities. Their parents have a history of discord, often with divorce, separation or death, and alcoholism. Violent people had poor rearing environments. Violence was an early, fixed pattern of interpersonal relationships. Also included are poor selfimage and depressive traits. The question remains of whether the psychopathology was caused by those situations or the children predisposed to it brought about some of the parental actions.

While not responding to punishment, a psychopath does respond somewhat to tangible rewards. He is a materialist. A study of imprisoned psychopaths found they responded as well as non-psychopaths to a loss of money as punishment.

In contrast to his low autonomic arousal, a psychopath is easily enraged. This is thought to be due to a chemical imbalance in the body.

Serial murderers seem to run counter to at least one conclusion about psychopaths. Studies showed that less intelligent psychopaths would commit more violent crimes as compared with intelligent psychopaths. Many of the tested serial murderers have normal or slightly above normal IQs, yet they commit very heinous crimes and many of them. Relatively few serial murderers have been studied on any psychological and biochemical aspects. This is an area of research that is desperately needed if we are to understand these criminals.

Physical Causes

Can a physical cause of psychopathology be found? Yes, a brain neurological defect in the language control center has been detected. Normally, a right-handed person's language center is in the left hemisphere of the brain. Studies suggest, in psychopaths, language is controlled equally between the right and left hemispheres. Thus, a psychopath can become extremely good at glibness and articulation, but he has no understanding of the emotional meaning of the words he uses. He can be charming and lie with equal ease.

Within the general population, from one to four percent of people are psychopaths, or about 1 in 300,000. A study from 2013 data ranked the forty-eight continental states and the District of Columbia by psychopathic personality traits. Washington, DC, had the most psychopaths, which tends to support the fact many psychopaths are not violent, but love power and controlling others. Males comprise at least eighty percent of all psychopaths.

What eighty years ago we considered the naivete of our forefathers may, in fact, have been correct. Researchers are again believe a psychopath is morally retarded. He appears to have the same psychological developmental stage of a preadolescent.

Also, evidence is present in violent or overly aggressive people of a temporal lobe dysfunction. Some studies have shown a significant correlation between electroencephalogram (EEG) abnormalities and such behavior. However, no distinct type of electrical irregularity is connected with violence.

Legal Definitions of Insanity

A psychopath is not insane. Traditional legal views held that the person who, at the time of trial, lacked the capacity to understand the proceedings and to assist in his own defense could not be tried for a crime. The person's criminal responsibility was not excused, but courts did recognize a person had a right to be present at his own trial. The legal definition was expanded later to cover new interpretations, including the role of psychopaths.

The American criminal justice system has four variations in declaring a person insane. First, the person who has a mental disability—does not know right from wrong or does not understand the nature of the act—at the time he committed the offense is considered insane. This is the M'Naghten test. It was expanded to a second version in some jurisdictions to include the "irresistible impulse" test. Third, the Durham test recognizes modern psychiatric knowledge. It states a person is not criminally responsible if his act was the product of a mental disease or defect, which goes beyond the right-wrong definition. Fourth, the Model Penal Code recognizes the person is not responsible for his actions if, as a result of mental disease or defect, he could not understand the wrongfulness of his act, or could not conform his conduct to meet the law. However, it sets provisions that psychopathic personalities, as repeat offenders or persons with antisocial conduct, do not meet the definition of "mental disease or defect." Psychopaths are, indeed, responsible for their conduct under legal guidelines.

As new research into the brain in conducted, can this requirement—that psychopaths are responsible for their actions—be upheld? Some people who have killed their victims have been found not guilty for medical reasons. These include people with certain forms of epilepsy producing psychotic episodes, tumors in various parts of the brain, or psychosis from a malfunction in the hypothyroid. Not all those found not guilty were set free; some were ordered to receive treatment in forensic psychiatric units or placed under strict probation with required medical treatment. However, these instances do represent cases where the criminal justice system recognizes organic medical problems that eliminate criminal responsibility for one's actions.

Serial Murderers and Punishment

Society wants revenge for a murder and has expected a perpetrator to be held personally accountable for his actions. Any attempt at an insanity plea, let alone a defense based on a biological excuse, is met with public indignation. Society can intellectually accept that such defenses exist but still feels someone must pay for the crime.

The question arises as to what punishment is appropriate for the serial murderer. If he has a genetic abnormality that leads to crime, is addicted to murder, or is a psychopath with a neurological malfunction, how responsible is he for his own actions in the face of his genetic or biological problems? This is not to say he should be set free with no payback to society. However, the question is what type of reprisal should be meted out.

Prisons are for punishing a person for his actions. They serve to incarcerate a person away from society as punishment for his deeds, which are only the symptoms of his real problems. Prisons usually do nothing to treat the cause of his criminal activity. Traditional rehabilitation programs have not been successful, as measured by the recidivism rates.

Why do prisons fail for serial murderers? As legal restrictions for being declared mentally incompetent are tightened, fewer people are sent to mental health institutions where they can receive treatment for their underlying problems. The rest of the people who are borderline cases for mental illness wind up in prisons. Because of budget cutbacks, few psychiatric treatment programs are available. Thus, the men spend their days incarcerated for their actions, but are never helped to overcome their problems.

A second reason may be the special nature of the psychopath. With his low autonomic response system, punishment by a prison term leaves no impression on him. He does not learn from the experience and does not improve his behavior when released. With the present prison system and traditional rehabilitation techniques, all the psychopath will have lost are a few years away from his criminal activities.

A New Approach

What may be needed is a new type of incarceration facility, or a change in traditional penal philosophy, as more and more biological causes of crime are discovered. Such a varied approach is already in progress for treating drivers who are repeatedly convicted of operating a motor vehicle while intoxicated. Instead of locking up such people in prisons, they are often sentenced to medical treatment programs, where they can receive counseling to help overcome their problem. This is a good example of punishment for their actions that also treats the origins.

Such an approach is needed with other types of criminals, especially psychopaths. In the general population, one to four percent are psychopaths. Their numbers appear to be rapidly increasing. This may account for the rise in the subcategory of serial murderers plaguing this country. While many psychopaths are never convicted of a crime, such as the shyster businessman who stretches all the rules but never enough to be arrested, a good proportion do become criminals.

A new treatment approach is under way in attempting to treat psychopaths. Based on the premise that their psychological development lags behind their age, the psychopaths are incarcerated in treatment programs with rigid, firmly enforced rules. The psychopath finds he cannot talk and con his way around the staff. For the first time in his life, his lies and verbal abilities get him nowhere. This process leads to his finally confronting his emotional emptiness. Then he can, hopefully, be taught to feel, to learn from experience, and to understand what it means to set goals for the future.

Even this program has some problems. If psychopathology is genetically or neurologically based, can an external behavioral treatment approach truly alter behavior? Are the psychopaths merely learning to act in a new style without really changing their basic thought processes?

Whether or not they receive psychiatric treatment, psychopaths' overt criminality usually lessens as they age. The drop off point comes around ages thirty-five to forty. Although they may become more social, it is noted their basic personality does not seem to change.

Other treatment approaches may be developed if medication can be useful. Currently, some former inmates are maintaining more normal behavior using monthly drug injections. These inmates are usually sex offenders receiving a chemical hormone to suppress their sexual aggression. If a biochemical imbalance is found to be part of a serial murderer's problem, then this type of treatment after release from a security facility might lessen the chances of repeat offenses. Also being developed are internally implanted medication pumps to supply continuous dosages of medicine, such as for acute diabetics who need consistent levels of insulin. Another alternative would be medicine patches worn next to the skin from which a drug dosage is absorbed through the skin on a continuous basis. Such medical procedures should be given serious consideration if they are found to help reduce criminal behavior.

The serial murder phenomenon is an extremely serious problem, especially in the United States. We do not know enough about these murderers to accurately assess how large the future incidence may ultimately become. We do know the family situation, genetics and/or biochemistry, and social pressures are involved. The genetic and biochemistry area is most in need of intensive research, for it is the topic least understood at this time. Society must alter its punishment of the symptoms of serial murder and determine its initial causes if any permanent solutions can be forthcoming.

The Whole Bloody Mess

In the biographies of the individuals who we have been discussing, we could not resist the periodic temptation to throw a rock at those we felt did not do their jobs or did not do them properly in dealing with serial murder cases. However, we have now reached the point where the system itself and how it deals with crime—not just serial murder but crime in the generic sense—must be scrutinized. We will look at its successes and failures.

Writers, like politicians, often tend to be social tinkerers. Each of us who feels we have the right to critique will usually also feel we have a better idea. In all fairness, it is quite possible there is no better mousetrap in dealing with crime. Many of the things that allow criminals to function in our society are also the very underpinnings of our much-vaunted freedoms.

In this chapter, we will comment upon some of these issues. It must be stated at the outset we are not and never will advocate restricting the lawful rights of a free people. Yet, for some, that temptation may be present. As was shown in Hitler's Germany, when you diminish the rights of one, you damage the rights of all. Unfortunately, this includes the rights of criminals and even serial murderers.

Criminals and Police

In considering questions of crime, it is obvious the most important actors in this entire drama are, in fact, the criminals and the police who apprehend them. Probably no function in society is more visible yet more misunderstood than law enforcement. One of the misconceptions contributing to contemporary cynicism about law enforcement is that the role of the police is to prevent crime. This is not true. The role of the police in our society is to apprehend criminals. Anything else is merely cosmetic. The prevention of crime is a byproduct, not the primary task of law enforcement.

It is striking to note most serial killers who are apprehended do not come to the attention of the police as the result of traditional law enforcement methodology. With extremely few exceptions, when serial killers are apprehended, it is because law enforcement personnel literally stumble across them. Some serial murder investigations, like San Francisco's search for the Zodiac Killer, have extended for decades without a significant break.

In recent years, the concept of the task force in dealing with serial murder cases has gained popularity. Yet, by and large, this approach and its concomitant abundance of manpower does not seem to be any more effective than traditional methods.

One of the historical complaints of law enforcement personnel has been the good guys have to play by the rules and the bad guys don't have any. There is a great deal of truth to this. They are, after all, criminals. Criminals are not restrained by concern about the rights of their victims. They virtually never worry about being sued by the police, their victims, or anyone else. Some radical writers in past decades have theorized the only truly free people in our society are criminals. If that is the case, then freedom does not seem to carry the value we have been taught.

To continue the analogy, not only do the bad guys not have to play by the rules, they frequently find ways to obtain the good guys' game plan. In no other society is access to information and education as easy and widespread as it is in the United States. Yet that access also has its price; the bad guys know a great deal more about what the good guys do and how they do it than vice versa. Even the most sophisticated of law enforcement techniques is publicly reported upon and available for study. We demand openness from our governmental agencies, even when it is not necessarily in our best interests.

The armchair quarterbacking of the news media, in addition to the vast quantity of public information available, provides the more sophisticated criminal with an important advantage over law enforcement agencies. It is impossible not to think of Ted Bundy sitting in his office at the Seattle/King County Crime Commission reading reports on rapes and murders and formulating the plan of action that allowed him to take the lives of dozens of young women.

It would be easy to advocate for all law enforcement investigations to be done in absolute secrecy. The United States Constitution and the citizens' right to know make that impossible. The accountability we demand from law enforcement plus the need to protect the rights of suspects makes the idea unrealistic.

Perceptions of Law Enforcement

Another and seldom-spoken reason why such secret investigations would be unacceptable to most Americans is our basic perception of law enforcement. After decades of stories about corruption and incompetence in major law enforcement agencies, we have been forced to confront the fact that Marshall Dillon is dead. No more John Waynes are available. If they ever existed, which is doubtful, they are gone.

It would not be accurate to portray all law enforcement officials as insensitive, inefficient, or dishonest. But we Americans, with our all-or-nothing attitude toward life in general, have not been able to completely adjust to the fact that law enforcement is a profession staffed by fallible human beings. We want our law enforcement officials to all be like Sherlock Holmes: superior in intelligence, unwavering in integrity, and unceasing in searching out wrongdoers. We are totally unprepared for the idea that cops are just like the rest of us. Like a ping pong ball, we bounce back and forth from one attitude to the other.

It is inevitable that the police will not rise to our expectations. They are, after all, as human as the rest of us. Peripherally, an area in which no research exists is the psychiatric effects of serial murder cases on the law enforcement people who investigate them. Our impression is these cases take a tremendous toll on the officers. We come away feeling that often the investigators will predecease the killers they seek due to the stress and emotional turmoil of the hunt. We have said the task force approach shows no higher success rate at capturing these killers than more traditional methods. However, it is obvious task forces are usually composed of the brightest and most dedicated investigators a police agency has. Therefore, it is not surprising that, when confronted with blind alley after blind alley, they tend to personalize the investigation and all its frustrations. Serial killers, more than most criminals, affect far more people than the actual victims.

Effect on Society

The serial killer, like his spiritual brother the terrorist, wins his greatest victories when he forces society and its members to change the way they live because of his actions. In a larger sense, no real difference is apparent between the impact of the Atlanta Child Killer and that of the 9/11 terrorists. They thrive on the creation and perpetuation of terror. Both are bringers of darkness. They prey on society, usually with impunity, and are virtually impossible to stop.

One of the problems we have had to overcome is the way in which the crime of serial murder has been conceptualized. We now know it is not enough merely to dismiss these situations as random, unrelated, or the acts of solitary madmen. These criminals, whatever their origin may be, are woven into the fabric of modern society. They have become a part of our everyday lives and cannot be dismissed as isolated. When we learn to think of them in their context, it will be possible for us to discover their antecedents, commonalities, and origins. Once that is done, it is possible, only possible, we can eradicate this horrible phenomenon from our society.

Traditional law enforcement by its very nature is handicapped when dealing with this type of individual. The time-proven methods of surveillance, forensics, and witness identification seldom work. These are techniques designed to cope with a visible criminal. Against a killer who reaches out from the dark, destroys his victim, and returns to invisibility, normal police methods have little chance for success.

Law enforcement agencies have seemed unable to grasp this new reality. For example, the Long Island serial killer took at least ten victims between 1996 and 2010 but is still at large. Since one theory is the killer may have a law enforcement background, it is likely he knows how to circumvent police strategy. Certainly, old-fashioned law enforcement does not seem to have made any significant inroads so far.

New Techniques Required

What is needed is the development of new and specialized techniques for investigating these crimes and apprehending these killers. The updates would include dramatically increased computerization, especially at the local level, and efficient nationwide computer linkups. These are two main areas where computer technology can be most helpful.

First, the computer as a tool in fighting crime has the usual blessing and curse. The blessing of the computer is it allows law enforcement to process vast amounts of information about certain individuals regarding specific crimes in a fairly short period of time and to put the information into a logical and coherent form. The downside is a computer is no better than those who operate it.

The old adage "garbage in, garbage out" takes on a new and frightening dimension in the pursuit of justice. Individuals who may have no role whatsoever in crime could find themselves subject to the harshest scrutiny as the result of a computer operator's error. In George Orwell's book, *1984,* Big Brother was an entity. In the real world of the twenty-first century, Big Brother could very well be a computer. Like any tool invented by man, it can be used rightly for good or wrongly to create great evil.

The second area with enormous potential for modern computer technology is in research. For the investigations to have any validity, we must again repeat our plea for further research and information into every aspect of the lives of the serial murderers in custody. We simply must know more than we do. It is possible the time may come when accurate profiles can be made available to law enforcement in their search for these individuals.

It also appears that a standing nationwide resource group of law enforcement professionals who have specialized in serial murder cases should be established. The hard-won knowledge and instincts of these individuals could then be made readily available at short notice to jurisdictions confronting this problem. It would require far more cooperation than has ever been provided in the past. The competitiveness and ego wars among law enforcement agencies must be put aside once and for all. It is far more important to protect the community than to worry about who gets their picture in the paper.

A frequently recurring problem with serial murder cases is the killers know they can further minimize their chances of being apprehended if they murder across jurisdictional lines. It is not even necessary to cross a county line. In a major urban area with multiple police precincts, the precincts themselves, although part of one law enforcement family, often provide minimal cooperation at best with each other. Vital information is lost. Work is duplicated. And the killers go merrily about their deadly business.

In their search for new methodologies to deal with serial killers, some law enforcement agencies have put forward the idea of preventive detention. Preventive detention is a concept whereby individuals who are suspected of crimes are taken into custody and detained based on that suspicion. This is not arrest; this is detention. Preventive detention is a way to circumvent habeas corpus. Under the habeas corpus concept, a charge must be filed to hold a person in custody. Under preventive detention, this is not the case. Further, bond or right to counsel would not be available for these individuals. They would simply remain in custody until charged or released.

It is a very small step from preventive detention to a point where citizens could be arrested because police thought they might commit crimes and, therefore, should be detained. It is interesting to note the dichotomy that we, living in the "bastion of freedom," should be toying with this idea while we continue to protest loudly when other countries declare martial law and imprison their citizens without benefit of due process.

Law Versus Liberty

Once again, we find ourselves with our noses pressed against the issue of law versus liberty. The founding fathers attempted to guide us through this morass, but they could not have been prepared for our modern times. No decent person wants crime on our streets. The question is: What price are we willing to pay to be crime-free? It is perhaps a quandary with no solution.

It is also true that a failure at any level of the criminal justice system affects the rest of the system. For example, a minor's so-called juvenile record of criminal offenses is expunged when he reaches the age of majority. As a result, when later courts deal with this individual, they do so as if he were a first offender. Thus, a juvenile offender with a history of chronic crime may find himself in front of a judge receiving a lighter than deserved sentence. Interestingly, one of the commonalities we found in most serial murder cases is that, while the killers may not have adult criminal records, almost without exception they had juvenile records or juvenile contact with police.

A few words must be said here about the role of the courts in the criminal justice process. We find, however, the concerns in this area tend to be somewhat generic. They are not specific to the role of the court in dealing with serial killers, but rather to the role of the court in dealing with criminal defendants.

It is not unusual to find pretrial delays of a year or more. The trial itself may last for years. This is not necessarily due to an exhaustive search for justice as much as to the grandstanding of both defense attorneys and prosecutors. Each legal motion generates a resistance, which generates a counter resistance.

It is impossible not to conclude much of this posturing is designed to provide content for the books that will be written. In virtually every major serial murder case, the prosecutor or the defense lawyer, and sometimes both, has written a book and made a profit. Many states enacted statutes to prohibit the accused from profiting by his crimes in any way. It is unfortunate a similar restriction has never been placed upon lawyers. Only the naivest would conclude such a situation is conducive to good justice. All the while the attorney is discharging his courtroom responsibilities, he is also playing to an unseen audience of readers.

Jurors and Trials

With the possible exception of a papal coronation, no social ritual is more complex and elaborate than a major American criminal trial. The lengthy trials are interspersed with complicated legal posturing. Observing all this and attempting to make a fair and valid decision are the twelve jurors charged with determining the fate of the defendant.

Some legal scholars have suggested the possibility of professional jurors. The idea is to create a pool of individuals who are already knowledgeable in forensics, basic criminal law, and human behavior. These individuals would then be on call to serve as decision makers in any jurisdiction. The concept has major constitutional problems but certainly, if implemented, would diminish the length of such trials and, concomitantly, the expense.

Jurors selected by traditional methods are usually poorly prepared for the rigors of a years long trial. Because of the economic burden placed on them and their families, most jurors at these trials tend to be retired persons or homemakers. They do not normally have a background that will prepare them for the intricate testimony they will hear. As a result, the attorneys spend enormous amounts of time educating the jury before presenting the facts.

These jurors are often required to listen to lengthy, elaborate, and obscure psychiatric testimony. It seems as if psychiatric testimony usually does nothing more than confuse the jury. Often the testimony that prevails is not necessarily the most accurate, but rather the most understandable. It sometimes appears psychiatric testimony plays a greater role in the determination of guilt or innocence than actual physical evidence.

As was seen in several of the cases we reviewed, psychiatric testimony usually revolves around a psychological profile. Psychological profiles are a major source of contention between prosecution and defense lawyers. The essence of the profiles is to provide a sort of psychological road map into the motivations and methods of the accused killer. These profiles are amazing documents. They start out as generic and vague. After the suspect has been arrested and interrogated by police, the profiles become considerably more specific. By the time of the trial, the psychiatrist/witness has had the opportunity to extensively review the history of the defendant. Suddenly, his original profile seems to contain everything but the defendant's shoe size and home address even though the psychiatrist has not necessarily interviewed the defendant. In our society, the statements of doctors and especially psychiatrists are given weight disproportionate to the content. Still, psychiatric testimony undoubtedly has an enormous influence on a jury.

Jurors are also educated in other areas. The jury that heard the Wayne Williams case probably knows as much about fiber evidence as anyone. It is incorrect to assume serving on a jury is an exciting, stimulating duty that keeps a person on the edge of his seat. Quite the contrary. Once past the gory descriptions of the actual deaths, most of what the jury hears is mundane and tedious. It is not unusual for jurors' attention to wander. A witness in the Gacy trial was distressed to see at least one juror sleeping through his testimony.

One of the most difficult and onerous responsibilities a jury has is to hear and examine the testimony of surviving victims. These individuals are forced to expose their pain and trauma to public scrutiny. Although this is vitally necessary to the administration of justice, it is tragic that the victims must be critiqued and displayed.

Sentencing Timelines and Appeals

Often at the end of this process, sentences are imposed that will never be carried out. Most serial murderers apprehended in America have been sentenced to death, yet few have been executed. Of the six serial murderers whose biographical overviews are in this book, only two were sentenced to be executed: Gacy and Bundy. Those executions were carried out only after many years of appeals. Corona and Buono died of natural causes while serving life sentences. Bianchi and Williams are still serving life sentences, having been denied parole a number of times.

The problem is the endless appeal process that plagues the American justice system. The appeal process is not designed to address the issue of guilt or innocence. Rather, it speaks to the question of whether the constitutional rights of the defendant have been protected. Any failure to protect those rights inevitably results in a mistrial and retrial, repeating the whole laborious process. Entire groups of lawyers in the United States have never tried a case as such, but they specialize in appellate work and in creating the need for new trials. Only a fool would say such a function is unnecessary in our legal process. After all, as legendary legal scholar Oliver Wendell Holmes once said, "I would rather see a hundred guilty men go free than witness the hanging of an innocent man." We are, indeed, that concerned with justice.

It seems as if the more serious the crime, the more likely the appeals will last for decades. Our concern for justice and doing the right thing has its price.

In Great Britain, by contrast, a convict gets one appeal, at which time he is expected to bring all his relevant facts before the court. When his issues are decided, that is the end of the matter, and no further appeals are permitted. For many, this approach is distinctly attractive.

Still, the other issue that must be addressed is the question of whether our concern over legal technicalities might in itself give rise to another kind of injustice. In the sterile, protected environment of a courtroom, it is easy to lose sight of the effects of crime in human terms. The courtroom has an odor of sanctity but does not provide the coppery smell and shocking sight of mutilated and bleeding bodies.

We have an irresolvable quandary here: the conflict between the letter of the law, the spirit of the law, and the search for justice.

All too often, justice is the loser. Justice is defined as a deserved reward or penalty. The law does not always provide for justice.

True Justice Versus Punishment

In a very pragmatic sense, one must ask how any murderer, especially a serial murderer, can ever receive justice. After all, John Gacy was sentenced to death on thirty-three counts, but he cannot be executed thirtythree times. One death cannot balance thirty-three. The very manner of his death is not fair or just if one is attempting to seek balance. When a murderer is executed, his body is not treated with the disrespect and contempt his victims suffered. The body of an executed killer is not tossed aside as if it were so much garbage or buried in a basement or thrown into a river.

The issue of the death penalty itself must be addressed as part of the concept of punishment. For many years, the standard rationalization for the use of the death penalty has been deterrence. Still, study after study has demonstrated no permanent deterrent effect in the death penalty. Other frequent arguments in favor of the death penalty include societal retribution and vengeance and economics. Many people consider the high cost of extended incarceration as a valid argument in favor of executing the offender. Although a morally reprehensible argument, it is one gaining in popularity. As the cost of incarceration continues to increase, it is quite possible this, more than any moral argument, will be critical in turning those few states that do not have the death penalty in the direction of executing these offenders.

In their excellent book, *Crime and Human Nature,* James Wilson and Richard Herrnstein cited a study involving a temporary decline in the number of homicides for about two weeks after a publicized public execution. The study seems to imply if we want to deter and if we want to execute, then it should be done publicly and in an open manner.

Executions in America over the last few decades have been anything but public. They are normally done at night, with only a few chosen observers present. We seem to feel guilty about carrying out these acts, and therefore, do them in darkness and semi-secrecy.

This temporary decline is hardly an argument in favor of the death penalty, because it is followed by an increase back to the average homicide rate. It seems any deterrent effect is short-term and probably statistically inconsequential. The only person permanently deterred is the one executed.

It is time for society to look objectively at the death penalty and to decide exactly what it is we are trying to gain. In the end, we will be forced to conclude what we want is not justice, law, or economics. What we want is vengeance, pure and simple. The vengeance principle in Western culture is as intrinsic to us as our desire for freedom. Tragically, hypocrisy is also intrinsic to us.

The Role of Prisons

Much emphasis has been placed on the role of prisons and incarceration in dealing with the crime problem. Hundreds of thousands of people are incarcerated in the United States. It is foolish to expect the American prison as it exists now to have much of an impact on crime generally and, certainly, on the specific type of crime we have been discussing. Prisons are overcrowded, underbudgeted, and understaffed. More importantly, they are designed to punish crime, not to prevent it. The naive, optimistic rhetoric of the 1960s, with its emphasis on treatment and rehabilitation, has been discarded in the harsher and more pragmatic times of recent decades.

While the numbers incarcerated and the length of sentences have increased, it is interesting to note the circumstances of incarceration have become progressively easier. Largely due to the so-called prisoners' rights movement of the last decades, incarceration in some states has taken on the element of a joke. Prisoners are frequently allowed to wear their own clothing, not required to work, and serve their time in cells wired for cable television and air-conditioning.

No one is advocating brutality or a lack of concern for basic human needs. However, one must question whether cable television is a basic human need. It is not unusual to be told by prisoners that they never had it so good on the streets as they do in the joint. Many things these same individuals could not afford or would not seek in the community are provided for them as a matter of course while they are imprisoned. What in past years were considered privileges for inmates who maintained good behavior have now become rights without any behavioral requirement.

At some point in history, it is hoped American criminal justice can make up its mind once and for all about exactly what it is that we expect from our prisons. As the late Lawrence LaBarge, long-term security director at the Iowa Men's Reformatory at Anamosa, Iowa, said, "If people would tell us what they want, we can provide it. We can provide security. We can provide treatment. We can provide privileges. We just need to know what's important and in what proportion."

Incarceration, in our opinion, should be humane but rigid. The entire issue of deterrence through incarceration should be discarded. Incarceration is done for the purpose of punishment and should be honestly acknowledged as such.

The FBI continues to maintain that nearly ninety percent of the crimes committed in this country are done by people who have already been in prison. Some law enforcement authorities think the answer is never to release anybody. One police official several years ago suggested the solution to the problem of crime was to "hang everything above a misdemeanor." He probably would have considered life incarceration as a reasonable, if somewhat weak-kneed, alternative. The cruel reality of the matter is crime, like poverty, will always be with us. We are doing nothing more than attempting to change the odds in our favor by seeking a workable response to crime.

The Media's Role

Much discussion in recent years has centered on the role of the media and, particularly, the broadcast media in the American criminal justice system. For many years, criminals and crime news have been a staple in the industry. Some people have even referred to the media as the "commercial companion to crime."

Much has been made of the issue of prime time crime. This is basically a belief that criminal behavior is learned from viewing television. No doubt Americans have become largely inured to crime and violence because of watching television. The exposure comes in two places: through entertainment programs, especially the traditional police shows, and through television news programs.

Many reputable organizations, including the National Parent Teacher Association (PTA), have criticized prime time crime. Their estimates of the numbers of homicides that a child has seen on television by the time he or she reaches the age of eighteen years old is in the thousands. Other crimes—burglaries, rapes, incest, robberies—probably multiply that number by many times. In the late 1970s, a Florida homicide case entitled *Ronny Albert Zamora v. The State of Florida* brought the issue to national attention. Zamora attempted to defend himself on a homicide charge by stating he had been "programmed" to criminal behavior by watching television shows. His defense was unsuccessful, and he was found guilty as charged. However, subsequent studies have not been successful at dispelling this concern over the impact of television.

These studies are a fascinating topic in themselves. They seem to be clearly divided in their conclusions along the lines of who funded the study in the first place. Studies by parents' groups show much of television programming as potentially harmful. Other equally elaborate studies funded by the networks show it has no impact at all, or the negative impact is limited to those with a predisposition for aggressive behavior. A proper analysis of this issue can only come from an objective, uninvolved source allowed wide latitude to examine and analyze over a considerable period of years. The single largest task such a study would face would be to isolate the effects of television from all other hereditary and environmental factors in order to make an accurate analysis of its impact.

Television news broadcasting has also played its role in this concern. Beginning with the daily coverage of the Vietnam War in the 1960s, television news has evolved into a stance reminiscent of the police gazette of years gone by. Crime news is usually presented in as graphic a manner as possible and has a direct relationship to ratings. The same streak of human morbidity that led nineteenth century Londoners to turn out en masse to watch the hangings at Tyburn Hill now brings us to the television for graphic coverage of the crimes in our communities. As we said above, every aspect of crime is presented except the punishment.

What can be concluded is that both television crime shows and the broadcast news programs produce an insensitivity to death. Television coverage of modern tragedies like the murders connected to O. J. Simpson and the bombings during the Boston Marathon were graphic in the extreme and far surpassed the legitimate news need. Using sophisticated communications systems, broadcast journalists are often on the scene of the crime as quickly as the authorities.

Every modern police agency knows it must factor in the effect of the media on its investigations. The most striking case of media impact and pressure in the area of serial murder cases has to be the so-called Atlanta Child Killings. The media succeeded in panicking a major metropolitan area and possibly having a negative effect on the ongoing criminal investigation.

Although our above comments have been limited largely to modern broadcast media, print media is also a factor in the issue of crime. The London newspaper coverage in the fall of 1888 of the Jack the Ripper murders set a standard of yellow journalism that has survived over a century. Their graphic drawings, extraordinarily detailed autopsy reporting, and elaborate descriptions of the wounds inflicted on the Ripper's five victims went beyond anything previously reported and far surpassed the normal view of Victorian good taste. It would be naive to say citizens do not have a right to know what goes on in the streets of their community. At the same time, one questions the need for the coverage to be as graphic and elaborate as it often is. Citizens are not informed in such situations; they are terrorized.

American media responds to such concerns by citing the First Amendment and the public's right to know. Responsible journalists will attempt to cover crime news in a dispassionate and objective manner. However, they are usually not the persons who set editorial policy and are sometimes overridden by other concerns.

The primary concern is something most of us do not often consciously think out: newspapers and television stations are profit-making entities. The business of newspapers is to sell newspapers. The business of a television or radio station is to sell advertising. It, therefore, becomes impossible, in our opinion, for these entities to be totally objective. As long as the reader, viewer, or listener is aware of this issue, the harm can be minimized. Unfortunately, media objectivity is not something to which most people devote any conscious thought. These warnings are not unique with us. As long ago as 1958, legendary broadcaster Edward R. Murrow, in a speech to the Radio and Television News Directors Association, warned of those dangers. Murrow said that, if the broadcast industry were not extremely cautious, the day would come when they would have no credibility at all.

Graphic crime news increases viewership. Viewership increases ratings. Ratings increase advertising. Advertising increases profits. Oft-raised moral concerns notwithstanding, few believe members of the American media will change their approach to crime and crime reporting.

One other aspect of the media's role in crime is the unusual relationship between police agencies and reporters. The police often find themselves in the position of manipulating the media to further their investigations. This is a two-way street. Reporters most amenable to loaded press coverage frequently get the best stories or get them first. This results in a subtle pressure on the media to prostitute themselves to law enforcement.

The above comments could probably be interpreted by some as being unfairly critical of the news media. In fact, this is not the case. We merely wish to point out the news media is often subject to invisible pressures that may affect the tone and quality of their work. If their bias is understood, readers can at least be aware other perspectives may exist to the story they are reading.

Society and Crime

We have discussed several disparate areas in society that, in one way or another, affect the issue of crime. Of necessity, our comments are vague and almost generic at times. Yet we must draw those comments together.

It has struck us repeatedly that one of the flaws in society's response to crime is a lack of an adequate, workable definition of crime. Crime was born the moment humankind banded together into groups. For people to coexist with each other, rules were necessary. Those rules became laws, but wherever law existed, law breakers also resided. The attempt to understand the phenomenon of crime led to human beings' first efforts to examine their own nature.

As we saw in the previous chapter, human biology is a leading candidate as a cause for crime. But we have been trained for many generations to equate crime with sin. Sin is conscious and deliberate. Biology is simply inborn. The truth probably lies somewhere in between. The tendency for criminality and homicide is quite possibly a result of our genetic makeup as much as the color of our hair and eyes. The environment in which we live encourages us or discourages us from actualizing that tendency.

Virtually every social institution created since humans first formed societies is the result of attempts to enforce certain types of behavior while excluding or eliminating other types. This even holds true with religions. If there were no need to control human behavior, there would be no need for civil or religious laws.

Such social institutions in their various ways can also enable and perpetuate crime. As we have seen in this chapter, even the societal mechanisms for punishing criminal behavior sometimes encourage it.

Until the time comes when we can resolve the question of the origins, functions, and place of crime in society, we are faced with a hopeless task. Crime will continue as long as society continues.

Is crime sin or sickness? If it is sin, the individual must bear all responsibility for his actions. If it is sickness, society must share the responsibility, and the role of the individual is diminished.

That being the case, the social institutions—police, courts, prisons, media—must share the guilt for crime. As Professor Hooten pointed out over seventy ago, the sharing of that guilt is unpalatable to society. We will continue to look at sociological and environmental factors as the be-all, end-all for criminal behavior. We are, as a society, unable to accept the fact the tendency for criminal behavior of any type exists in all of us given the right set of circumstances. Until we can divest ourselves of those illusions, we will never make any real headway against the Ripper's children.

Now consider for a moment how we would make that headway should we be willing to accept the truth. The social planner with unlimited resources and unnumbered years would attempt to create a society absolutely nonconducive to crime. The practical man would, most probably, take the quicker and most expedient route of attempting to breed criminality out of the species.

Speculative writers, such as Aldous Huxley in Brave New World, have attempted to show a society where that had been accomplished. The vision is frightening. Thus, we continue to ignore our biological criminality and look elsewhere for reasons and solutions.

It may seem we have gone somewhat far afield in our attempt to understand serial murderers. It is not so. We have found it necessary to look in many places for our answers. Serial killers belong to our species and society as much as anyone else and must be seen and understood in that context. They are the best and brightest of criminals, but criminals none the less. They may indeed be the next evolutionary step in criminal behavior.

Afterword
A Season in Hell

Nothing on earth is colder than a prison in winter. Buff-colored limestone and green painted bars chill the spirit. The Iowa Men's Reformatory in Anamosa is a huge, aging, Gothic building that looks more like Ivanhoe's castle than a prison. It seemed far more likely that those walls would be guarded by archers than men with guns. For a hundred years, it has dominated the rolling hills and rural landscape.

The air was filled with snow on 30 January 1969, and the walls loomed up brown on the white earth The police cruiser had carried me two hundred miles from home to leave me in prison. I had done my best after being arrested to accommodate and please my captors. I had gone from being a tough street hood and burglar to being a wimp in one fell swoop. Fear will do that to you. My first Christmas and New Year's locked up had done nothing to ease my mind.

As I got out of the car in handcuffs and chains, the officer stuck a five-dollar bill in my pocket and said, "Just do your time, keep your mouth shut, and you'll be fine." He walked me in the prison door, unfastened the cuffs, removed the leg irons, and handed me over to two guards.

Obeying orders, I stepped through the first set of barred doors. The clang they made behind me was the loudest sound I'd ever heard. After the second door shut, I was marched to a receiving area to be handled and processed like livestock. I was showered and sprayed, had my hair cut, got photographed, and had fingerprints taken. The last of my free-world clothes were taken away and destroyed. I went in one door a man and came out the other a convict.

My first walk across the yard revealed the colorless world of prison. The ground and the sky were the same—pasty gray and featureless. The faded denim uniforms of the other convicts added no life, and their pale faces blended into invisibility against the background. I felt as if I had walked into a black and white photograph from which I could not escape.

As I looked at the walls, I realized that in each of the towers was a man with a gun whose job it was to keep me inside those walls. I decided there and then not to test their sense of purpose.

The first night in prison brought no sleep.

The next morning, I had my first meal in the prison Dining Hall. The food was plentiful but tasteless. Behind the serving line was a moon-faced man dressed in white, ladling scrambled eggs onto steel trays. He looked at me and smiled. "New man, eh? Don't be so scared." He could obviously see the fear on my face. "You'll be fine." Reaching across the steamtable, he shook my hand. "I'm John Gacy. Look me up when you get on the yard."

Having heard all the stories in jail about older cons and what they do to new "fish," I was not eager to look him, or anyone else, up when I got in the yard. At the same time, he possessed something engaging, almost fatherly, about him even though he was only five or six years older than I.

The days and nights spent in the Orientation Unit before I went to the yard were almost endless. Each new man lived alone in a tiny cell that measured forty-four square feet. The bed, sink, toilet, mirror, and shelves could all be touched without taking a step. Steel bars, chipped paint, and smelly toilets were part of my new home. For the first thirty days, that was my world.

Living in a prison cell is a lot like living in a glass house. Absolutely no privacy exists for anything. You sit on the toilet and people walk by four feet away, looking in. Everything you own and everything you do are under constant scrutiny. Not just from guards, which is bad enough, but from other inmates. Some of those guys seem dedicated to appraising the resale value of everything in the cell, including your body.

We new cons were separated from the other cons by a steel gate, but we could see and hear everything that went on. The Orientation Unit was on the ground floor of the cell house. Ranging above it were three more tiers of cells. The inmates who lived in those cells could come to the railing at the edge of their tiers, lean over, and look down at the new men walking on the flagstones below. Catcalls and obscene suggestions were nonstop.

The cell house had been occupied for over a century. Built by convict labor, one wall was part of the outer wall of the prison, and the free standing cell block contained over two hundred prisoners. Hundreds of nameless men had resided in that building. Some lived, some died. But all left behind their loneliness, misery, and pain. The walls oozed sadness.

The sounds of a cell house at night are never forgotten. Twenty or thirty amateur guitarists playing "Folsom Prison Blues" or singing the lyrics "I turned twenty-one in prison doing life without parole." In the darkest hours, the sound of a guard's heels clanked on the steel catwalks. The muffled sound of men weeping in the night stabbed my soul.

When my first month was finished, I was released into what is called the general population. You never saw a finer collection of murderers, rapists, robbers, and thieves. Seven hundred men lived on thirteen acres of steel and concrete.

The first day out, I was reassigned to the cell house where I would live for the next two years. I carried my few belongings into Cell House D and placed them in Cell 2–20, my new address. After I'd unpacked, I headed for my new job on the prison yard gang.

The yard gang is the lowest job assignment in the prison. In the winter, you spend your days chipping ice and shoveling snow. In the summer, you spend your days picking up other people's cigarette butts and mowing the grass.

As I came around the edge of the cell block and headed out the door, a large, dramatically ugly, black man grabbed me by the arm and pulled me into the corner. Suddenly I found myself with a razor-sharp X-ACTO knife under my chin.

"You know what you're going to do for me, white boy!"

If I had had any doubts, the knife certainly explained the situation. That little knife looked to me like a machete. In a moment of pure fear, I jumped what seemed at the time to be eight or ten feet straight into the air, wet my pants at the top of the leap, and slammed against his shoulder when I came down. I knocked him off balance, and he stumbled back a couple of steps.

A large push broom was standing along the edge of the cell block near me. Grabbing it, I swung it with all my strength. I got lucky. The head of the broom caught him under his jaw. The knife clattered onto the flagstones, and he fell to the floor. Insane with fear, I hit him again and again and again.

At that moment, two other inmates came around the edge of the cell block. Sizing up the situation, one of them said to me, "Hey, man, you've dealt with it. If you hit him anymore, you'll be doing fuckin' life in here." Taking me by the arms, they marched me briskly away, leaving the would-be rapist bleeding and unconscious. "Welcome to prison, kid."

Nothing was ever said about the incident again. I found out later that the guy was serving fifty years for second-degree murder.

Those who have never lived inside prison walls are forced to rely on secondhand information about what it's like to do time. Most of that information comes from films like *The Longest Yard* and *Cool Hand Luke*. While entertaining, these are not accurate portrayals of prison life.

Prison life is largely divided into two sections: boredom and fear. Boredom fills most of the days and nights. Convicts are constantly looking for anything to entertain or divert their attention. The only thing that really changes in prison is the date on the calendar. At the same time, fear lies over everything like soot on snow. After all, this is not a resort in the Bahamas, and nobody ever went to prison for being a nice person.

The long Iowa winter dragged on. A few weeks later, I found myself sitting in the recreation hall looking for something to do, passing the hours playing solitaire. Suddenly, I felt a hand on my shoulder. I jerked around, ready to fight. In prison, nobody ever touches you. If they do, somebody's likely to wind up dead. Behind the walls, everybody has the "Colgate shield" protecting them all the time.

The intruding hand belonged to the moon-faced guy from the kitchen who had spoken to me the first day. "Hey, you're Cornell?"

A fairly safe assumption since my name and number, 26578, were stenciled on my shirt in large black letters.

"I'm John Gacy. Do you remember me?"

I acknowledged that I did.

"Hey, do you play bridge?"

I replied that I had never played bridge in my life.

"You want to learn?"

Desperate for something to do, I said I did. By the end of the day when we went back to our cells, I felt I had made my first friend in prison. His name was John Wayne Gacy Jr.

John had been born and raised in Chicago and had gotten busted in Waterloo. He readily admitted that he was serving time under the Iowa sodomy laws, but said it was for showing pornographic films to teenage girls. In a prison of seven hundred men, all of whom are constantly thinking about sex, it seemed like an almost insignificant crime. He said that the real reason he was in prison was because some political bigwigs wanted to get rid of him as he knew too much about their illegal activities and sexual indiscretions. It would be over a decade before I found out the truth about his life in Waterloo.

As we were going down the sidewalk, a fellow coming the other way greeted Gacy and called him "Colonel." Gacy said that was his nickname because he had owned some Kentucky Fried Chicken stores and was an honorary Kentucky colonel. I was impressed. I'd never been an honorary anything.

In the days that followed, two friends of mine from the streets also came into prison. Soon, Larry, Duane, Gacy, and I were an inseparable foursome, each of us looking out for the others and protecting the others' backs. We walked the yard together, took our meals together, played cards, and talked incessantly.

Spring in prison is a strange time. You wake up in the morning and you can feel the new life on the other side of the wall. The sounds and scents of spring are present, but you're separated from them by forty feet of limestone.

One April day, unable to resist the temptation, I took off my shoes and socks and walked barefoot through one of the small plots of grass in the prison yard. Pure sensual pleasure. From out of nowhere, a guard appeared and screamed, "Hey, yard bird, put your goddam shoes and socks back on and get your ass off the fuckin' grass!" I was crushed.

One of the few things that helped me keep my sanity was the daily conversations with Gacy. Walking the yard, we talked for endless hours. I told him how I came to be in prison, growing up in poverty, married, and a father at eighteen. I had nothing. Like many young men, providing for my family and my two small children was more important than obeying the law.

John, in return, told me the story of his life. Mostly he spoke of his father. Gacy told of him with a mixture of reverence, fear, and hatred. The Old Man worked as a machinist, could make his own tools, and fixed everything around the house. He was also an alcoholic. Coming home from work, his father would lock himself in the basement, where he proceeded to get blind drunk. The family had to wait supper upstairs, while The Old Man screamed and thrashed around in the basement beneath their feet.

Raised by an alcoholic stepfather myself, I understood much of what he felt.

Nothing John had ever done satisfied his father. When he brought one of his friends home, The Old Man had said the boy looked like a "queer" and accused John of being one, also. He would scream at John, tell him he was no good, and beat him with his fists. When his mother tried to protect him by reminding The Old Man of John's bad heart, his dad would call him a "sissy" and a "momma's boy."

John said that he had had a lot of health problems, including fainting spells. He told us he had to take it easy and be careful of his heart. That's why he liked working in the kitchen. It was obvious that he also enjoyed the protection running with the three of us gave him. Our reward was his generosity with prison food.

We endlessly circled the exercise yard as the days began to warm. Around and around we'd go, at least two hours every day.

At that point, I remember thinking that perhaps prison wouldn't be so bad after all. As winter broke and spring came, I at least had friends and people to talk to. We traded books and magazines, loaned each other cigarettes, went to the weekly movie together, and continued to play cards in the evening. I did not know that my education in prison life was far from over.

One April evening, sitting on the yard with some friends, I was once again reminded of what prison is really like. A few feet away, three young black men sat talking. Suddenly an older con, a hard rock known as Gene, appeared out of nowhere, grabbed one of the blacks by his hair, lifted him to his feet, jammed a knife in his belly, and ripped upwards.

Stunned by the sight, the scene became a slow-motion drama. The only thought I had was one of amazement as I watched the blood spurt three feet into the air. I never knew human beings had that much blood in them.

As if to hammer the message home, a few days later I came around the cell block where I had been accosted previously. There, on his knees, was a young, blond inmate performing fellatio on an older con. Never having seen men having sex with each other before, I stopped. The older guy looked up and grinned at me. He ejaculated into the kid's mouth then, and before the kid could get to his feet, kicked him as hard as he could in the face with his heavy, Brogan shoe. Wordlessly, he brushed by me and went back out to the yard. Part of my soul died at that moment. I looked down at the young man, no more than eighteen years old, lying weeping on the cold stones. His face was covered with blood and semen. I wheeled around and fled like a frightened rabbit.

In mid-May 1969, I had my first hearing before the Iowa Board af Parole. I had nourished the hope that I would be one of those rare inmates released early. Despite the fact I was serving two concurrent ten-year sentences, had only been in prison a few months, and was guilty of several hundred burglaries for which I had never been charged, I dreamed on.

The day came. I was escorted into the Parole Board room and seated alone on a hard wooden chair. Facing me, seated behind a massive walnut table, were three men. They rocked slowly in their high-backed leather chairs. It was clear to me now that I was no longer the master of my own destiny. They nodded and smiled at my pleas for freedom and said they would see me in a year.

John sometimes seemed more of a counselor to me than a fellow inmate. He pulled me through that letdown. We took endless turns around the prison yard, talking, watching John smoke another of his forty or fifty small cigars a day, trying to make some sense out of who I was and how I'd gotten there. His insights and compassion made him easy to open up to and easy to trust.

John, on the other hand, continued his discourse on his childhood and the complex relationship he had with his father. It was easy to see that he loved and loathed his father at the same time. In a strange way, I envied him that, for I had never known my real father.

Gacy talked about his many accomplishments, about his time in the Marine Corps, and the fact that he was wealthy while still in his early twenties. He implied that he was married to the daughter of Colonel Harlan Sanders, founder of the Kentucky Fried Chicken chain. He also boasted of his sexual conquests and complained endlessly about how he had been railroaded into prison.

His complaints about the wrongs done to him usually led to long, philosophical monologues on the nature of justice. He talked about how the poor and the weak were always victimized by the system and how wrong that was. He made it clear that he thought it was the responsibility of an honorable man to protect those who could not protect themselves, even from the depredations of the law itself.

Younger and unsophisticated, I was enthralled by his eloquence on the subject. More than any other aspect of our friendship, that part of John caught and held my attention. I remembered everything he said on the subject, and it would change my life.

John appeared to be a devout Catholic. He renewed my interest in the Church. We both served as lectors at the Mass, alternating Sundays.

Gacy seemed indestructable. Working eight to ten hours a day in the kitchen, he had also joined the Reformatory Jaycee chapter and had become one of the directors. In June, I had finally made enough money from my new job in the prison library that I could afford the fifteen dollars for dues to join myself. The Junior Chamber of Commerce is one of the largest civic organizations in America. Few people know that almost every prison in the country has a Jaycee chapter. The Jaycee projects in prison include providing movies to inmates, planting flowers, and attempting at every opportunity to humanize the sterile environment of prison.

I looked forward to the weekly meetings on Wednesday nights. At John's urging, I became one of the most active Jaycees in the joint. John liked to be the big man and wanted to be around those in power. Thus, he encouraged his friends to extend themselves.

In the fall of 1969, Gacy, tireless and inquisitive, pulled a master stroke for the Jaycees. He had read in the paper that an elderly couple in central Iowa who had run a miniature golf course for many years wanted to retire and were looking for someone to whom they could give the golf course equipment. He wrote them a letter and convinced them that the miniature golf course would be well used and much appreciated as a recreational activity by the men in prison. The couple agreed to donate the golf course to the reformatory. Gacy, in a supreme feat of salesmanship, convinced the warden to allow the Jaycees to install the course on the prison yard. He also convinced a local department store to donate several hundred yards of indoor-outdoor carpeting.

After eight months in prison, John had adjusted to his environment better than anyone could have imagined. His unbelievable ability at salesmanship, his bright and concerned approach, and his phenomenal manipulative skills had made the short, fat guy from Waterloo a power to be reckoned with in the inmate population.

John was now lead cook in the prison kitchen. Under his talented hands, the quality of the food had improved enormously. Never one to allow a void in power, John had developed a network second to none. The base of his power was something that most of us take for granted: food.

Those in prison can't go out to a restaurant or order a pizza. As a result, a steak sandwich or extra fruit becomes a bargaining chip of major importance. On the other hand, mess with the cook and you're likely to get ground light bulb in your mashed potatoes.

One particularly obnoxious guard learned a hard lesson. Assigned to Dining Hall security, he went to one end of the room, leaving his tray of food at the other. Certain modifications were made in his absence. A hearty eater, he returned to his tray heaped with mashed potatoes, picked up his fork, and stabbed in. A small squeak issued forth. In his absence, someone on the kitchen staff had placed a dead rat under the potatoes. The pressure from his fork forced the last air from its dead lungs, causing a postmortem squeak. He was never seen eating in the Dining Hall again.

Inmates and guards alike came to Gacy for favors. The warden made certain that John had a plentiful supply of his favorite cigars. Unlike the rest of the population, who were clad in blue shirt and baggy denim jeans, Gacy always wore a white shirt and his trousers were neatly pressed, an accommodation from the prison laundry. He walked the yard like a king.

John seemed to be able to roll with the punches as well as anyone. In August, he was called to his counselor's office and curtly told that his wife had divorced him. John had often spoken of his wife and children. After that day, when he did speak of them, he did so as if they were dead.

Soon John achieved Minimum Custody status and was allowed to go outside the walls on speaking trips and panels for the Jaycees. At his suggestion, I also sought this privilege and was eventually successful. We traveled far and wide, speaking to high school classes, church groups, and civic organizations. John was always the man with the words. He was able to verbalize what the rest of us could only feel. We talked about the loneliness, the boredom, and the fear that make up prison life. For some, those trips into the free world were a brief vacation from prison. For Gacy, they were an agonizing reminder of what he had lost.

In September, I stood for election to the Inmate Council, again largely at Gacy's suggestion. The Inmate Council is somewhat like a student body council for convicts. We met weekly with the warden and other administrators to discuss problems. I had spent most of the previous year learning how to speak in public and to articulate what I felt. More than anything else in my life, I wanted to be able to talk like John Gacy.

That same month, my wife divorced me. I had lived each day in prison hoping that when I was free again I could go back to my wife and my children. That hope was now dashed. It was a cold and rainy September, which suited my mood perfectly. For the first time in my life, I thought about suicide. I sat inside the walls of a prison, thinking how my wife had found another man and my children were callling somebody else "Daddy."

Gacy, ever alert to the moods of others, quickly picked up on what was happening to me. We had become so busy and involved with projects that the daily card games had ceased. Still John, in the midst of all the other things with which he was dealing, found time to help me through my depressions and the feelings of hopelessness. Again we walked the endless square of the prison yard, hour after hour.

"Cornell, it'll pass. It's not worth dying for. You've got everything in the world going for you when you get out of here. You can't look back. Why don't you go to college and get an education? You should use your head for something beside a hat rack."

The feelings of hopelessness remained and have remained to some degree to this day. You can get the man out of prison, but you never really get the prison out of the man. Still, the depressions ended and I moved on.

As my second winter in prison began, John made certain that all of us had plenty to do. He'd gotten the warden's agreement to allow the Jaycees to run a "Toys for Tots" program for poor kids in the area. We collected used and worn-out toys, repaired and painted them in the kitchen basement, and wrapped them so they would sit under the Christmas trees of children we would never see.

At the same time, John had decided to give his friends a special Christmas party. Under the drain in the kitchen basement, John was brewing his Christmas gift to us. He had carefully collected five gallons of cherry juice, added yeast and sugar, and allowed it to ferment. The homemade "rook" would be ready before Christmas.

After the toys were finished, the Reformatory Jaycees had a Christmas party on 20 December 1969. Every prison, like every high school, has at least one rock and roll band. Ours played in the prison auditorium, now decorated with red and green streamers. Thirty homemade pizzas were the food for the one hundred Jaycees. John had hidden six additional pizzas for his close friends to take back to their cells later.

We made certain that none of the guards had a taste of our potent punch. While the two officers were engaged in conversation, Gacy would make a hootch run to the basement to refill the punch bowl, which he had borrowed from the warden's wife. As soon as it was full, the cons would empty it again so the guards never knew about the booze.

During the course of the evening, John made a point of spending a little time with each of us who had worked on the project, politicking and thanking us for the work and the help we had given. That evening was the warmest, most congenial time I ever spent with John Gacy.

As we wobbled back to the cell house that night, John threw his arm around my shoulders and said that he considered me his friend and would never forget me.

A few days later, John Gacy's world collapsed. The Board of Parole reviewed his case just before Christmas. John had been planning his release for a year. He devised the most elaborate parole plan anyone had ever seen. He had saved money, had gotten a commitment for a job at a Chicago-area restaurant, and planned to live with his mother. Everything was prepared, everything was organized, everything was ready. The board said no.

Gacy put a brave face on it and immediately began making plans for an attempt at a special parole in the spring. It was not a good Christmas for him.

The holiday season in prison is an especially tense time. More fights, more suicides, and everyone on edge. Christmas in prison is the loneliest thing a human being can endure. Christmas without hope, Christmas without love.

A couple of days later, I was walking across the yard, headed for my job in the iibrary, when I saw John Gacy coming toward me. His face was as white as his shirt. Tears ran down both pudgy cheeks. He brushed by me as if I were not there. Shocked and concerned, I asked around and discovered that he had just been told The Old Man was dead.

Like a thread running through John's life, his deeds, and his conversations, The Old Man had always dominated him. More than anything else, John wanted a chance to be free and to vindicate himself in the eyes of his father. He had arranged for an inmate artist to paint a portrait of his father from a photograph. The Old Man never saw John's last Christmas gift to him. In the space of a few days, John had lost both his chance at freedom and his father.

Suffering from the blues myself, I spent most of the remainder of the season in my cell. I didn't see John again until after the first of the year, when we resumed our regular Jaycee meetings.

It was 1970, a new year, a new decade, a new chance. By then, I had adjusted to prison life and had convinced myself that I might very well be in prison for ten years, the length of my sentence. If that were the case, I would make the best of it. I began reading every book I could get my hands on and took two college classes at night.

Shortly after the beginning of the year, I began my campaign for president of the Reformatory Jaycee chapter. Little did I know that my opponent would be my friend, John Gacy.

John found out that I was running against him before I knew of his campaign. Where once he had been my friend, now he was my competitor.

Unknown to all of us, something inside John Gacy had snapped with his father's death. The compassionate, concerned Gacy was gone and would not return. Frustration and anger took the smile from his face and replaced it with a snarl. Where once he had been a negotiator and a problem solver, now he was angry, bitter, and confrontive.

The first real evidence I had of the changes in John came in the

Dining Hall. Going through the serving line one evening, I saw ahead of me a well-known and extremely effeminate homosexual prisoner. Gacy was standing behind the steamtable, ladling out hot chili. Fairy Frank, as he was known, came to Gacy's station and extended his tray. John poured steaming hot chili over his hands. Frank dropped the tray and splattered food all over himself. Gacy merely smiled.

Other things surfaced. The Inmate Council began to hear rumors about how Gacy had "declared war on the queers." Any inmate assigned to the kitchen that Gacy thought was homosexual or merely suspected of being homosexual was systematically harassed into seeking another job assignment. Gacy did this while hiding behind his relationships with guards and his inmate friends.

A few weeks later, John and his three friends—Larry, Duane, and I—were walking the yard. We had had a break in the winter weather, the snow had melted, and everyone was outdoors. On the sidewalk ahead of us, a "prison turn-on" approached. At that moment, a basketball from the nearby court bounced in front of John. Seizing the ball, he slammed it at the approaching homosexual. The ball struck him in the forehead and rebounded to Gacy. He seized it for a second shot and threw it with all his force. Scary Gary, now warned, dodged the ball.

Cocking his hand on his hip, Gary pursed his lips at John and said, "Missed me, missed me, now you've got to kiss me!"

Gacy broke into a run, raging anger on his face. He forgot about his alleged heart condition and pursued the fleeing youth with all his might. Only Gary's relative youth and Gacy's extra weight averted murder. For the first time, the dark face under my friend's mask had been revealed. That was not the benign John Gacy, but another person altogether.

As he turned back toward us, his features were rigid and set, and his eyes seemed ready to explode from his face. Anger and hate consumed him. Not a word was said, but he had lowered his barriers for a split second, allowing us to glimpse inside.

That little exchange had far-reaching implications. Word spread quickly through the yard that the way to get the great John Gacy's goat was to imitate the mincing walk and lisping speech he hated so much. If John had gotten a dollar for every time he heard that phrase, "Missed me, missed me, now you've got to kiss me," he could have retired wealthy the day his sentence ended.

Time passed and John continued to work on his second parole plan. He now hoped to be released in the summer of 1970. He filled his idle hours working on the golf course, which was now nearly completed and ready for play. He had become incredibly authoritarian and rigid in his dealings with the other inmates. He ordered them about as if they were his employees, indeed, his slaves. Where once he had been admired, he was now avoided. Where once he had been respected, he was now disliked. The change effected his friendships with Larry, Duane, and me. On several occasions, he nearly came to blows with Larry, who had once been his greatest admirer.

It seemed as if nothing was going right in his life. When the Jaycee election came in March, Gacy lost his bid for the presidency by seventy or eighty votes. It was obvious that his friendship with me was at an end.

I was approaching my second parole review date, having served nearly a year and a half on my sentence. Where once I could have gone to John for practical advice, I was now proceeding on my own.

I took the advice he had given me the year before, sat through the ACT test, and, to my astonishment, scored extremely well. I wrote letters to several colleges and went through the application process to become a student in the fall. Amazingly, I was not only admitted, but Drake University in Des Moines offered me a scholarship to study history. When I went to John to show him the letter, he merely grunted and walked away.

After my election as president of the Jaycees, I was also asked to serve the remainder of a term as president of the Inmate Council for an inmate who had been released. John had never succeeded in being elected to the council.

An opening came shortly afterward in the hierarchy of the Jaycees. In April of 1970, I appointed John Wayne Gacy as official chaplain of the chapter. He also served as parliamentarian.

A few days later, we went together as the inmate representatives to the annual Jaycee conference and awards ceremony in Independence, Iowa, one hundred miles away.

That year, the most recognized and acknowledged Jaycee chapter in Iowa was the Reformatory Jaycees. Largely because of the efforts of John Gacy, we were voted the Outstanding Chapter and garnered more awards than any other chapter. His recruiting efforts had increased the size of the Reformatory Jaycees from thirty members to 250. Because of his organizational skills, the miniature golf course had been completed, the Toys for Tots program was an outstanding success, and we had even received publicity in the form of a picture article in the *Des Moines Register*. Never before or since have the Reformatory Jaycees enjoyed the prestige and respect they had as a result of John's efforts.

May came. Once again, I was reviewed and denied by the Parole Board. I was depressed and angry but, thanks to John, I had developed the strength to deal with those things like a man. In one of our last times together, he urged me not to give up but to continue my efforts in any way possible to be on campus in the fall.

In June, the golf course was ready, a new president was elected for the council, and the activities of the Jaycees slowed down for the summer. On warm summer evenings, we played a few rounds on the miniature golf course we had worked so hard to create, but the friendship and camaraderie were gone. Now we were just doing time, waiting for our releases.

The last week in June 1970, the Iowa Board of Parole granted parole to John. As he waited for the papers to be processed, he finalized his plans to return to Chicago.

In the meantime, I had been reclassified as a clerk to the minimum-security Riverview Release Center in Newton, Iowa, only a few miles from my home. That meant I would be living in minimum security, would be eligible for furloughs home, and, most importantly, would no longer be living behind the wall.

On the morning of 9 July 1970, I had breakfast with John. My belongings were packed, and I would be leaving in a few hours. John was waiting for a friend to pick him up later that day and drive him to Chicago.

After breakfast, we stood on the sidewalk for a few moments and said goodbye. We shook hands, and I walked away. I did not see John Gacy again for ten years. We exchanged a few phone calls, a few Christmas cards, but each of us knew that the other was part of a past we both preferred to forget.

At the Riverview Release Center, I worked as an inmate clerk for the counselors. I was fortunate enough to be assigned a correctional counselor who took a true interest in my case. Seeing my college scores and discovering that I had not only been admitted to the university but actually offered a scholarship, a thing unheard of for a person coming out of prison, he moved heaven and earth in order to get me on campus that fall.

Within a short period of time, I had been classified for Work Release status. I was allowed to live in a halfway house in Des Moines and go to school. All the pushing and dreaming had finally borne fruit. I had gone from convict to college student in a few short weeks.

It was a wonderful time to be on a college campus in America. The Vietnam War was grinding down, but the sexual revolution and the counterculture of the 1960s and 1970s was in full sway. I let my hair grow down to the middle of my back, grew a beard, sported fringed jackets, and rode a bicycle. The word "hippie," which had been such a negative term in prison, was an accolade on campus.

The college courses were difficult but engrossing. I rediscovered in myself a need and an ability to learn that I had forgotten. Every course I took fascinated me in some way. The most difficult ones seemed to bring out the best in me and, unlike most of my fellow students, I knew what the alternatives to an education and a good job were: poverty, crime, and prison.

I also took time to experiment with the drugs so prevalent then. I tried LSD, mescaline, and peyote. A bad experience with some mescaline laced with strychnine cured me of my interest in pharmaceuticals.

I took all the psychology courses available on campus but found many of them asinine and distracting. It's much easier to speculate about the motivations of rapists and murderers, criminals and psychopaths, if you have never had to live among them. They are most safely studied at a distance, where one can maintain objectivity. When one has lived with and befriended them, it is considerably different. They lose the anonymity of statistics and become thinking, feeling human beings.

By 1973, as I approached graduation, I found myself interested in many things other than the criminal justice system, which had held me for so long. The study of history, of human behavior at its finest, had taken the place of crime and criminals. I sought my teaching degree, gained it, and began applying for jobs.

After hundreds of applications had been sent and many interviews given, I was finally offered a job teaching history in Wisconsin. A few weeks before I was scheduled to leave, a call came that would change my life. After having made application for a job as ombudsman for the prison system, a part of a new agency called the Iowa Citizens' Aide, I had forgotten about the position and had moved on to other things. Finally, the call came informing me that I was the final candidate and offering me the job.

The position entailed doing something that I had not seriously thought I would ever care to do, to return to prison. Only now I would be in the position of a problem solver and a prisoner's representative in dealing with the administration of justice. More importantly, I would be able to leave at the end of the day.

I took the job, indicating to my new wife that I would stay for only one year and then move on to something else. My wife, a gentle Iowa farm girl, hated every moment of the job. As soon as I was appointed and sworn in, I began a travel schedule that was extremely grueling. Three, sometimes four, days a week I was on the road visiting various prisons, interviewing inmates, and working with correctional administrators to solve their problems. My wife and I quickly drifted apart and, within six months after the job began, it was obvious that my second marriage was on the rocks.

While I began the Iowa ombudsman job, John Gacy moved to Chicago in July of 1970 and lived at 8213 West Summerdale Avenue. The Iowa parole board continued in blissful ignorance of Gacy's behavior. In October 1971, they discharged him from parole and recommended that his citizenship rights be restored. In less than two months, his first victim would die.

By the end of 1972, Gacy and Carole's marriage was almost at an end. His erratic behavior and other issues were driving them apart.

Back in Iowa, life was not going very well for me either. After three years in the ombudsman's office, my second marriage ended in a divorce caused largely by the pressures of the job. I had come to the reluctant conclusion that, in one way or another, my life would always be dominated by the issues of justice and imprisonment. The hunger for justice given me by John Gacy sometimes bore bitter fruit.

On Labor Day weekend 1976, my brother, a bright, troubled, Vietnam veteran, was arrested and charged with first-degree murder in Iowa. When he came home, he had brought the war with him. A violent argument with a friend led to murder. My brother marched him into the woods and blew his friend's brains out. Violence and death are contagious; they always lead to more violence and death.

My stature as a professional had become such that, when I attempted to resign, my resignation was refused.

On the afternoon of 22 December 1978, I was sitting in my office in the Capitol Complex in Des Moines. The phone rang and on the other end was a reporter from the *Chicago Sun Times*. Eileen Ogentz had previously worked for the *Des Moines Register*, a Pulitzer prize-winning Midwestern paper. She had gone to the *Sun Times* to cover their crime beat.

I was surprised to hear from her and even more surprised when she asked me to comment on the Gacy matter. Not knowing any better, I thought perhaps John had been nominated for governor of Illinois. Not knowing that John and I were friends, she told me that six bodies had been dug out of his basement and it was suspected there might be as many as twenty more. For the first time in my life, I fainted. The days and nights that followed saw an enormous barrage of nationwide publicity in graphic and ghastly detail. I read every word and watched every broadcast, hoping against hope that it was all a gigantic misunderstanding.

In February 1979, I was contacted by the Illinois Department of Criminal Investigation. Searching through John's personal effects, they had found my name, address, and a photograph taken a decade before in prison. When they contacted me, they were surprised to discover that I had become a senior correctional official and an investigator. The call was brief, and they informed me that I undoubtedly would be contacted by the defense. The rules of discovery in criminal cases require that all the evidence and information the prosecution possesses must be revealed to the defense.

Sure enough, in mid-May I was contacted by the defense and told that I might be called as a witness on John's behalf, a prospect I did not relish. After the rather tense phone call, the defense decided not to use me as a witness.

During the days and then weeks that followed, Gacy's house

was searched, excavated, and demolished. By early 1979, John Wayne Gacy Jr. was charged with more individual counts of homicide than any individual in American history: thirty-three. Although the trial would not begin for over a year, one of the most exhaustive and expensive pretrial investigations ever conducted had begun.

In August 1979, I continued to work on my routine cases. I did an early release case that would change my life again.

The man had been convicted of several crimes but had been illegally denied credit on his sentence. He was in jail for assault with intent to commit murder. I obtained that time for him, allowing him to be released nearly a year early. His name was Fred Lewis Lamp.

In early September, my superiors were contacted by the Illinois Department of Criminal Investigation asking that I be temporarily detached and made available to them to assist in interviewing background witnesses from Gacy's prison days. They saw this as doubly useful, because I was a trained corrections professional and also an ex-con who had known John and the other witnesses in prison.

The next month, I was flown first to Chicago, then to South Carolina, in order to help locate and interview prospective trial witnesses. The trip was emotionally difficult and forced me to remember the prison days I had tried so hard to forget. Even then, no one seemed certain whether I would actually be called as a witness at the trial. My doubts were resolved when I received a subpoena commanding me to be in Chicago on Monday, 25 February 1980.

That cold morning of 25 February, I took the red-eye flight from Des Moines to Chicago. I had been informed that I would be met when my plane landed at the Chicago O'Hare International Airport. As I came through the gate, I saw a large mustached man obviously looking at a photograph and scanning the crowd. When he noticed me, he came up and said, "Are you Ray Cornell?"

I admitted I was.

He looked at the photograph again and then smiled. "Do you know that you fit the description of twenty-two of John's thirty-three victims? They were short, muscular, and had blond hair."

That was bad enough, but his next sentence was, "Our new theory of the crime is that you were such a lousy card player that Gacy's been killing you over and over again all these years." He laughed uproariously.

He introduced himself as Greg Bedoe, a Cook County Sheriff's investigator. Greg would be my constant companion for the next week. He and his partner, Detective Hein, had been among the first into the Gacy death house.

The ride from the O'Hare Airport to the hotel on the Loop was the first time in my life I had ever ridden in the front seat of a police car. It beat the hell out of riding in the back seat.

They checked me into a room and informed me that, for the next few days, my movements would be closely monitored, as were those of all the witnesses. At all costs, I should avoid the press or any approaches by defense attorneys or their investigators.

The following morning, 26 February, I was taken to the Cook County Court House on California Avenue. I was introduced to the prosecutor's staff and the main prosecution attorney, Terry Sullivan. For the next three days, I worked with them in preparing my own testimony and also in preparing what were called the Iowa witnesses. All of us had known Gacy a decade before, when the violence and murder were nothing more than a shadow of a dream. Each of us, with the possible exception of young Voorhees who lived with the memory of his encounter with Gacy, had difficulty making the transition from John then to John now.

I was asked to examine the documents pertaining to John's incarceration in Iowa. The single document that stood out the most was his psychiatric evaluation from the University of Iowa Psychopathic Hospital in the summer of 1968. A psychiatrist at the hospital had made the only accurate prediction of John's future. He saw him as amoral, dangerous, unlikely to change, and unsafe in the community. Reading that document, I wondered if perhaps that psychiatrist, unlike most of his colleagues who seemed to work with crystal balls, actually had some insight into human behavior. He certainly seemed to predict well.

Finally, on the morning of 29 February 1980, Leap Year Day, I was awakened early and told I would testify that morning. I had suspected the day before that my time had come to face my friend and to help damn him. I had gone out that night, gotten drunk, and picked up a girl in a bar. During the night, I gave her a drunken soliloquy on how hard it was to betray a friend, even one who had turned into a monster. Despite what he had done, I couldn't forget what he had been. I sent her home at dawn and awakened a few hours later to prepare.

At the Cook County Courthouse, the witnesses were individually sequestered. Since not enough holding rooms to separate each witness were available, I was asked to wait in a holding cell until my turn to testify. It took all my strength of will to walk into a cell and listen to the door locking behind me.

As I sat alone for hours, I realized that the cell also contained some of the physical evidence used earlier in the trial. The crawlspace had been mounted vertically on casters and a library cart held the thirty-three body books, each of which contained the in situ photographs of one victim.

I finally looked at each body book. An attempt had been made to arrange the books in the order in which the victims had died. The first few showed only skeletonized remains, empty eye sockets, and gaping jaw bones. Bones, a reminder of human mortality. Then, book by book, they progressed to rotting flesh, dripping tissue, and the glistening look of dead flesh.

While I looked at the photographs, the room seemed to fill with the sickly sweet aroma, the coppery smell, of death.

The last five volumes were the river bodies—bloated, blackened flesh that bore little resemblance to human beings. The eyes and extremities had been picked at by fish and, on each of the bodies, a swollen gigantic erection, a final acknowledgment of how and why they had died.

To that point, I had not seen John. Now I wondered if I could ever see him again without those images imprinted over his face.

In court, my testimony covered our lives in the Iowa prison. I was questioned closely about the incidents involving John and the homosexual prisoners. A defense attempt to impeach my testimony based on my felony convictions was thwarted when I produced a certified copy of my full pardon given by the governor of Iowa several years before. It was hot in the courtroom and snowing outside. Some of the older jurors seemed to be nodding off. It struck me that perhaps they could absorb no more details about death.

The nightmare was not over for me. Ten weeks to the day after my testimony in the Gacy trial, my sixteen-yearold sister headed home from a friend's house around ten p.m. She was kidnapped at gunpoint from a Des Moines Street. She was taken to a secluded location and brutally raped. The assailant, apparently unsatisfied because she was having her period, stabbed her twice in the stomach and threw her naked onto a country road in the rain that chilly May night.

She crawled two hundred yards before she was found. Almost as if she knew what to do, she gave law enforcement officers what is called a dying declaration, "I know I'm dying, and I want you to know who did this to me." Her description of the man and his vehicle led to the arrest a few hours later of Fred Lewis Lamp. He had killed at least twice before taking my sister's life. Only her courage and tenacity stopped him from becoming another John Gacy.

I was consumed by guilt. I had betrayed a friend and also freed the monster who killed my sister. The cycle of blood and pain seemed endless; one serial murderer off the street, and another begins his career.

At the end of 1980, I once again found myself a prosecution witness in a murder trial. Fred Lamp was convicted and sentenced to life. This time, his fate would not be in my hands. He was transferred to a prison in another state. This was done partially as a way of easing my situation and partially because my brother, still in the Iowa penitentiary serving life for murder, was waiting for Lamp to appear. Lamp's death would have followed in moments of his being released into general population.

Now I was the one sitting around drinking myself stupid and considering eating my pistol. I crawled into a bottle and stayed there for nearly three years. The nightmares from Gacy and the nightmares from my sister's death were constantly with me. It seemed as if the world was nothing more than a great cosmic charnel house and God a bloody-minded trickster.

The pain eased over time. The memories are always present. I do not fear the dark any more than others do, but I understand that fear. I know what's out there waiting.

The chapter on John Wayne Gacy Jr. was especially hard to write. Having once been his close friend, I cannot pretend my reaction to his crimes is objective. I attempted to put forward a balanced and a fair perspective. Even now, in a way I cannot describe, my revulsion for his crimes is still tempered with a compassion for how he came to be what he was.

Indeed, with John and the other serial murderers described in this book, it is very easy to forget that, like their victims, they, too, have friends and families and, at least part of the time, attempted to lead normal lives. Perhaps this is the most horrible aspect of all.

As much as we would like to see them as outsiders, the serial murderers are a part of our society, our communities, and our lives. Mixed with the anger, confusion, and sadness will always be present what they could have been and what they became.

Raymond Cornell

ABOUT THE AUTHORS

Raymond Cornell has lived an unusual life. Born into extreme poverty, he has been a cat burglar, convict, college graduate, and Iowa's first prison ombudsman. He is also a pardoned ex-offender and a trained hostage negotiator. Cornell worked as a private investigator on dozens of murder cases and other major felonies. Besides testifying as an expert on federal prison cases, he has consulted on numerous other murder cases around the country. Also, he is the brother of a murder victim and of a convicted killer. Recently, he consulted on and appeared in two television specials, "John Wayne Gacy: Devil in Disguise" for NBC and another John Wayne Gacy show due to appear on Netflix in April 2022. Now writing in retirement, he is working on a history of prisons in America and an autobiography. Cornell spends his spare time studying the cases of Sherlock Holmes and raising corgis and coleus with his wife Sandra.

Ilene W. Devlin was born in Winterset, Iowa. Attending the University of Iowa, Devlin obtained a BA in anthropology and an MA in archaeology and museum training. Afterward, she worked in museums in Nebraska, Tennessee, and Alabama. Since 1986, Devlin has lived in San Antonio, Texas. Her freelance articles and essays have been published in newspapers in San Antonio and Iowa. She is the author of three books: *Cherry Tree Dares: Essays on Childhood; Emma's World: A World War II Memoir;* and *Truth and Fiction: Essays & Short Stories on Life.*

Bibliography

Aamodt, M. G. (2016, September 4). Serial Killer Statistics. http://maamodt.asp.radford.edu/serial killer information center/project description.htm.

All That's Interesting. (2021). Who Was Ted Bundy? Inside the Life of America's Most Notorious Serial Killer. https://allthatsinteresting.com/who-is-ted-bundy.

Alot Living. 15 Notorious Serial Killers and Why Everyone's Obsessed With Them. https://living.alot.com/entertainment/15-notorious-serial-killers-where-did-they-grow-up--16950?isLong=0&isVertical=1.

ArchiveNewsFootage. (2015). Ted Bundy Takes Stand. https://www.youtube.com/watch?v=VVV3XeAevc8.

ArchivesNewsFootage. (2019). Ted Bundy Newsreel. https://www.youtube.com/watch?v=WDdvhcM_KhE.

Ardrey, R. (1966). The Territorial Imperative: A Personal Inquiry Into the Animal Origins of Property and Nations. New York: Atheneum.

Atlanta Child Murders: Committee to Stop children's Murders. Maynard H. Jackson unpublished personal papers. https://radar.auctr.edu/islandora/object/auc.075%3A00119.

Baldwin, J. (1985). The Evidence of Things Not Seen. Austin, TX: Holt, Rinehart & Winston.

Barcella, L. (2018). Was Serial Killer Wayne Williams Really the Atlanta Monster Who Murdered Dozens of Black Kids? True Crime. https://www.aetv.com/real-crime/wayne-williams-atlanta-monster-child-murders-black-serial-killer.

Baumann, M. (2021). "Am I Getting Too Close to the Serial Killer I'm Tracking?" An Advice Column for TV Cops. The Ringer. https://www.theringer.com/tv/2021/1/12/22225004/tv-cops-advice-column-chasing-serial-killers-prodigal-son.

Belmonte, A. 17 of the Most Notorious Female Serial Killers. Insider, July 1, 2018. https://www.insider.com/most-notorious-female-serial-killers-2018-6.

Bond, M. (2016, March 31). Why Are We Eternally Fascinated by Serial Killers? BBC, Health. https://www.bbc.com/future/article/20160331-why-are-we-eternally-fascinated-by-serial-killers.

Bonn, S. A. (2014). 5 Myths about Serial Killers and Why They Persist. Scientific American. https://www.scientificamerican.com/article/5-myths-about-serial-killers-and-why-they-persist-excerpt/.

Bonn, S. A. (2017). How the Police Can Create "Monsters." Psychology Today. https://www.psychologytoday.com/us/blog/wicked-deeds/201705/how-the-police-can-create-monsters.

Bonn, S. A. (2018, May 12). Why Many Serial Killers Crave Public Notoriety. Psychology Today. https://www.psychologytoday.com/us/blog/wicked-deeds/201805/why-many-serial-killers-crave-public-notoriety.

Buffalmano, L. The Madonna-Whore Complex: What It Means to You. The Power Moves. https://thepowermoves.com/madonna-whore-complex/.

Cahill, T. (1986). Buried Dreams: Inside the Mind of John Wayne Gacy. New York: Open Road Integrated Media.

CAVDEF. "Atlanta Child Murders." http://www.cavdef.org/w/index.php?title=Atlanta_child_murders.

Campos, R. A. (2013). Ted Bundy Interview (1977). https://www.youtube.com/watch?v=AEWsxCrMM1U.

CBS Television. (2018, June 7). Wayne Williams – Serial Killer. https://www.youtube.com/watch?v=Mze_gc9chaU.

Chase, J. (2011). Psychological Triggers and Obsessions of the Serial Killer Mind. Author Jennifer Chase. https://authorjenniferchase.com/2011/04/22/psychological-triggers-and-obsessions-of-the-serial-killer-mind/.

Chavez, S., and A. Gorman. (2002, September 22). Hillside Strangler Dies at 67. The New York Times. https://www.latimes.com/archives/la-xpm-2002-sep-22-me-hillside22-story.html.

Churchland, P. S. (2013, May 7). Criminal Genes and Criminal Brains: Are We There Yet? Psychology Today. https://www.psychologytoday.com/us/blog/neurophilosophy/201305/criminal-genes-and-criminal-brains.

Coletta, S. Serial Killers by States – FBI Stats – How Many Live Near You? Sue Coletta, Inside the Mind of a Crime Writer. https://www.suecoletta.com/serial-killers-by-state/.

Cornwell, P. (2002). Portrait of a Killer: Jack the Ripper Case Closed. New York: G. P. Putnam's Sons.

Corry, J. (1985, February 10). TV View: "The Atlanta Child Murders": A Trial by TV. The New York Times. https://www.nytimes.com/1985/02/10/nyregion/tv-view-the-atlanta-child-murders-a-trial-by-tv.html.

Cray, E. (1973). Burden of Proof: The Case of Juan Corona. New York: Macmillan Publishers.

Crepeau, M. (2017, July 19). Second Long-Unknown Gacy Victim Identified as Boy from Minnesota. Chicago Tribune. https://www.chicagotribune.com/news/breaking/ct-john-wayne-gacy-victim-haakenson-20170719-story.html.

Criminal Justice. Biological Theories of Crime. http://criminal-justice.iresearchnet.com/criminology/theories/biological-theories-of-crime/.

Criminal Minds Wiki. Carl Panzram. https://criminalminds.fandom.com/wiki/Carl_Panzram.

Crime Museum. Ted Bundy. https://www.crimemuseum.org/crime-library/serial-killers/ted-bundy/.

Criminology. Understanding Criminology Theories. https://www.criminology.com/understanding-criminology-theories/.

DeLong, W. (2018). 50 Years Before Ted Bundy, Earle Nelson Was the Most Prolific Serial Killer in American History. All That's Interesting. https://allthatsinteresting.com/earle-nelson.

DeLong, W. (2020). Wayne Williams and the Mystery of the Atlanta Child Murderers. https://allthatsinteresting.com/wayne-williams-atlanta-child-murders.

Dettlinger, C. (1983). The List. Atlanta, GA: Philmay Enterprises, Inc.

Dodgson, L. (2018, October 4). The Main Differences Between Male and Female Psychopaths. Insider. https://www.insider.com/male-and-female-psychopaths-how-they-are-different-2018-9.

D'Orban, P. T., and J. Dalton. (1980, May). Violent Crime and the Menstrual Cycle. Psychological Medicine, 10(2): 353–359. http://dx/doi.org/10.1017/s0033291700044123.

Duncan, J. (2018). 10 Twisted Facts about the Hillside Strangler. Listverse. https://listverse.com/2018/10/03/10-twisted-facts-about-the-hillside-strangler/.

Easteal, P. W. (1991, January). Women and Crime: Premenstrual Issues. ResearchGate. Trends and Issues in Crime and Criminal Justice. https://www.researchgate.net/publication/228145096_Women_and_Crime_Premenstrual_Issues.

Epstein, G. (1987, August 30). From 1987: Atlanta Child Murders: Williams "Very Like" FBI Profile. The Atlanta Journal-Constitution. https://www.ajc.com/news/crime--law/atlanta-child-murders-williams-very-like-fbi-profile/IKyewPxrv06NXcUWz98F9J/.

FBI News. (1980, June 26). Atlanta Child Murders. FBI Records: The Vault. https://vault.fbi.gov/Atlanta%20Child%20Murders/Atlanta%20Child%20Murders%20Part%201%20of%2024/view.

FBI News. (2013). Serial Killers: Part 3: Ted Bundy's Campaign of Terror. https://www.fbi.gov/news/stories/serial-killers-part-3-ted-bundys-campaign-of-terror1.

FBI News. (2014). Serial Killers: Part 5: Wayne Williams and the Atlanta Child Murders. https://www.fbi.gov/news/stories/-serial-killers-part-5-wayne-williams-and-the-atlanta-child-murders.

FBI News. (2014). Serial Killers: Part 8: New Research Aims to Help Investigators Solve Cases. https://www.fbi.gov/news/stories/serial-killers-part-8-new-research-aims-to-help-investigators-solve-serial-murder-cases.

Garrity, A. (2020, October 2). 25 True Crime Documentaries on Netflix That Are Too Scary for Primetime. Good Housekeeping. https://www.goodhousekeeping.com/life/entertainment/g27047877/best-true-crime-documentaries-netflix/.

Gaudette, E. (2017, November 21). How Many Serial Killers Are in the United States? One Scientist Believes It Could Be Thousands. Newsweek. https://www.newsweek.com/serial-killers-united-states-how-many-718232.

Gibian, R. (2017, October 29). 10 of the Most Notorious Female Serial Killers. InsideHook. https://www.insidehook.com/article/news-opinion/notorious-female-serial-killers.

Goleman, D. (1988, January 10). Inside a Psychopath, a Morally Retarded Child. *Chicago Tribune.* https://www.chicagotribune.com/news/ct-xpm-1988-01-10-8803210461-story.html.

Guy, F. (2016, Apr 10). The Warrior Gene: Genetics and Criminology. Crime Traveller. https://www.crimetraveller.org/2016/04/the-warrior-gene/.

HellHorror.com. Female Serial Killers: List of Famous Serial Killers: 59 Notorious Female Serial Killers List. https://hell-horror.com/female-serial-killers/.

Ho, R. (2020, April 8). Four Decades Later, HBO Digs Deep into "Atlanta's Missing and Murdered Children" Case. The Atlanta Journal-Constitution. https://www.ajc.com/blog/radiotvtalk/four-decades-later-hbo-digs-deep-into-atlanta-missing-and-murdered-children-case/3UBB0F5AWkfSY-eVdjr128M/.

Howard, C. R. (2020). It's Time to Demystify the Serial Killer. CrimeReads. https://crimereads.com/its-time-to-demystify-the-serial-killer/.

Insanity. (n.d.) *The People's Law Dictionary.* (1981–2005). https://legal-dictionary.thefreedictionary.com/insanity.

Interview with Evil. Episode 8: The Secrets They Keep. (2020). https://www.interviewwithevil.com/episodes/episode8/thesecretstheykeep-fdxx6-j7xtg.

Interview with Evil. Episode 7: Bundy Raw 2. (2020). https://www.interviewwithevil.com/episodes/episode7/bundyraw2-fdxx6.

Interview with Evil. Episode 6: The Archive. (2020). https://www.interviewwithevil.com/episodes/episode6/thearchive.

Ishak, N. (2021, May 1). Inside the Gruesome Atlanta Child Murders – And Why This Case Remains Unsolved. All That's Interesting. https://allthatsinteresting.com/atlanta-child-murders.

John Wayne Gacy – Investigation. https://www.liquisearch.com/john_wayne_gacy/investigation.

Kneeland, D. E. (1971, June 16). For Yuba City Suspect, Early Prosperity Ended in an Unsuccessful Plea for Welfare. The New York Times. https://www.nytimes.com/1971/06/16/archives/for-yuba-city-suspect-early-prosperity-ended-in-an-unsuccessful.html.

Knight, S. (1984). Jack the Ripper: The Final Solution. Detroit, MI: Treasure Press Publishing.

Krouse, W. J., and D. J. Richardson. (2015). Mass Murder with Firearms: Incidents and Victims, 1999–2013. Congressional Research Service. Washington, DC. https://sgp.fas.org/crs/misc/R44126.pdf.

Larsen, R. W. (1980). Bundy: The Deliberate Stranger. Upper Saddle River, NJ: Prentice Hall.

Last 9 Gacy Victioms, Still Unidentified, Are Buried. (1981, June 14). New York Times. https://www.nytimes.com/1981/06/14/us/last-9-gacy-victims-still-unidentified-are-buried.html.

Lee, W. (2018, December 16). John Wayne Gacy Was Arrested 40 Years ago in a Killing Spree That Claimed 33 Victims and Shattered the Illusion of the Safe Suburban Community. Chicago Tribune. http://graphics.chicagotribune.com/john-wayne-gacy-murders-40-years-later/

Leyton, E. (1987). Hunting Humans: The Rise of the Modern Multiple Murderer. Toronto, Canada: Seal Books.

Lin, S., R. Umbach, and A. Raine. (2019). Biological Explanations of Criminal Behavior. Psychology, Crime & Law, 25(6), 626–640.

Linedecker, C. L. (1986). The Man Who Killed Boys. New York: St. Martin's Paperbacks.

Lunde, D. T. (1976). Murder and Madness. San Francisco: San Francisco Book Co.

Madonna–Whore Complex. (2015, October 3). PSYCH 424 [Web log post]. Pennsylvania State University. https://sites.psu.edu/aspsy/2015/10/03/madonna-whore-complex/.

Madriga, E. (2021). 32 Creepy Facts about Serial Killers I Learned from the "Mindhunter" Book. Thought Catalog. https://thoughtcatalog.com/emily-madriga/2018/04/32-

creepy-facts-about-serial-killers-i-learned-from-the-mind-hunter-book/.

Masters, R. D. (2018). Neurotoxicity and Violent Crime: Linking Brain Biochemistry, Toxins, and Violent Crime. MedCrave Group LLC. https://medcraveebooks.com/view/Neurotoxicity-and-Violent-Crime-Linking-Brain-Biochemistry,-Toxins-and-Violent-Crime.pdf.

Matthews, M. (2018, June 21). Here's Where the Most Psychopaths Live in the U.S. Men's Health. https://www.menshealth.com/health/a21748745/heres-which-state-has-the-most-psychopaths/.

Miller, A. (2014, February). The Criminal Mind. Monitor on Psychology, 45(2). http://www.apa.org/monitor/2014/02/criminal-mind.

Mills, S., and J. Meisner. (2011, November 29). DNA Identifies Gacy Victim. Chicago Tribune.. https://www.chicagotribune.com/nation-world/ct-xpm-2011-11-29-ct-met-gacy-victim-identified-20111130-story.html.

Montaldo, C. (2020). Biography of Ted Bundy, Serial Killer. ThoughtCo. https://www.thoughtco.com/profile-of-serial-killer-ted-bundy-973178.

Montaldo, C. (2021, February 28). The 10 Biggest Criminal Cases of the 21st Century. ThoughtCo. https://www.thoughtco.com/biggest-criminal-cases-4150497.

Morley, K., and W. Hall. (2003). Is There a Genetic Susceptibility to Engage in Criminal Acts? Trends & Issues in Crime and Criminal Justice, no. 263. Canberra: Australian Institute of Criminology. https://ww.aic.gov.au/publications/tandi/tandi263.

Morton, R. J., J. M. Tillman, and S. J. Gaines. (2014). Serial Murder: Pathways for Investigations. Washington, DC: U.S. Department of Justice. https://www.fbi.gov/file-repository/serialmurder-pathwaysforinvestigations-1.pdf/view.

Morton, R. J., Ed. (2005). Serial Murder: Multi-Disciplinary Perspectives for Investigators. Washington, DC: U.S. Department of Justice. https://www.fbi.gov/stats-services/publications/serial-murder

Mosbach, M., S. Conrad, and A. McCollum. (2011). Earle Leonard Nelson: "The Gorilla Killer" and "The Dark Strangler." http://maamodt.asp.radford.edu/Psyc%20405/serial%20killers/Nelson,%20Earle%20Leonard.pdf.

Moser, W. (2011). John Wayne Gacy, Runaways, and the Decline of the Serial Killer. Chicago Magazine. https://www.chicagomag.com/city-life/october-2011/john-wayne-gacy-runaways-and-the-decline-of-the-serial-killer/.

Moskowitz, C. (2011, March 4). Criminal Minds Are Different From Yours, Brain Scans Reveal. LiveScience. https://www.livescience.com/13083-criminals-brain-neuroscience-ethics.html.

Murrow, E. R. (1958, October 15). Speech to Radio Television Digital News Association, Chicago, IL. https://www.rtdna.org/content/edward_r_murrow_s_1958_wires_lights_in_a_box_speech#.VDrbgNTF8X4.

National Organization for Rare Disorders. (2012). XYY Syndrome. Rare Disease Database. https://rarediseases.org/rare-diseases/xyy-syndrome/.

O'Brien, D. (1985). Two of a Kind: The Hillside Stranglers. New York: Dutton Adult.

Oliver, M. (2020). How the Hillside Stranglers Kenneth Bianchi and Angelo Buono Terrorized L.A. in the Late '70s. All That's Interesting. https://allthatsinteresting.com/hillside-strangler-kenneth-bianchi-angelo-buono.

Olsen, L. (2021, January/February). Undetected. Texas Observer. https://www.texasobserver.org/undetected/.

People v. Gacy, 103 Ill. 2d 1 (1984). https://law.justia.com/cases/illinois/supreme-court/1984/53212-6.html

People v. Gacy, 125 Ill. 2d 117 (1988). https://law.justia.com/cases/illinois/supreme-court/1988/64382-7.html#:~:text=This%20case%20involves%20the%20petition%20of%20the%20defendant%2C,convicted%20of%20murdering%2033%20boys%20and%20young%20men.

Priebe, H. (2015). Here Is What a Madonna-Whore Complex Looks Like in 2015. Thought Catalog. https://thoughtcatalog.com/heidi-priebe/2015/06/here-is-what-a-madonna-whore-complex-looks-like-in-2015/.

Quora. What Percentage of People Are Psychopaths/Sociopaths? https://www.quora.com/What-percentage-of-people-are-psychopaths-sociopaths.

Ramsland, K. (2021). The Forgotten Serial Killer: A Case for Our Times. Psychology Today Blog, May 19, 2021. https://www.psychologytoday.com/us/blog/shadow-boxing/202105/the-forgotten-serial-killer-case-our-times.

Robins, B. (2019, September 6). How Many Active Serial Killers Are in the US? Grunge. https://www.grunge.com/165267/how-many-active-serial-killers-are-in-the-us/.

Robins, B. (2018, February). Traits That Most Serial Killers Eerily Have in Common. Grunge. https://www.grunge.com/190380/the-most-notorious-female-serial-killers/.

Rosenthal, N. (2020, June 3). John Wayne Gacy's Kids: What Happened to Michael and Christine Gacy? Grunge. https://www.grunge.com/214543/john-wayne-gacys-kids-what-happened-to-michael-and-christine-gacy/.

Rosewood, J. (2018). 9 Early Warning Signs of a Serial Killer. Insider. https://www.insider.com/warning-signs-of-serial-killers-2018-5.

Ruch, J. (2021). New DNA Testing in Atlanta Child Murders to Begin Within 60 Days, Police Say. Reporter Newspapers. https://reporternewspapers.net/2021/01/21/new-dna-testing-in-atlanta-child-murders-to-begin-within-60-days-police-say/.

Rule, A. (1981). The Stranger Beside Me: Ted Bundy: The Shocking Inside Story. New York: Simon and Schuster

Rumore, K., and K. Bentle. (2018, December 17). Here Are John Wayne Gacy's Victims. Chicago Tribune. https://www.chicagotribune.com/history/ct-john-wayne-gacy-victims-20181215-htmlstory.html.

Schwarz, T. (1981). The Hillside Strangler: A Murderer's Mind. New York: Doubleday.

Scott., S., L. Fleury, and K. Sabat (Executive Producers). (2021, August). Invisible Monsters: Serial Killers in America. [Television 6-part series]. New York: A&E Television Networks, LLC.

Serial Killer Shop. (2018). Carl Panzram: America's Most Repulsive Serial Killer. https://serialkillershop.com/blogs/true-crime/carl-panzram.

Sewell, D. (2019, February 9). 30 Years Later: Exclusive Interview with Serial Killer Ted Bundy. Associated Press. https://canoe.com/news/crime/30-years-later-exclusive-interview-with-serial-killer-ted-bundy.

Silverman, E. (2019, March 5). Juan Corona, the "Machete Murderer," Dies in Northern California Prison at 85. The Mercury News. https://www.mercurynews.com/2019/03/04/juan-corona-the-machete-murderer-dies-behind-bars-at-85/.

State v. Bundy, 589 P.2d 760 (1978). https://law.justia.com/cases/utah/supreme-court/1978/589-p-2d-760.html.

Stout, D. (2019, March 4). Juan Corona, 85, Convicted as Killer of 25 Farm Workers, Dies. The New York Times. https://www.nytimes.com/2019/03/04/obituaries/juan-corona-dead.html.

Tanos, L. (2021). The Hillside Strangler Murders Explained. Grunge.com. https://www.grunge.com/473410/the-hillside-strangler-murders-explained/.

Ted Bundy – Identified Victims. Murder Murder Murder. https://www.murdermurdermurder.com/ted-bundy-victims.

Tehrani, J. A., and S. A. Mednick. (2000). Genetic Factors and Criminal Behavior. Federal Probation Journal, 64(2). https://www.uscourts.gov/sites/default/files/64_2_4_0.pdf.

Ton, G. (2018). Law and Horror: Cops Who Became Serial Killers, and Serial Killers Who Were Obsesses with Cops. True Crime Buzz. https://www.oxygen.com/martinis-murder/cops-who-became-serial-killers-ted-bundy-ed-kemper-golden-state-killer.

Torpy, B. (2020, April 15). Opinion: "Missing and Murdered" Cases: 40 Years later, Still Divisive. The Atlanta Journal-Constitution. https://www.ajc.com/news/local/opinion-the-missing-and-murdered-years-later-still-divisive/2FNszgQkkUK6AV6VtItYHP/.

True Crime Magazine. Revisiting the Atlanta Child Murders. https://www.thecrimemag.com/revisiting-the-atlanta-child-murders/.

True Crime Magazine. Revisiting the Hillside Strangler Murders. https://www.thecrimemag.com/hillside-strangler-murders/.

Turner, J. (2020, October 14). 9 Currently Active Serial Killers: Unsolved Cases in 2021. Serial Killer Shop. https://serialkillershop.com/blogs/true-crime/9-current-serial-killers-still-at-large.

Villalon, C. (2020, February 25). Are We Obsessed with Serial Killers? The Gale Review [Web log post]. https://review.gale.com/2020/02/25/serial-killers/.

Wasserman, D., A. Asch, J. Blustein, and D. Putnam. (2017, Fall). Cognitive Disability and Moral Status. In E. N. Zalta (Ed.), The Stanford Encyclopedia of Philosophy. https://

plato.stanford.edu/cgi-bin/encyclopedia/archinfo.cgi?entry=cognitive-disability

Wertz, J., et al. (2017). Genetics and Crime: Integrating New Genomic Discoveries into Psychological Research About Antisocial Behavior. Psychological Science 29(5): 791–803. http://dx/doi.org/1177/0956797617744542.

Wikipedia. Caryl Chessman. https://en.wikipedia.org/wiki/Caryl_Chessman.

Wikipedia. Hillside Strangler. https://en.wikipedia.org/wiki/Hillside_Strangler.

Wikipedia. Juan Corona. https://en.wikipedia.org/wiki/Juan_Corona.

Wikipedia. Ted Bundy. https://en.wikipedia.org/wiki/Ted_Bundy.

World Population Review. Serial Killers by State 2021. https://worldpopulationreview.com/state-rankings/serial-killers-by-state.

WTF Detective. (2019). The Final Interview of Ted Bundy in Words. https://wtfdetective.com/ted-bundy-interview/.

Willson, J., and R. Herrnsein. (1998). Crime and Human Nature. Tampa, FL: The Free Press Publishing Company.

Wilson, J. W. (2011). Debating Genetics as a Predictor of criminal Offending and Sentencing. Inquiries, 3(11), 1. http://www.inquiriesjournal.com/articles/593/debating-genetics-as-a-predictor-of-criminal-offending-and-sentencing.

Zamora v. State, No. 77-2566 (361 So.2d, 1978). https://www.leagle.com/decision/19781137361so2d77611012.

Raymond Cornell and Ilene W. Devlin

Raymond Cornell and Ilene W. Devlin

Made in the USA
Las Vegas, NV
12 September 2021